Paul Gaulot, Frances Cashel Hoey

A Friend of the Queen

Marie Antoinette, Count Fersen

Paul Gaulot, Frances Cashel Hoey

A Friend of the Queen

Marie Antoinette, Count Fersen

ISBN/EAN: 9783337322199

Printed in Europe, USA, Canada, Australia, Japan

Cover: Foto ©ninafisch / pixelio.de

More available books at **www.hansebooks.com**

A FRIEND OF THE QUEEN

(MARIE ANTOINETTE—COUNT FERSEN)

FROM THE FRENCH OF
PAUL GAULOT

By MRS. CASHEL HOEY

With Portraits

LONDON
WILLIAM HEINEMANN
1895
[*All rights reserved*]

PREFACE

THE personal history of Count Fersen, and the part which he played at the Court of France, have been only vaguely known up to the present time; but the documents which were necessary to complete our information respecting the Count have been supplied by a recent work. Baron R. M. de Klinckowström, a Colonel in the Swedish army, and grand-nephew of Count Fersen, has given to the world *Le Comte de Fersen et la Cour de France*, compiled from extracts from the papers of Count John Axel Fersen, Grand Marshal of Sweden.

Although this work is incomplete, it throws so novel and unexpected a light upon the Count in the first instance, and also upon certain portions of the history of the closing years of the eighteenth century, that I have thought it well to retrace the life of Count Fersen, by the aid of these documents and others which I have succeeded in procuring elsewhere, and to add a narrative of the events with which he was so closely associated.

A strong additional inducement to attempt this task of historical reconstruction existed for me in the fact that Marie Antoinette is revealed in these documents in her real character, just as she actually was; so that I am enabled to restore its true physiognomy to a fascinating image, which has hitherto been falsely presented, whether for good or evil, by the legends that have been almost universally accepted as true portraiture.

I am of opinion that after the lapse of a century the truth may be written concerning the revolutionary epoch, and the people of that epoch, even though it should displease those who regard history as only (to quote Fontenelle) "*la fable convenue.*"

PAUL GAULOT.

CONTENTS

CHAPTER I.

France during the last years of the reign of Louis XV.—Mme. du Barry—The Dauphin and the Dauphiness—A ball given by the Dauphiness on the 10th January 1774—Count John Axel Fersen—The masked ball at the Opera—Shrove Tuesday at Versailles—A despatch from Count Creutz to Gustavus III.—The Fersen family—Count Frederick—John Fersen at Turin and Strasburg—Voltaire at Ferney—Count Fersen in London—His return to Sweden. . . . 1-25

CHAPTER II.

Count John in Sweden—Gustavus III.—The Count's second visit to France—The Queen recognises him and is pleased at seeing him again—Mutual liking—Count Creutz's despatch to the King of Sweden—A project of marriage attributed to Count Fersen—Mdlle. de Leijel—He starts for America . . . 26-39

CHAPTER III.

The English colonies in America—The heavy yoke of England—The first upheaval—Washington—Enthusiasm in France—Franklin—Count John Fersen is attached to the expedition as aide-de-camp to M. de Rochambeau—He leaves Paris—From Brest to Newport—Incidents—The Duc de Lauzun—Interview between M. de Rochambeau and Washington—General Arnold's treason—The feeling among the insurgent population—Spies—Williamsburg—The capitulation of Lord Cornwallis (19th October 1781)—Philadelphia—The approaching peace—Count Fersen leaves America—Boston—Porto Cabello—Return to France (June 1783) 40-77

CHAPTER IV.

A letter from Gustavus III. to Louis XVI.—Count Fersen at the Court of France—Mdlle. Necker—An abortive project of marriage—Stedingk and Staël—Gustavus III. in Germany, in Italy, and in France—Count Fersen's return to Sweden (1784)—Political events—Preludes to the Revolution—Queen Marie Antoinette—Unpopularity—The French Court—The Comtesse Jules de Polignac—Baron de Besenval—The Duc de Lauzun—The Duc de Coigny—The diamond necklace—The louis-d'or of Strasburg—M. de Calonne—"The King has sent in his resignation"—The Assembly of the Notables—Count Fersen's impressions—Sweden in 1788—Finland expedition—Count Fersen's mission in France—Mme. de Chicogne—Valenciennes and Paris—Revolutionary agitation 78-117

CHAPTER V.

The 5th of May at the door of the Menus-Plaisirs—The States-General—The taking of the Bastille—Count Fersen's impressions—October days—The mob at Versailles—The Queen in danger—The Royal Family returns to Paris—The Journal of Louis XVI.—Count Fersen at Aix-la-Chapelle—Baron Taube—The Fête of the Federation—Political news—Incidents of the 18th of April 1791—Preparations for departure—Uneasiness among the people—Vigilance of Citizens Buscbi and Hucher—The 21st of June—M. Lemoine enters the King's bedchamber—It is empty—Disappearance of the Royal Family—Commotion in Paris—*Au bœuf couronné* 118-142

CHAPTER VI.

Flight contemplated—The plan of M. de Breteuil—The Marquis de Bouillé—Count Fersen is charged with the negotiations—Intervention of the Emperor of Germany—Movements of troops on the frontier—Baron de Goguelat—Forces at the disposal of M. de Bouillé—Plan of journey—Reims to be avoided—Stages so far as Montmédy—Goguelat reconnoitres the route—The King's commands transmitted to Bouillé—Preparations in Paris—Baroness Korff—The berline

CONTENTS

—Meeting of Count Fersen and the Duc d'Orléans at Vincennes—The Tuileries watched—Doors made in the wood panelling—Persons associated with the projected flight: Count Fersen, Madame Sullivan, Colonel Crawford—Lafayette—Mesdames de Tourzel, Brunier, and de Neuville—The body-guards, Messieurs de Valory, du Moustier, and de Maldent—The 20th of June in Paris—The final preparations—Count Fersen at the Tuileries—A chest of pistols and bullet-casting—Leaving the Tuileries—Incidents—Count Fersen disguised as a hackney-coachman—At Bondy—Separation—First relay—*Pourboires* too liberal—The royal family think they are out of danger—A saying of Louis XVI.—His imprudence—He is recognised by various persons—Pont Sommevesle—Commotion caused by the presence of the detachment commanded by Choiseul and Goguelat—Sainte-Menehould—M. d'Andoins—He warns the King to hasten onward— —Drouet the postmaster and Guillaume—A quartermaster escapes and pursues, but does not come up with them—Clermont—M. de Damas—Drouet arrives at Varennes at a quarter to twelve o'clock—The Procureur of the commune is warned—The bridge barred —The berline arrives and cannot pass—Arrest of the travellers—The alarm-bell—The National Guard in arms—M. Destez—The King makes himself known— The night at Varennes—Goguelat attempts to deliver the King—Louis XVI. tries to gain time—M. de Bouillé does not appear—Arrival of Messieurs Romeuf, aide-de-camp to Lafayette, and Baillon—Departure from Varennes for Paris—Incidents—Murder of M. de Dampierre—Meeting at Epernay with the three commissaries sent by the National Assembly, Barnave, Latour-Maubourg, and Pétion—Pétion's narrative—Paris re-entered—The attitude of the population —The King's Journal 143-209

CHAPTER VII.

Count Fersen at Mons—False news—"The King is saved!"—Count Fersen meets Bouillé at Arlon— "All is lost!"—M. de Mercy-Argenteau at Brussels —"He takes the gloomiest view"—Notes from Marie Antoinette—The Princesse de Lamballe—Mme. de Polignac—News from Paris—Dejection of the King —The King and Queen are interrogated by Tronchet, Duport, and d'André—Indictment of the authors of the "Abduction of the King" and their accomplices—Count Fersen's sojourn in France interdicted—M. de Damas, M. d'Audoins, M. de Choiseul, and M. de Goguelat—Courageous bearing of the three bodyguards—Letter from the Marquis de Bouillé to the National Assembly—Displeasure of the Royalists remaining in France—The King of Sweden at Spa—Count Fersen at Coblentz—The Princes: Monsieur and the Comte d'Artois—M. de Calonne—Count Fersen at Vienna—Interview with the Emperor Leopold—"The accursed Florentine"—The political interest of the House of Austria in the degradation of the House of France—A contemplated landing in Normandy—Louis XVI. accepts the Constitution—The Queen accused of allowing herself to be led by Barnave—Her double game—Letters to Fersen—Political and private communications . . 210-252

CHAPTER VIII.

Gustavus III. renews his efforts for the deliverance of the royal family—A scheme of flight—Count Fersen is commissioned to communicate with the King and Queen of France—Obstacles to his return to Paris—The Queen consents—Difficulties concerning passports—His journey, postponed at first, is accomplished in February 1792—Departure from Brussels—Disguise—Arrival in Paris—First visit to the Tuileries—Interview with the King—Departure from Paris—Incidents of the return—Fersen's report to the King of Sweden 253-273

CHAPTER IX.

Sudden death of Leopold II.—Rumours of poison—The emigrants rejoice at the death of the Emperor—Francis II.—News from Sweden—Convocation of the Diet at Gefle—Dissatisfaction of the Swedish nobility—Superstitious credulity of Gustavus III.—The vision of Charles IX.—In the Haga Park on an evening in January 1792—Plot against the life of the King—The conspirators—Ankarstroëm—Lieutenant-Colonel Liliehorn—The 16th of March—At the masked ball—"*Bonjour, beau masque*"—Gustavus is wounded by a pistol-shot—His last hours—His death—The doom of Ankarstroëm—Count Fersen's grief 274-297

CHAPTER X.

The situation in France—Isnard's words—A summons to the Electors of Trèves and Mayence, and to the other Princes of the Empire, to put an end to the massing of troops upon the frontier—The reply of Francis, King of Bohemia and Hungary—Declaration of the "State of War"—Satisfaction of the Queen and Count Fersen—Correspondence in cipher—*M. Rignon*—The 20th of June—The Queen's despatches—"It is said, but I do not believe it"—Lafayette proposes a plan of flight—The arrival of the Marseillais—A manifesto by the Duke of Brunswick—M. de Limon's text modified by Count Fersen—It is proposed to ask for a declaration by the King of England in favour of the Royal Family of France—The 10th of August—The National Assembly and the Temple—Lafayette is made prisoner—The September massacres—The death of Mme. de Lamballe—Manuel's words—M. de Mercy—Dumouriez—Valmy (20th September 1792)—Sufferings of the troops and the emigrants—The Duke of Brunswick's retreat—Count Fersen leaves Brussels—Jemmapes (6th November 1792) . 298-323

CHAPTER XI.

News from Paris—The trial of the King—The 21st of January—The Will of Louis XVI.—Attitude of the Princes and emigrants—Indifference of foreigners—Attempts to escape made at Paris—Toulan and Jarjayes—The Stamp—Agreement arrived at between Dumouriez and the Prince of Coburg—Hopes of Count Fersen, appointed Ambassador to King Louis XVII.—Note of the 8th of April 1793—The defection of Dumouriez—Interview of the General with Count Fersen at Brussels—Inaction of M. de Mercy—Hostility of M. de Thugut—Drouet—The Queen transferred to the Conciergerie—The Chevalier de Rougeville—Details of the captivity of Marie Antoinette—A last effort in favour of the Queen—Novere, the dancing-master, and Ribbes, the banker—The trial of the Queen—Marie Antoinette at the National Window—Count Fersen's grief . . . 324-357

CHAPTER XII.

Consequences of the Queen's death—The Regent of Sweden deprives Count Fersen of his diplomatic post—Recognition of the French Republic—The son of Gustavus III.—Reactionary policy—The majority of Gustavus IV. is proclaimed (6th November 1796)—Count Fersen at the Congress of Rastadt—General Bonaparte's speech to Fersen—Return to Sweden—The strong protest of Gustavus IV. against Napoleon is attributed to Count Fersen—The fall of Gustavus IV.—The Duke of Sudermania is proclaimed King under the name of Charles XIII.—Adoption of Prince Christian of Holstein-Augustenburg—Sudden death of the Prince—Rumours of poison—Accusations against Count Fersen, and against his sister, Countess Piper—Popular excitement—Moral complicity of the King—Funeral ceremony of the 20th of June 1810—Popular feeling against the Grand Marshal—Count Fersen is massacred in the courtyard of the Hôtel-de-Ville 358–371

A FRIEND OF THE QUEEN

CHAPTER I.

France during the last years of the reign of Louis XV.—Mme. du Barry—The Dauphin and the Dauphiness—A ball given by the Dauphiness on the 10th January 1774—Count John Axel Fersen—The masked ball at the Opera—Shrove Tuesday at Versailles—A despatch from Count Creutz to Gustavus III.—The Fersen family—Count Frederick—John Fersen at Turin and Strasburg—Voltaire at Ferney—Count Fersen in London—His return to Sweden.

THE well-known saying of Pope Benedict XIV., "Can any further proof of the existence of a Providence be desired than the prosperity of France under the reign of Louis XV.?" was merely a splenetic phrase. With all the good-will in the world, it would be difficult to see anything else in it, for France had rarely been less prosperous.

The worthless sovereign who had occupied the throne of France from his earliest childhood had allowed everything to become disorganised by degrees, and to dissolve in his hands. The ruin was general and lamentable. Not an institution had escaped the universal decay; no, not even the institution of royal mistresses, which the sovereigns who preceded him had hitherto so vigilantly defended.

Louis XV. gave Jeanne Vaubernier, ill-disguised under her new title of Comtesse du Barry, as a successor to the Duchesse de Châteauroux and the Marquise de Pompadour; and "court and city," so the phrase still ran, had observed the left-handed misalliance with astonishment, and also with some disgust.

This was a very different matter from the decorous adulterous relations of Louis XIV., and accordingly respect died out. One day, the King, in talking about his new love affair, deigned to acknowledge that he was not Du Barry's first admirer.

"It is X. whom I succeed," said Louis.

And some one present had the boldness to reply—

"As your Majesty succeeds Pharamond."

The King had some excuse to plead; he was bored to death. When Louis XIV. was growing old, he took to devotion; Louis XV. tried to dispel his incurable ennui by new sensations. What a strange malady was that for a man whose destiny it was to reign over a nation numbering many millions of souls! The remedy was stranger still, and, moreover, it did not cure. The most it ever did was to afford him some passing diversion. It appears that the descendant of Henri IV. derived keen pleasure from being treated like any other of her lovers by a common woman, and gladly encouraged her in her vulgar familiarity. Not indeed that she required encouragement; that is plain from some of her sayings which have been recorded by history, as, for instance, "Hi! France! your coffee is cutting away!" (The *tutoiement* gives this speech peculiar point and insolence.)

What the King did not see was that the monarchical idea was imitating his coffee in rapidly "cutting away," and preceding the fall of the ancient house of France. He did indeed say, "After us the deluge;" but by that he merely meant difficulties, worries, crises, perhaps a few revolts; he neither foresaw nor divined that great thing which came of his faults, and was the issue of his shameful life—the Revolution.

It must always be a cause for regret that events were not precipitated, and that Louis XV., the guilty, was not also the punished person.

Nevertheless, it may be that he was, for he was not brave in the face of either danger or death. This was amply proved on the occasion of the abortive attempt of Damiens to assassinate him. The doctors assured him that the scratch he had received was of no importance, not the slightest anxiety was felt by anybody, but he continued to tremble, was convinced that he was about to die, and insisted on being repeatedly given absolution by the Abbé de Rochecour, the almoner of the district, who was summoned to attend him. Of a surety, he must have suffered intensely when he knew that he was in the grip of the fearful malady which carried him off. A fetid odour was exhaled from his skin for several days before the end came. The knowledge that he was an object of horror and disgust to all who approached him must have sorely wounded his pride, and this, added to the superstitious terror of his craven soul, might have consoled those who regretted that he escaped the popular fury, by suggesting that he probably believed himself to be stricken by divine justice.

He had only one son, Louis, who died in 1769. The eldest of his grandsons, the Duc de Berry, who was then hardly fourteen years old, became Dauphin and heir-presumptive. It was a strange chance of the law of heredity, which has been fatal alike to France and to the royal family, that a child was called to succeed an old man, and thus a great nation's destinies were left to the hazards of two kinds of feebleness. The reign that was drawing to a close was expiring amid general discontent; the reign that was imminent inspired many hopes impossible of realisation. All the more was expected of the new Dauphin because the people grew increasingly wretched under his grandfather.

It was, however, necessary that the future king should have the qualities requisite for the part which he would have to play. In person, the Duc de Berry was a big boy, short of stature and clumsy, without any kind of prestige, devoid of those external gifts which the populace look for and like to recognise in the descendants of royal families, and which seem to justify the privileges of birth. His eyes were lustreless, his glance was vague, his voice was shrill, and, notwithstanding his age, occasionally high and sharp, breaking into vulgar and disagreeable falsetto; his gait was heavy and ungraceful. He was only moderately intelligent, and he displayed no real aptitude except for bodily exercises. He excelled in handicraft, especially of the rougher kinds, taking the greatest pleasure in forging iron, mixing mortar, and raking rubble. If his evil destiny had not made him a king, he would have been the best mechanic in the realm. He did, however, care for hunting, and willingly joined in that more elevated pastime; but if he expended his strength in these "violent delights," he speedily recruited it, and something more, for his appetite was formidable, and he never lost or failed to satisfy it even in the most terrible crises of his life.

He had indeed none but passive qualities, but at least he could be kind, although not always judiciously kind. Perhaps education might have rendered the prince worthy to fill the throne of France, by teaching him how to conduct himself wisely in the midst of the turbulence of his reign; but in this respect he had been truly unfortunate; the guidance of his youth was intrusted to the blindest and least adroit of preceptors. The Duc de la Vauguyon, who was as vain as he was noble, as full of self-sufficiency as he was devoid of ideas, once in his life did a clever thing. His ambition to attain a position in which he might gratify his pride and realise his desires, suggested to him to suborn one of the valets in the service of the Dauphin (the son of Louis XV.).

"The valet conveyed to him every morning the title of the book which the Prince had just been reading," says the Comte d'Allonville in his *Mémoires Secrets*. "The Duc de Vauguyon procured the book, read it rapidly, and retained so much of its contents as he knew to be on the moral, political, and religious lines of the august personage. Then he would skilfully contrive to turn the conversation upon the subject of the book, and make the Prince believe in his vast and wholesome erudition. The Dauphin soon came to look upon the Duc de la Vauguyon as the very man to bring up his son."

That the Dauphin was not a very wise person must be admitted, but what lessons had he ever been taught? One little feature of the royal education of those days reveals a great deal. The young princes were given as "headlines" for their copies such sentences as the following: "Kings are gods upon the earth; they can do all that they will." The Duc de la Vauguyon was not the man to change this deplorable system; he contrived to make it worse, and of more ruinous effect.

All that might have developed and formed the mind and heart of the royal youth was rigorously excluded from the singular programme of his education, and as to all appearance the blood of Henri IV. and Louis XIV. did not run freely and warmly in the veins of their descendant, the result proved all that was to be feared and expected. The mild and passive nature of the Duc de Berry led him to accept whatever he was taught without question. The pupil never rebelled. Petty practices, pious reading, rigorous discipline had done their work so well, that when the time came for his marriage to be considered, the young prince was as little fitted to be a husband as he was to be a king. And yet the Duc de la Vauguyon was not completely satisfied; he did not think he had fully succeeded. During the early years of their marriage he took the most ridiculous precautions to keep the young couple apart, even to arranging with the architects that the husband and wife were to have separate apartments. And when he could not avoid leaving them together—as seldom as possible—he even condescended to play the spy to the extent of listening at keyholes in order to overhear the conversations between his charge and the Dauphiness, at the risk of being surprised in that equivocal attitude, a catastrophe which occurred one day, to the great confusion of all three.

As for the poor little Princess of fourteen, taken away from her mother and her country, what must her impressions have been on finding herself the wife of one whom the Prince de Ligne described as "the best but not the most attractive youth in his kingdom"?

Gay, lively, laughter-loving as a child—and indeed she was no more—ignorant, inexperienced, confiding, she was thrust into a gloomy and sullen *milieu*, surrounded in a hostile Court by persons by no means kindly disposed towards her. She could only have one protector, her husband; but he, privately disinclined towards a marriage made up by Choiseul, and retaining, in spite of everything, a certain distrust of this Austrian princess, had neither the wish nor the capacity to protect her. And Marie Antoinette, educated by the Abbé Vermond, a Frenchman who possessed every kind of *esprit* except the religious, had nothing in common with the pupil of the Duc de la Vauguyon.

Was it surprising that she, who had no guide, no supporter, should be guilty, if not of faults, at least of imprudent actions? Had she not a ready-made excuse in her natural desire to amuse herself, in her need of "distraction"? She has been mercilessly blamed for this by some, and warmly defended by others. Those who have regarded her as a Messalina have been met by having her represented as a saint. On both sides there has been ridiculous exaggeration: Marie Antoinette was neither the one nor the other. She was a woman in the full acceptation of the word; sometimes she seemed to be a mere coquette, sometimes she displayed real feeling. In her day of good fortune she had the levity and the grace which beseemed her sex; in her evil fortunes she had the resignation and greatness of soul that became her rank. Amid all the personages who composed the royal family of France she shines with an imperishable lustre, presenting herself to history adorned with the twofold crown of beauty and misfortune.

For close upon four years Marie Antoinette

had been Dauphiness, passing her time in the surface-stir and profound monotony of a future queen's existence, in, but not of the Court, where Madame du Barry reigned, and where Louis XV., then near his death, could barely drag himself about, when a trifling event, whose future consequences no one, not even the parties interested, foresaw, took place at a ball given by her on the 10th of January 1774. The ambassador from Sweden to the Court of France presented to the Dauphiness one of his countrymen, a young Swede, who was travelling to complete his education—Count John Axel Fersen.

The daughter of Maria Theresa could not fail graciously to receive the young foreigner, whose presence promised to dispel a little of the dulness of the ceremonial entertainments prescribed by etiquette; especially as the personal merit of this foreigner, the bearer of an illustrious name, whose renown had reached France, justified his welcome.

Count Fersen, who was then in his nineteenth year, attracted attention by his manly beauty and fine expression, although the latter was rather cold; but, as Tilly remarks, "Women do not dislike impassive faces when they may hope to animate them." The young Swede's countenance was of this kind. His large, limpid eyes, shaded by thick black lashes, had the calm outlook of the Northern people, the impress of whose melancholy he bore; but this did not always or completely conceal the warmth of a generous nature quite capable of passion. He had a small mouth, with expressive lips; a straight, well-formed nose; the fine, thin nostrils that are sometimes a sign of shyness, or, at least, of caution and reserve. His manners bore the impress of nobility and simplicity; his attitude was in every respect that of a true gentleman.

Fersen was about the same age as Marie Antoinette. He was born on the 4th of September 1755, and the Dauphiness on the 2nd of November in the same year. Both were hardly more than children when their first interview took place, and the impressions which they received from it were both keen and light, as sentiments generally are at that age. Fersen was naturally flattered by the welcome he received, and charmed by the grace and beauty of the future Queen of France. The ball began at five o'clock, and was prolonged until half-past nine. Count Fersen was one of the last to leave the ballroom.

A few days afterwards, on the 30th of January, chance contrived for him a second meeting, under less commonplace circumstances than the first, and to this the girlish spirits of the young Princess lent a striking interest.

It was at the masked ball at the Opera. Fersen, like every intelligent foreigner who wishes to see and learn, had included the pleasures of the capital and the study of Parisian manners in his programme. Besides, at this epoch, the Opera balls were the resort of the highest, if not the most staid, society. On that evening there was a crowd. The Swedish gentleman wandered about among the masks, looking and admiring, when a domino approached and began to coquet with him gracefully. The form was elegant, the voice was charming; he lent himself willingly to the adventure which offered itself; perhaps he had been seeking one. Although his conversation was not usually animated, it must be supposed that he acquitted himself well on the occasion, as the fair mask talked to him for a long time.

There was whispering around them: who was his unknown? At last, as usual, the secret came out, and to his astonishment he recognised the Dauphiness herself, who took as much pleasure in making herself known as she had derived from preserving her incognito.

Unfortunately, the crowd also had recognised Marie Antoinette, and it gathered around the two with the ill-bred eagerness of curiosity which embarrasses but is not embarrassed. The Dauphiness, to escape from this, had to retire to her box, where the Dauphin and the Comte de Provence, who had accompanied her on that evening, were awaiting her. Fersen left the scene at three o'clock in the morning, bearing away a more deep and vivid remembrance of this second meeting than of the first, and in his mind a new-born secret sympathy with the radiant Princess.

The favour that had been shown to Fersen by the Dauphiness did more for him probably than the distinction of his name and his personal merit. He was invited everywhere, and the openly-displayed favour of Count Creutz, the ambassador of Gustavus III. to the Court of France, gave him the *entrée* of the foreign salons also. He dined with M. Bloome, the Danish Minister, supped with the Duchesse d'Arville, and frequently visited the Spanish ambassador, the Princesse de Beauveau, Mme. du Deffand, and the Comtesse de la Mark.

He attended a ball at the Palais Royal, where he was "surprised, on entering, to see all the women dressed as shepherdesses in gauze and taffety, and the men in rich coats, embroidered on all the seams."

The spectacle was quite novel to him, and it shocked him a little for a moment. "I thought," he writes, "that it was a public ball, and that the dancers were women of the town."

He corrected this first impression, and speedily learned to regard the ladies whom he met there with different eyes. He particularly admired "Mme. de l'Olstein, indisputably the best and prettiest dancer in Paris."

Nevertheless, his observant turn of mind suggested some reflections upon certain traits of character, and certain sayings which struck him. "As I went away," he remarks, "I was thinking that the French do not know how to amuse themselves; they have a bad habit of always saying, 'I am bored,' and this poisons all their pleasures."

Did Fersen, in making this remark, show much discernment? We take leave to doubt it, for the French at all periods, and those of that particular time more than those of the present day, do not always say what they think. Without quoting the too well-known saying of Talleyrand concerning the charm of life prior to the Revolution, we may refer to the memoirs of that epoch for the proof that there was not much boredom in it.

Fersen was as much at Versailles as in Paris, that Versailles where royalty had taken up its abode since Louis XIV., and sat enthroned far from the real people, amid a world of courtiers. Fêtes followed each other in rapid succession. He had the pleasure of seeing Marie Antoinette again on Shrove Tuesday, the 15th of February.

The occasion was a ball, attended by the greatest personages, next to the old worn-out King, who preferred solitude with Mme. du Barry. The Dauphiness was there, also her two sisters-in-law, the Comtesse de Provence and the Comtesse d'Artois, and a young widow whose beauty had captivated Louis XV. to such an extent that for a while some believed and others feared he would marry her. This young widow was the Princesse de Lamballe.[1] Among the men were the Dauphin, the Comte de Provence, the Comte d'Artois, M. de Ségur, and M. de Coigny, "all wearing the Henri IV. costume, which is the old French dress."

The young Swede remarked that the Dauphin danced very badly; that his brother, the Comte de Provence, did likewise; that the others were better, some of them even good, dancers; also that the spectacle was charming.

We may fully believe him.

[1] Her husband was the son of the Duc de Penthièvre

Madame was tall and dark, with black arched eyebrows: there was something hard in her countenance and haughty in her demeanour. The Comtesse d'Artois, Madame's sister, was very short, and her fine complexion and pleasing expression hardly atoned for the extreme length of her nose. But then there was the Princesse de Lamballe to attract all observers by the sweet expression of her angelic face, her refinement and grace.

But, above and beyond all, the young Dauphiness shone with a radiant lustre. A future queen by the right of her marriage, she already wore the crown by right of her beauty. "Let us picture to ourselves a dazzlingly fair complexion, in which the tints of the earliest summer roses are blended; large, prominent eyes of azure blue; a forehead crowned with luxuriant fair hair, bearing the impress of majesty and frankness, gave the noblest expression to her whole countenance. This was enhanced by the perfect shape of her nose. The only defect in the face of the lovely Princess was the slight protrusion of the lower lip; but this was a distinctive feature of the house of Austria, and reminded all that she was the daughter of Maria Theresa. Her figure was shapely and tall for her age; her neck and bust were perfect; her hands beautiful; her legs and feet worthy of the Venus de Medicis. Her movements were easy and graceful, her whole person was delightfully harmonious, so that none could behold her without admiration, because she always desired to please all whom she saw."

We need not be surprised or shocked by the mention of the legs and feet of Marie Antoinette, for this portrait is drawn by an artist who was privileged to observe them, the famous dressmaker, Mdlle. Bertin.

These details justify the eulogium of the writer; but according to contemporaries the general aspect of the Princess deserved even greater admiration. Count Tilly, who was one of her pages, sums up the common impression. He writes:—

"She had that which is of higher price upon the throne than perfect beauty, the face of a Queen of France, even at those moments in which she sought to appear only as a pretty woman. She had two ways of walking—one was firm, rather quick, and always noble; the other more leisurely and balanced—I might almost say it was a caressing movement, but it never tempted any to forgetfulness of respect. Never did woman curtsey with such grace, saluting ten persons by one bend of her body, and giving each his or her share by the movement of her head and eyes. In a word, it would have come as naturally to every man to bring forward a throne for her as to offer a chair to any other woman."

Notwithstanding the pleasant manner of the Dauphiness and her frank and familiar reception of him, Count Fersen maintained the perfect reserve of a great gentleman, who always bears in mind that it is for princes to attract their inferiors to them, and not for the latter to assert themselves. He admired the Princess none the less fervently, however, and it may safely be affirmed that on leaving France he carried within his breast the germ of that deep attachment which made him in later days the Queen's most ardent defender, and the woman's most devoted servant.

For he had to depart before long. His programme of travel included a visit to London; and however strong the attraction that detained him might be, he was obliged to obey his father's instructions. He left Paris on the 12th of May. The fêtes, too, had come to an end; not because Lent had begun—he remarks in his Journal that the fair Parisians do not observe the penitential season so strictly as to forego "dancing suppers"—but because Louis XV., who had fallen sick of confluent small-pox on the 28th of April, died on the 10th of May.

A few days after Count Fersen's departure, Count Creutz sent the following despatch to Gustavus III. :—

"The young Count Fersen has just left Paris. Of all the Swedes who have been here in my time he has been the best received in the great world. He has been extremely well treated by the royal family. No one could possibly have behaved with greater discretion and decorum. With his handsome face and his intelligence he could not fail to succeed in society, and he has done so completely. Your Majesty will assuredly be glad to hear this; but what will make Count Fersen especially worthy of your Majesty's favour is that he possesses singular nobility and elevation of mind."

It may seem strange that the sojourn of one of his subjects in France, and the conduct of a young man of nineteen, should so deeply interest a king as to occupy a place in the diplomatic correspondence of his ambassador; but the youth in question was the representative of one of the highest and most ancient families among the Swedish aristocracy, and although no one could have foreseen the part which he was destined to act in the future, every one regarded him as capable of playing a distinguished one.

The Fersen family was of old Livonian origin, and had made its mark in Swedish history in the successive reigns of Christina, Charles X., and Charles XI. Three of its members were distinguished in the Council of the kings, and were made senators, three in the army; each of the latter became a Field-Marshal.

Political parties in Sweden in the eighteenth century were divided into two great branches, that of the *Hats*, which was favourable to French, and that of the *Caps*, which represented Russian, influence. The Fersens, with almost the whole of the nobility, took the side of the *Hats*, and Count Frederick Axel Fersen, Count John's father, became the head of the party.

His influence was considerable; he was equally active and eloquent, and it certainly required all his skill to lead the liberal opposition in its conflict with the royal power, which was tending more and more to confiscate the national liberty and ignore the authority of the laws, in order to transform itself into a despotism equally prejudicial to the nation and opposed to the fundamental compact of the Constitution.

Count Frederick Fersen had lived out of

B

Sweden for a long time. (Is it not marvellous to observe the readiness with which the longest journeys were undertaken at an epoch when the means of locomotion by land and sea were so defective?) He came to France in the beginning of the reign of Louis XV., and remained there for several years; he even took service in the French army and attained the rank of major.[1] After he returned to his own country, his military abilities were recognised and utilised by his being given a command in Pomerania.

He was three times Marshal of the Diet, and played a great part in the Assembly of the States in 1736. Some time previously he had married Countess Hedwige Catherine de la Gardie, who bore him one son, John, and two daughters. The latter became respectively Baroness Klinckowström and Countess Piper.

At that time it was the custom that the descendants of great families should make a journey in Europe, and this was called "the grand tour." The patriotic "idea" had not then entered upon the acute and jealous phase which it has assumed in our day, and service in foreign countries was considered the most natural thing in the world; gentlemen of every nationality being held to belong, after a fashion, to all the sovereigns. Thus, Count Frederick Fersen obtained for his son the rank of lieutenant "attached to" or "with" the Royal Bavière regiment[2] in the French army, although Count John was a lieutenant in the Småland cavalry.

[1] Maréchal-de-camp. [2] Lieutenant à la suite.

The honorary title did not carry the obligation of residence, for Count John, going to fulfil its functions, took the proverbial "schoolboy's road." He left Sweden in 1771, and went in the first instance to the Brunswick Military School at Turin, sojourning for some time afterwards at Strasburg.

He then visited several countries, and in the course of his peregrinations he had an opportunity of meeting a man whose unequalled celebrity had made him popular throughout the whole of Europe, and who certainly deserved that a traveller should turn aside from his direct road, if it were only to obtain a glimpse of him. Voltaire, in his retirement at Ferney, enjoyed the renown which is rarely accorded to a great man until after his death. He was both clever and lucky. Although he was a very middling poet, his tragedies were applauded to the echo; although he was occasionally a superficial writer, his slightest productions were discussed and praised, and he had contrived to secure concurrently the dislike, the admiration, and the friendship of the greatest personages of his day, in proportions admirably calculated to spread his fame.

Posterity, which frequently pulls down those who have been highly favoured by their contemporaries, has not been too hard upon Voltaire, and illustrious writers have judged him with the serene impartiality of genius. It will not be out of place here to recall Lamartine's remarks in *L'Histoire des Girondins:*—

"Voltaire possessed the genius of criticism,

the mocking negation that blights all that it overthrows. He had made human nature laugh at itself; he had struck it down to raise it up again; he had displayed before it all the prejudices, all the errors, all the iniquities, all the crimes of ignorance; he had driven it into insurrection against established ideas, not by enthusiasm for the future, but by scorn of the past. Destiny had given him eighty years of life in which to decompose the old world slowly; he had had time to fight against time, and when he fell it was as a conqueror. Courts, Academies, and Salons were peopled by his disciples."

This was true, and were a proof of its truth needed, where should we find one more convincing than the following remarks of a contemporary whose turn of mind and intellectual culture were all unlike, indeed opposed to, the genius of the terrible jester?

The Comte de Ségur met Voltaire one day at his mother's house, and he records the impression made upon him in an almost lyrical passage.

"When I saw Voltaire, he realised my ideal portrait of him. His meagre frame bore the traces of his life of labour; his antique and singular costume reminded me that he was the last survivor of the age of Louis XIV., the historian of that century, and the immortal painter of Henri IV. His piercing eye glittered with genius and satire; in its glance one recognised the tragic poet, the author of *Œdipe* and *Mahomet*, the profound philosopher, the acute and ingenious narrator, the witty and satirical observer of mankind; his slender bent body was but a thin, almost transparent covering, through which his soul and his genius shone. I was filled with pleasure and admiration."

What enthusiasm concerning a man who never felt any! And how simple-minded young Ségur must have been to praise in such terms "the author of *Œdipe* and *Mahomet*," and to call the maker of bad rhymes who had written *La Henriade* "the immortal painter of Henri IV."!

It is amusing to compare the few lines which Count John Axel Fersen devotes to the great man on the occasion of his visit to Ferney, with the foregoing effusion. There is none of the young Frenchman's poetry in those lines; the calm, observant mind of the young Swede is completely manifested in the simplicity of his narrative and in the moderation of his sentiments.

Count Fersen, being at Geneva with his "governor," Bolemanny, on the 30th of October 1771, took advantage of the opportunity to obtain a sight of "the man of the age." M. Constant, an intimate friend of Voltaire, gave the two gentlemen a letter of introduction; this, however, did not do much for them: on presenting themselves at the philosopher's pretty house they were refused admittance. The master had "taken medicine." He habitually resorted to this pretext when he did not wish to receive visits; he might have found a better, but the matter was too small for consideration by so great a mind.

The travellers had to wait until the morrow, " and thus we were obliged to remain one day more," remarks Fersen in his Journal.

Were they compensated for this alteration in their plan by the pleasure they derived from the visit when it did come off? It would seem, at least in so far as Fersen was concerned, that his curiosity only was satisfied. His brief record of the incident manifests no enthusiasm :—

"We were received at the appointed time, and we talked with him for two hours. He was dressed in a scarlet vest with embroidered button-holes; no doubt, his father and grandfather had worn it. An old wig, not curled; shoes after the antique; woollen stockings rolled up over his breeches, and an old dressing-gown completed his toilet. It harmonised admirably with his deeply wrinkled face; but we were struck by the beauty of his eyes and the vivacity of his expression. The face, taken as a whole, is entirely satirical.

"He has in his house Père Adam, a Jesuit, and his valet, who knows all his master's library by heart. M. de Voltaire does a great deal of good in his village; he collects all the clockmakers from Geneva, and allows them to work at his house; the part in which he had set up a theatre being now converted into a series of lodging-rooms which he has placed at their disposal. He has also provided for their immediate needs."

This is all. John Fersen was evidently not thinking either of the writer or the philosopher while writing these lines. He did not recognise either in the man.

From Geneva he had proceeded to Turin, where he was presented to the King, "a little, wrinkled old fellow, walking with the help of a cane," who advised him "to profit diligently by the teaching of the Academy."

Passing by way of Milan, he saw the Arch-Duke, who "talked to him for a whole quarter of an hour." This did not prevent his recording that "the number of visitors who formerly stopped here has greatly diminished," and that "visitors, wanting to escape from the trouble of a presentation at Court, which involves three days' formalities at least, hasten away from Milan so soon as they have seen its curiosities; a custom not amusing for the Milanese."

The traveller cared little for any of these things; his eager desire was to reach France. At last, on the 1st of January 1774, he was present at the Mass of the Holy Ghost, and he paid a visit to Mme. du Barry.

These two duties—unequally prescribed by moral rules and those of etiquette—accomplished, the young Count was free to do as he liked. We have seen how he used his freedom, and what were the events, very small in appearance, but big with consequences, which marked his sojourn in Paris and at Versailles.

He left Paris on the 12th of May, arrived in London on the 26th, and remained in England four months. His impressions are influenced by the comparison with his recollections of France which he was constrained to institute.

He was presented to Queen Charlotte, who

received him graciously; but he remarked that "she was not at all pretty."

He was not charmed by English "high life," in which he naturally moved, owing to his social relations. The French, he observed, would protest, while amusing themselves, that they were bored, while the English, although really bored to extinction, said nothing.

He was taken by Count X. to Almack's. To his great surprise, he saw all the ladies seated on benches to the right and left of a wide gallery, waiting for the men—who preferred remaining at their clubs as late as possible—and they were not even talking among themselves.

The supper was less dull than the rest. Perhaps this more favourable impression may be attributed to the fact that Fersen was seated by the side of one of the handsomest girls in London, "who talked pleasantly with him." But when a few days afterwards he met her again and addressed her politely, "she did not even answer him."[1]

[1] The entry in Count Fersen's Journal relating to this incident is as follows:—

"*Thursday, 19th May* 1774.—I have been presented to the Queen, who is very gracious and amiable, but not at all pretty. In the evening I was taken by Comte —— to Almack's, a subscription ball which is held during the winter. The room in which they dance is well arranged and brilliantly lighted. The ball is supposed to begin at ten o'clock, but the men remain at their clubs until half-past eleven. During this time the women are kept waiting, seated on sofas on either side of the great gallery in great formality; one would fancy oneself in a church, they look so serious and quiet, not even talking amongst themselves. The supper, which is at twelve o'clock, is very well served,

What a difference between this sort of thing and Parisian society! We may safely conclude that when he returned to Sweden at the beginning of 1775, of all his recollections, that of his meetings with the Dauphiness was the most vivid and the sweetest, and that it remained in his memory a gleam of light. Did not after events prove that so it was with him?

During his absence grave events had occurred in France. A demise of the crown had taken place, the Dauphin was now Louis XVI., and the domino who had so prettily puzzled Count Fersen one evening at a masked ball at the Opera was Queen of France.

and somewhat less dull than the rest of the entertainment. I was placed by the side of Lady Carpenter,* one of the handsomest girls in London; she was very agreeable, and conversed a great deal. I had occasion to meet her again some days later, when, to some civil remark I addressed her with, she did not even reply. It surprises one to see young girls talking unreservedly with men, and going about by themselves; I am reminded of Lusanne in this, where also they enjoy complete liberty."—*Translator's Note.*

---

* Lady Almeria Carpenter, daughter of Lord Tyrconnel.

CHAPTER II.

Count John in Sweden—Gustavus III.—The Count's second visit to France—The Queen recognises him and is pleased at seeing him again—Mutual liking—Count Creutz's despatch to the King of Sweden—A project of marriage attributed to Count Fersen—Mdlle. de Leijel—He starts for America.

ON his return to his own country, Count Fersen found himself obliged by his position to lead the idle and futile life of a courtier.

The King of Sweden, being full of the memory of Louis XIV., was exclusively bent upon imitating "the great monarch," and as imitation of him in big things was out of the power of Gustavus, he fell back upon little things, endeavouring by display, entertainments, and prodigality, to reproduce the splendour of the "Sun-King" in his chilly realm.

Such a life could not be pleasing to Count Fersen, perhaps not only because it was idle, and out of harmony with his tastes, but also because his travels in other lands had introduced him to other modes of existence, and he now had new ideas and aspirations.

How could he fail to regret France, and, with France, all that had contributed to make the time he had passed there the most agreeable period of his life?

He might, however, have expected that his King would share his admiration for her who occupied so large a place in his mind, in anticipation of the time when she was to be deeply rooted in his heart.

Gustavus III. had been in France; he had seen the Dauphiness; but—a strange thing—no sympathy had been felt by one for the other. Quite the contrary, indeed; there was nothing to indicate that the future would one day contradict the past, and that of all the sovereigns of Europe the King of Sweden would be the most generous, ardent, and chivalrous champion of the cause of Marie Antoinette.

But this disinterested sentiment, which arose from an innately lofty, rather than a modern, conception of the rights and the duties of princes, had not yet been awakened. Gustavus, who was at that time Crown Prince (he received the intelligence of the death of his father on the 1st of March 1771, while he was in Paris), had excited only a certain amount of curiosity. He was of middle height, had dull blue eyes, and did not make a "success." He talked readily, and indeed too much; he was polite rather than affable, and was supposed to be indifferent to the charms of the fair sex. Now, women really care only for men who care for them. Notwithstanding his cold reception, Gustavus professed a warm admiration for France. The ignominy of the later years of Louis XV. had not destroyed the supremacy which our country, strong in the great memories of its might and majesty in the past, and still stronger in the glorious expectation of its future destinies, maintained over the whole world. Rosbach had not effaced

Fontenoy. Gustavus III. regarded Count Fersen's wish to return to fair France as quite natural, and, Sweden being in the enjoyment of profound peace, he could safely consent to the absence of the young gentleman who had become captain "attached" to the King's Light Horse. His Majesty therefore confirmed the paternal permission, and Count Fersen retraced his steps towards France with the utmost alacrity.

He arrived in the middle of August 1778. Three years had elapsed. The Count did not indeed suppose that he had been altogether forgotten, but he was not prepared for the welcome that awaited him. He proceeded at once to Versailles, and had himself presented to the royal family as though this were his first appearance at Court. A voice exclaimed, "Ah, an old acquaintance!"[1]

Marie Antoinette had recognised him. We may conceive the pleasure with which Count John received this precious token of royal kindness. A courtier would have been overwhelmed with joy: he was a man of feeling, and it touched him deeply. The grace of the Queen's spontaneous recognition was enhanced by his speedy conviction that it was not due to the caprice of the moment or the hazard of a fortunate meeting. The Queen took pleasure in giving him some daily token of her regard. He informs his father of this with delight.

"The Queen, the prettiest and the most

---

[1] He adds, in his account of this incident to his father, "The rest of the royal family did not say a word."

amiable princess whom I know," he writes on the 8th of September, "has had the goodness to make frequent inquiry for me; she asked Creutz why I do not come to her reception (*jeu*)[1] on Sundays, and having been told that I did go, on a day when the reception did not take place, she made me a kind of apology."

Their mutual relation was no longer as it had been during the Count's first visit, kindly, with a touch of familiarity on the occasion of the masked ball; it had become almost intimate. The Queen and the Count met very often. She, whom Mme. du Barry called "the little redhead," now Queen of France, had lost her youthful shyness, and being less restrained in her sayings and doings, she made no secret of her liking for amusement; and at the risk of horrifying the Comtesse de Noailles, whom she jestingly nicknamed "Madame l'Etiquette," she gave herself up to the joy of living, and asked no better than to lead the life of a mere *bourgeoise*, far from the obligations of the Court, and free from the boredom of supreme rank.

This was easy for Marie Antoinette, because she now possessed a retreat in which she might lay aside her greatness and escape from tiresome folk. The King, awkwardly kind and clumsily gallant, had made her a present on New Year's Day, 1774. "You love flowers?" he said to the astonished Queen. "Well, then, I have a bouquet to give you: it is the Little Trianon."

[1] Trictrac, quinze, and billiards was played at *le jeu de la Reine*.

Thenceforth, Marie Antoinette, being free to select her own society, began little by little to indulge in fancies, which, although very natural on the part of a young woman, could not fail to expose a Queen of France to adverse criticism.

The representatives of the old French families were shocked by her ways—even her habit of according a ready welcome to foreigners offended them; but what did she care? It was so pleasant to have friends and not mere courtiers about her, or only—for she was not apt at discerning the difference—courtiers whom she took to be friends.

Fersen was certainly one of the most favoured of this limitedly-intimate circle. Encouraged by Marie Antoinette herself, " the most amiable princess whom he knows," he attended her receptions frequently, and on each occasion she noticed his presence, and addressed him with graceful and gracious kindness, by which he was profoundly affected.

One day somebody alluded before the Queen to the Swedish uniform of the young captain of Light Horse; she immediately took a fancy to see him in that costume, and expressed her wish. A few days afterwards Fersen, happy to obey her, appeared in the private apartments wearing his handsome uniform.

He attended the *soirées intimes* at Trianon, and figured at the fêtes given in honour of the Queen by Mme. de Lamballe and Mme. de Polignac.

By degrees the intimacy between Marie

Antoinette and Count John increased; notwithstanding his reserve and his apparently cold nature, it was evident that his admiration had given place to a more tender feeling. Fersen was deeply in love with the Queen.

She, whose imprudence had kindled the flame, was neither frightened nor surprised. She liked to see the young Swede; she knew he loved her, and she was not displeased; nay, more, touched by the sentiment she had inspired, she came very near to returning it; how could she fail to be moved by a passion so profound, so discreet, so respectful? Her heart was softened, and many signs betrayed the young Queen's predilection for the adorer who dared not tell his love, to the sharp eyes of some of her familiar associates.

One day, when she was singing to her harpsichord, Fersen was by her side, and she was betrayed by her own music into an avowal which song made easy. Her eyes sought the Count's while her voice uttered the passionate words of some fashionable opera, and his ill-disguised emotion emphasised an evident allusion.[1]

Less than this would have sufficed to gain the credit of a royal "*bonne fortune*" for the brilliant Swedish officer. Did he not possess

---

[1] M. Geoffroy states, in his *Gustave III. et la Cour de France*, that Count Fersen's friend and travelling companion, Stedingk, was also received in the Queen's intimate circle. The compromising couplet of the above anecdote was the following, from the now-forgotten opera of "Didon":—

"Ah! que je fus bien inspirée
Quand je vous reçus dans ma cour."

—*Translator's Note.*

all the attributes of a hero of romance, and had not she, who was thenceforth regarded as his "conquest," an excuse in advance of the fact for yielding to the promptings of her heart? The beautiful young Queen had found neither the majesty of a king nor the affection of a husband in her consort, and the personal relations of the royal couple were well known.

From the first, Marie Antoinette, whose womanly pride was hurt by the Dauphin's indifference to her, formed a "poor notion (*mince idée*) of the character and intellect of her husband." M. de Mercy, who transmitted this impression to the Empress Maria Theresa, wrote that in his opinion her daughter's notion of Louis was too poor; but was he a good judge, and would he not have agreed with the young Princess afterwards if he had seen the King elsewhere than at the solemn function of a reception of the Austrian ambassador? If he could have read the journal of the personage whom Marie Antoinette once called "poor man!" he would have been convinced, and forced to recognise that her estimate of her husband was just. What is to be thought of a prince who, in the very month of his marriage, finds nothing more sentimental or interesting to set down than the following :—

Sunday, 13.—*Left Versailles. Supped and slept at Compiègne at the house of M. de Saint Florentin.*
Monday, 14.—*Interview with Madame la Dauphine.*
Tuesday, 15.—*Supped at La Muette. Slept at Versailles.*
Wednesday, 16.—*My marriage. Apartment in the gallery. Royal banquet in the Salle d'Opéra.*
Thursday, 17.—*Opera of Perseus.*

Friday, 18. — *Stag hunt. Meet at La Belle Image.* *Took one.*
Saturday, 19. — *Dress-ball in the Salle d'Opéra. Fireworks.*

The month's chronicle ends with this characteristic record :—

31.—*I had an indigestion.*

For seven years, Marie Antoinette's sole wifely privilege was the beholding of her stupid husband as he ate, drank, hunted, and did his locksmith's work. Is it to be wondered at that she was wounded to the heart by such extraordinary indifference, and that she sometimes allowed bitter and sarcastic words to escape her lips; for instance, when she impatiently answered one of her ladies, who urged her not to go out riding—

"For God's sake, leave me in peace, and know once for all that I am not endangering an heir!"

The following passage from a letter written at this period by the Queen to the Comte de Rosenberg Orsini throws a strong light upon the feelings of the neglected wife:—"I shall never trouble myself about the stories that go to Vienna," she writes, "so long as you are told of them. You know Paris and Versailles; you have seen and judged. If·I had to excuse myself, I should readily confide in you; indeed, I would candidly acknowledge more than you say; for instance, that my tastes are not the same as those of the King, who cares only for hunting and blacksmith's work. You will admit that I should not show to advantage in a forge.

I could not appear there as Vulcan, and the part of Venus might displease him even more than my tastes, which, however, he does not dislike."

The result of such a situation, so prolonged, was that, when Louis XVI., yielding to the remonstrances of his brother-in-law, the Emperor of Austria, and comprehending at length that he owed it to the crown of France to give it an heir, became the husband of his wife, it was too late for him to gain her affection. Her heart was still to be won, and the prize fell to Fersen.

But, at the very moment when he might regard himself as the fortunate winner of a woman and a queen, well accustomed to homage, and to whom vows, far less discreet and respectful than those of the Swedish gentleman, were offered, Fersen proved, by his absolute devotion and self-abnegation, how worthy he was to inspire such a sentiment.

Calumny had already been busy with Marie Antoinette, who was doubly exposed to its malice by her position as a neglected wife, and by the free and independent ways which her life at Trianon facilitated. These attacks had hitherto been vague; we may therefore guess how glad the enemies of the Queen were when distinct indications and real facts enabled them to speed their darts with a truer aim.

Every day of her life the Queen was under the scrutiny of eyes sharpened by curiosity, jealousy, or enmity; she could not keep her dangerous secret, and her preference for the noble foreigner soon became the common topic of her calumniators.

In this state of things the pregnancy of the Queen was announced, and immediately became the subject of malicious insinuations. The cabal, led by the Comte de Provence, who hated his sister-in-law with brotherly hate, thenceforward pursued its abominable task of foul-mouthed slander with increased energy. Why should it have laid down arms? Had not the heir-presumptive, the natural supporter of the throne, bestowed his powerful patronage upon calumny by casting the most offensive accusation that could be brought against her upon the young mother, in the Cathedral of Notre Dame itself, at the baptism of her infant daughter, Marie Thérèse?

The King of Spain was the godfather of the newly-born princess, but the Comte de Provence acted as his Majesty's proxy, and presented her at the baptismal font. The Grand Almoner, who officiated, having asked what name was to be given to the child, Monsieur answered: "But we don't begin by that; the first thing is to know who are the father and mother." The sardonic tone in which these words were spoken gave them emphasis that could not escape anybody's attention; and besides, they were let fall on well-prepared ground!

Fersen was far too observant not to see what was passing around him, too clear-sighted not to feel that his presence was harmful to the Queen. Then did he prove himself chivalrous enough to save her, and heroic enough to do this at the cost of the hardest of sacrifices.

There was only one way in which he could

give the evil-speakers the lie; it was by absenting himself from the Queen, from the Court, from Paris, Versailles, France. And to prevent his departure itself from being malignantly interpreted, he would have to find a motive lofty enough to appear natural, and sufficiently plausible to appear spontaneous.

Circumstances strangely favoured his generous plan. The struggle between Great Britain and her colonies had just begun. France, already feeling the impulse of her great destiny, thrilled at the mere words " Independence " and "Liberty." Enthusiasm was aroused among all classes; it was of a strangely blind kind among the nobility, while the enthusiasm of the people was a perhaps unconscious instinct. That aid and succour should be carried to the "brothers" in America was the demand of all, and as the oppressors were the English, always regarded as the enemies of our nation, there was nothing to check the general impulse.

Count John Axel Fersen announced his approaching departure for America, and begged to be enrolled in one of the corps formed by Lafayette and Rochambeau. This brave resolution had its dangers also, for it shed a lustre round him who was capable of forming it. Marie Antoinette, deeply touched by so great a sacrifice, was no more able to hide her sorrow than to conceal her attachment from the persons about her. While the latter rejoiced that they were to be rid of the object of their envy, the Queen could not put such restraint upon herself as to look upon the friend whom she was about to lose, it might be for ever, with composure, and her grief, sincere and deep, betrayed itself by her irrepressible tears.

Fersen, firm in his purpose, resolutely advanced its realisation, and the moment soon arrived when he was to leave Paris to join the corps to which he was attached at Brest. He could not go away without apprising his father and his sovereign: they learned the fact from himself, but it was another who informed them of the true reason.

The fate of queens, whose greatness forbids them even to weep in privacy, is sad. It is through a diplomatic "act," by an ambassador's letter preserved among the papers of Gustavus III. in the archives at Upsala, that history is now placed in possession of the secrets of a royal woman's heart. What does it matter? They do her no discredit.

On the 10th of April 1779, Count Creutz addressed the following secret despatch to the King of Sweden :—

"I must confide to your Majesty that the young Count Fersen has been so well received by the Queen, that several persons have taken umbrage. I own that I cannot help thinking she has a liking for him; I have seen indications of this too certain to be doubted. The young Count has behaved, under these circumstances, with admirable modesty and reserve, and his going to America is especially to be commended. By absenting himself he avoids danger of all kinds; but it evidently required firmness beyond his years to resist such an attraction. During the last days of his stay, the Queen could not take her eyes off him, and as she looked they were full of tears. I entreat your Majesty to keep their secret for yourself and Senator Fersen.[1]

"When the approaching departure of the Count was made known, all the favourites were delighted.

"'*How is this, Monsieur?*' said the Duchesse de Fitz-James, '*you forsake your conquest!*' '*Had I made one,*' he replied, '*I should not forsake it; I go away free, and unfortunately without leaving any regrets.*'

"Your Majesty will own that the Count's answer was wise and prudent beyond his years. The Queen, moreover, behaves with much more self-restraint and prudence than formerly. The King not only entirely complies with her wishes, but shares her tastes and her pleasures."[2]

It was just at this time that a project of marriage between John Fersen and Mdlle. de Leigel, the daughter of a Swedish noble who was naturalised in England, and lived in London, was entertained. The match would have been suitable, for the young lady inherited the fortune of two of her uncles, who were members of the East India Company.

Although John Fersen had corresponded with his father on this matter, and the latter had approved, it would seem that things did not go very far. Fersen probably lent himself to

---

[1] The father of Count John.
[2] *Gustave III. et la Cour de France*, par M. Geoffroy.

the project, in order to have it believed that he was not averse to marriage; but that he was not in earnest about it is proved by the fact that he went away to America without coming to any conclusion, and during his absence Mdlle. de Leigel married one of her new-made countrymen.

This episode, which is revealed by the Count's correspondence, does not appear to have been known in France at the time. At all events, it occasioned him neither solicitude nor regret.

For the second time Fersen bade adieu to France; but under what conditions? We admire Titus and Berenice for immolating their love to a policy which prohibited it. Why should we not admire these two who sacrificed a pure and lofty sentiment to one still higher, and who likewise parted *invictus, invicta?*

CHAPTER III.

The English colonies in America—The heavy yoke of England—The first upheaval—Washington—Enthusiasm in France—Franklin—Count John Fersen is attached to the expedition as aide-de-camp to M. de Rochambeau—He leaves Paris—From Brest to Newport—Incidents—The Duc de Lauzun—Interview between M. de Rochambeau and Washington—General Arnold's treason—The feeling among the insurgent population — Spies — Williamsburg — The capitulation of Lord Cornwallis (19th October 1781)—Philadelphia—The approaching peace—Count Fersen leaves America—Boston—Porto Cabello—Return to France (June 1783).

Towards the middle of the year 1773, the town of Boston became strangely disturbed. The East India Company, being encumbered with a great quantity of tea, sent several ships carrying cargoes to that port from London. Now, the English colonies in America had pledged themselves to use no more English merchandise in consequence of certain disputes with the metropolis. At the sight of the ships the population rose, and gave vent to their indignation; while fishermen, disguised as Indian "braves," and urged on by the crowd, boarded the vessels, seized upon the chests of tea, stove them in, and flung them with their contents into the sea.

The English Government heard with amazement of this violent resistance to their will. Lord North immediately had a bill passed closing the port of Boston, and depriving the province of Massachusetts of the right to appoint its own magistrates.

Intimidation was of no avail. The metropolis resists? So be it. The Colony accepted conflict but not chastisement, proclaimed itself in insurrection, and appealed to the neighbouring States. The latter approved of the conduct of Massachusetts, and the Congress of Philadelphia (September 1774) formed the union of all against the claims of England.

This was the prelude to hostilities. England ought to have been prepared for the course of events. Her American colonies were not like her other dependencies, and it was easy to predict that they would be by no means disposed to accept the fate of the unhappy natives of Hindostan. These colonies had been founded by well-to-do and well-educated Puritans, who had not left their native land to seek their fortune, but in order to enjoy the religious liberty which England denied them, and they had no notion of enduring oppression from the mother country, which to them had never been a mother, and had now almost ceased to be a country.

The result of the Boston incident and the Philadelphia Congress was that the thirteen provinces formed a confederation, under the grand name of the United States. They then had the supreme good fortune to find a man who was equally able as a politician and capable as a general, and he, combining all its powers, became the soul of the revolt. A great soul, if ever one existed, was George Washington.

In the meantime, the revolted provinces sent

forth appeals to all generous spirits the whole
world over, while negotiating secretly with the
enemies of England. We know there never was
a lack of the latter; so that Europe, while caring
but little about the colonies in insurrection, but
very glad to injure Great Britain, hastened to
lend her moral support to the new United
States. France placed herself in the van of this
movement.

It is difficult for us to realise nowadays the
enthusiasm which our nation felt and proved for
the cause of "these Spartan Protestants"—more
Protestant than Spartan, by the way. Not only
did the populace espouse the cause of the rebels,
but the "noblesse," being desirous of effacing
the disgrace of the last war and the humiliation
of the Treaty of 1763, bestirred themselves, and
many of them proclaimed their readiness to start
on this novel kind of crusade. Such being the
disposition of all classes, the public mind was
puzzled by the undeniably logical opposition of
Louis XVI. and his brother-in-law, Joseph II.,
who was then in France. There were persons
who were actually astonished at this, and even
said so.

"But, Madame, it is my business to be a
royalist," was Joseph's reply to one of these
persons. The sweet reasonableness of this
humorous rejoinder, made by a sovereign, was
not fully understood. On the other hand, when
Franklin appeared, the general enthusiasm knew
no bounds. Everybody wanted to see him, to
speak to him, to admire him at close quarters.
He produced a favourable impression.

"I was very young when I saw the illustrious Franklin," writes the Duc de Lévis; "but the candour and nobility of his face, and his beautiful white hair, I shall never forget."

Anybody who discovered "candour" in Franklin must indeed have been very young. He was an ardent patriot, he neglected nothing that could be of utility to his country, and he contributed to the success of its cause, but not by methods remarkable for frankness. On the contrary, Franklin displayed consummate skill, extreme acuteness, and his simplicity was too much studied ever to be candid. He prepared everything, even to the smallest details of costume, or, so to speak, scenery and stage management, with sedulous care, and if he appeared amid the elegant and refined society of that period in the plainest attire and with unpowdered hair, he did so because he desired everything about him to attract attention, as a means, he believed, of securing sympathy.

The French Government, under the pressure of public opinion, signed a Treaty of Commerce with the United States, which soon became a Treaty of Alliance (6th February 1778), and after this it had no right to oppose the departure of any Frenchmen who wished to go to America with the intention of helping the cause of independence by their swords.

Lafayette had already set out. A new corps was in process of formation under the command of Rochambeau, and Count Fersen had asked leave to join it.

The thing was not done without difficulty. In fact, a considerable number of gentlemen solicited the favour of accompanying the corps about to depart; but what could be done with them? They were not required as officers—they were not on the strength; accordingly, the requests of most of them were refused.

Fersen had better fortune. Owing to the reputation of his father, who, as we know, had formerly taken service in France, and also to the support of M. de Vergennes, obstacles were smoothed away for him, and better still, Rochambeau consented to attach him to his personal staff as aide-de-camp, to the great joy of the recipient of so marked a favour.

It was no easy matter in those days to transport, not to say an army, but even a troop of any numerical importance to America. The voyage might be long, the vessels being at the mercy of the winds; and then there was the risk of meeting the English fleet, which was cruising in the seas to prevent the arrival of European reinforcements. Rochambeau's command numbered 7000 men; the force was to muster and embark at Brest. The departure was fixed for the beginning of April, from the 1st to the 4th.

Among those who, like the fortunate young Swede, had obtained leave to accompany the expedition, was the brilliant and almost famous Duc de Lauzun, equally renowned for his love adventures and distinguished by his birth. He was of a daring and versatile disposition, and after having served with distinction in America, he went wrong, but made a good end. It was the strange destiny of this noble Duke to become a republican general and to die on the scaffold.

At this juncture there was no foreshadowing of such a future for him, and the war, in which he took part, gave him an opportunity of displaying all his qualities; hearty good-humour and sprightliness in the first instance, and distinguished gallantry so soon as it was called for.

He has drawn amusing sketches of some of his comrades. A sketch of his chief and the officers of his staff deserves to be reproduced at this point.

"M. de Rochambeau, major in command of the vanguard, talked of nothing but war, manœuvred, and occupied positions in the open, in the room, on the table, on your snuff-box if you took it out of your pocket. He is exclusively occupied with his business, and understands it thoroughly.

"M. de Caraman, dressed to the pitch of perfection, soft-spoken, fidgety, stopped everybody in the street whose coat was buttoned awry, and gave them little military lessons with an air of interest; he was an excellent officer, highly informed and active.

"M. Wall, major, an old Irish officer, was very like Harlequin, with the addition of humour, liked good eating, drank punch all day, said that everybody was right, and did not meddle in anything.

"M. de Crussol, major, had a crooked neck, and not too straight a mind."

The other generals were the Marquis de Jaucourt and the Marquis de Viomesnil, the latter a very indifferent officer. The other two were more meritorious, or at least had a better reputation.

The convoy, prepared to carry the troops, was to be escorted by twelve vessels accompanied by an adequate number of frigates, and placed under the command of M. Duchaffand. But the delays inevitable in such a case prevented the sailing of the convoy on the appointed day; moreover, of the 7683 men mustered for embarkation, only 5088 could be taken on board the ships in the port; 2595 had to be left in France. Thus the small force under command of M. de Rochambeau was seriously reduced "by the negligence and ineptitude with which everything is now done in this country," adds Count Fersen.

The convoy fleet numbered only seven vessels instead of twelve. Rochambeau, with his aide-de-camp of longest standing, sailed in the *Duc de Bourgogne*, a great ship of eighty guns. Fersen embarked on the *Jason*, Lauzun on the *Provence*. The expedition carried a great deal of artillery, a considerable siege train, and victuals for eight months.

On the 4th of May, one month after date, the anchors were lifted and the fleet sailed. The voyage was tedious. From Brest, the convoy proceeded to the Gulf of Gascony, where it encountered a gale, then doubled Cape

Finistère, to the north-west of Spain. In sight of the cape, Fersen wrote the following short note to his father :—

> "*At Sea, 16th of May (Monday)* 1780,
> *On board the Jason, in sight of Finistère.*

"I have only time to write a few words, to tell you that I am well. I have not suffered from the sea. We have already had rough weather, which dismasted one of our vessels. The wind is fair, and I think we may reach America in forty days. We have just seen a large ship very far off; we do not know whether it is a friend or an enemy. I have no time to write more."

The fleet kept on its course towards the south until the 27° of latitude, then steered to the west. On the 20th of June, off the Bermudas, it sighted five English vessels and a frigate, and they exchanged fire for two hours, but at a great distance, so that the hostilities were harmless. The night separated the combatants; at dawn the English ships had disappeared.

The French fleet was preparing to land in Chesapeake Bay, and on the 4th of July was within fifteen leagues of the mouth of the bay, when eleven ships hove in sight, evidently meaning mischief.

It would have been mad to risk a fight, and almost certain destruction to the troops under convoy; therefore the commander immediately ordered the ships' course to be changed, and steered towards the north. Seven days afterwards, the fleet anchored in the harbour of

Rhode Island, and the landing was effected in the island of Newport. This was accomplished only just in time. Shortly afterwards twenty sail appeared, and the newly landed troops were blockaded.

The story of the War of Independence does not come within the scope of this work; its purpose is only to record, in its proper place, the part which Fersen played, and the impressions made upon him; and to this effect his correspondence must be largely drawn upon.

The French set to work at once to form a camp at Newport and to surround it with earthworks. Strict discipline was maintained, and, as always happens at the beginning, the army treasure-chest and the soldiers' purses being well furnished, the inhabitants were paid in ready money for all the provisions purchased from them. "The discipline is admirable," remarks Fersen; "it fairly astonishes the natives, who are accustomed to being pillaged by the English troops and their own."

Although the blockading fleet had gone away, the French had apparently no chance of an immediate transfer to the mainland, and the prospect of passing the winter at Newport was not attractive.

"You know the French, my dear father," writes Count John, "and what are called Court-people well enough to imagine the dismay with which our young fellows of that class contemplate the prospect of a quiet winter at Newport, far from their mistresses and the pleasures of Paris—no suppers, no plays, no balls! They are in despair; nothing short of an order to march against the enemy can console them.

"This is a charming country, with a superb climate. We went to the mainland a week ago with the General. I was the only one of his aides-de-camp who accompanied him. We stayed two days, and we saw the fairest land in the world, well cultivated, with beautiful sites, well-to-do inhabitants, but without lavishness or show; they are satisfied with a scale of living which in other countries is adopted by a less elevated class; their clothing is simple but good, and their morals and manners have not yet been spoiled by European luxury. It is a country which would be very happy if it might enjoy a long period of peace, and if the two parties by which it is now divided did not inflict the fate of Poland and that of so many other republics upon it. These two parties are called 'Whigs' and 'Tories.'"

It is evident that Fersen was led into the error, common to all travellers, of supposing himself capable of forming a sound judgment of a nation at first sight, after he had passed two months in a small island off the coast, and two days on the mainland. He afterwards learned the wisdom of distrusting his first impressions.

In the meantime hostilities had begun with varying fortunes. Fersen sent all news to his father. General Gates had been beaten by Lord Cornwallis, and nothing was said about going to the assistance of the defeated commander. Far from this, indeed, action was deferred until the arrival of the second division —that of the men left at Brest. And so "the garrison of Newport began to be very dull and depressed."

However dull the duty may have been, thanks to the industry characteristic of the French, the garrison found means to cheat the demon of ennui to some extent. Lauzun was not of Fersen's opinion. He made no secret of this, and when he had to go over to the mainland, Rochambeau having ascertained that the resources of Newport were not sufficient, received his orders from his chief with a touch of melancholy.

"The want of forage obliged him to send me into the wilds of Connecticut, eighty miles away. . . . I did not leave Newport without regret; I had found very agreeable society there."

He evidently included Count Fersen, his comrade in arms; the two were on very intimate terms. Between these two admirers of Marie Antoinette—admirers with the difference arising as much from their characters as from their nationality — there were points in common. The young Swede had been attracted by the sprightliness and graceful manners of the Duke.

"Opinions are divided respecting him," wrote Fersen to his father; "you will hear both good and evil said of him. Those who speak well of him are right, the others are wrong. He has formed a friendship with me, and asks me, in the frankest way in the world, to accept the post of colonel-commandant of his legion. . . . The Duc de Lauzun has written on the subject to the Queen, who shows him great kindness, as she does to me also. I, too, am writing to her about this."

Of course he eagerly seized upon such a pretext, which was a welcome relief to him, but not sufficient to dispel his ennui. His inaction was beginning to weigh upon him, and the whole of the little army felt as he did. There was too much difference between that which they had come to do, and that which they were doing. Fersen's calm and observant mind understood this, and his reflections on the subject are full of good sense.

"Far from being useful to the Americans," he writes, "we are a burden to them. We do not reinforce their army, for we are twelve days' march from it, separated by arms of the sea which it is impossible to pass in winter, when they are encumbered with floating ice. We are an expense to them, because, by increasing consumption, we make provisions more scarce, and by paying cash we depreciate their paper money, thereby depriving General Washington's army of the facility of procuring victuals, which the purveyors refuse to give for paper.

"Our condition is better than our position; we brought with us only two million six hundred thousand livres, one half in ready money and the rest in drafts on Mr. Holker, a banker in Philadelphia. We should have brought double that sum; the lack of specie in a country where one wants money in one's hand at every turn obliges us to practise great economy, while magnificence and profusion are required. This ruins our credit."

Besides, idleness is an evil counsellor. "The generals are not agreed among themselves. The whole army is discouraged by being left so long without doing anything" (16th October 1780).

The commander-in-chief was aware that such a state of things could not be indefinitely prolonged without danger, that it must be remedied as speedily as possible; but how was this to be done without aid in men and money from France? It was urgently necessary that he should inform the Government at once of the bad condition of affairs and the necessities of the moment In order to do this, Rochambeau determined to detach a frigate from the fleet, and to send a trustworthy officer to bear his just demands to the King and his Ministers.

Every officer of any exceptional importance in the expeditionary corps cherished a secret unspoken hope that he might be the one selected. Long months passed in idleness, and the prospect of a winter equally devoid of occupation, rendered such a desire more than excusable. The best of it was that each believed himself to be the chosen emissary. Fersen makes no concealment on that point.

"Everybody names me," he writes; "several of the general officers, M. de Chatelux and Baron de Viomesnil, have spoken of me as one fitted to carry out the intentions of the General in this matter. I do not know what the result will be, but I shall take no step to influence it, neither shall I refuse the proposal if the General should make it to me. Nevertheless, I would rather not be charged with this task. Something interesting might happen during my absence, and I should be in despair at having missed it."

Lauzun, too, states in his Memoirs that his name was put forward. Perhaps those two were not the only candidates. In any case, they were all disappointed, and Rochambeau finally appointed his son. This was quite natural, for whatever may have been the confidence of the commander-in-chief in the other officers, he was still more sure of his son, and the communications with which the latter was charged were of the utmost gravity. In fact, Rochambeau had had an interview with Washington himself.

A meeting between the two generals had been arranged for the beginning of October at Hartford in Connecticut. The English must have been relying just then upon the winter to paralyse the movements of their enemies, for they do not appear to have watched the coming and going of the leaders at all closely. Rochambeau, accompanied by the Admiral, the commanding officer of engineers, his son, and two aides-de-camp, had not even an escort on his way from Newport to Hartford, a distance of forty leagues. Fersen, who was one of the two aides-de-camp selected, was sent in advance to announce the arrival of the French general, and thus he was the first to see Washington, the hero of Independence, who produced a profound impression upon the Count, as upon all who approached him. Fersen writes:—

"His face, handsome and majestic, but at the same time kind and gentle, completely corresponds with his moral qualities; he looks like a hero; he is very cold, and says little, but he is polite and frank. There is a sadness in his countenance which does not misbecome him, and renders him more interesting."

Washington had consumed three days in coming to Hartford, but as "he passed through a country filled with enemies," he had taken an escort. We cannot believe that these enemies were very numerous, for the escort was composed of only twenty-two dragoons, and no accident or unpleasant encounter befell the party. Yet this would have been a good opportunity for laying hold of the leaders of the revolt, for, in addition to Washington and Rochambeau, Lauzun was there; but, as Lauzun remarks in reference to the fact, "The English, throughout the whole course of that war, seemed to be struck with blindness; they always did what ought not to be done, and failed to avail themselves of the clearest and most certain advantages."

The three generals and the Admiral began their conference. Lafayette's presence was doubly useful, for he acted as interpreter. General Washington did not speak or understand French.

What passed during that interview? The

secret was well kept. All that can be related is, that the three parted well pleased with each other; "at least they say so," adds the cautious Swede.

That they should be pleased with each other was very natural—the energies of all were directed to the success of a common object; but it is doubtful whether they were content with the situation and with events. At this precise conjuncture they were informed of a formidable danger to which the cause of Independence had just been exposed.

General Arnold, one of the best officers in the American army, had turned traitor, and that his treachery was baffled before it had caused irreparable misfortune, was due solely to an extraordinary coincidence.

Arnold, who was brave to the point of heroism and bold to the point of temerity, had distinguished himself by deeds which had made him famous. Being ordered in 1775 to help Montgomery to take Quebec, he set out from Boston with a thousand men, plunged into uninhabitable country, and led his small force by an unknown route, in spite of innumerable obstacles, to the front of the city, arriving before Montgomery. No sooner had the latter joined him than the assault was attempted. The daring of their chiefs electrified the soldiery. The besiegers were, however, already weakened; a discharge of grapeshot killed Montgomery. Arnold rallied his troops, but was struck down by a ball which broke his leg. He was forced to retreat, and the valiant general, wounded, and exhausted by fatigue and pain, mustered the remnant of his little army and retired, beaten and glorious.

After such proofs of courage and patriotism, who could have doubted Arnold?

When a general was to be appointed to the command at Westpoint, Washington thought he could not do better than to select Arnold, and he gave him the post with entire confidence. Westpoint, which was one of the most important positions—so important that it has been called "the Gibraltar of America"—was a fort built upon a promontory that juts out into the Hudson, and commands the course of that river.

This citadel, in the neighbourhood of New York, was the centre of resistance, and regarded as impregnable. The English knew what an advantage it would be for them if it should fall into their hands, and as they could not take it by force, they tried stratagem. They have always known how to use with skill the aptly-named "cavalry of St. George," and indeed what is this but putting in practice the time-honoured axiom of Philip of Macedon, that "no place is impregnable if a mule laden with gold can be made to climb into it."

This must be a truth—true in all ages and in every country, since a traitor was found in Westpoint, and that traitor was Arnold! How was it that the commander of the English forces, Sir Henry Clinton, who was acquainted with the great reputation of the American general, ever ventured to reckon upon such a hero's being capable of such a "falling-off;" how could he believe the thing to be, if not feasible, at least possible? This would appear incredible did we not know what respect the Englishman professes for the power of gold, and what contempt for the weakness of conscience. At all events, the fact was that Sir Henry Clinton had directed one of his aides-de-camp, Major André, a brave and talented young officer—he was only twenty-four—to place himself in communication with Arnold.

Major André, holding that no task is unworthy of a soldier provided it be useful to his country, set to work at once with such success, that for eighteen months secret relations had been in existence between Clinton and Arnold.

What induced Arnold to listen to these proposals, and then to accept them? How did this brave man, who had so often risked his life for his country, allow himself to grow familiar with the idea of selling his country? We can answer only that herein lies a mystery of the human heart, which is more earthy than the body itself, and in which the mud sometimes comes to the surface, when regrets for useless sacrifices arise, and when unruly appetites for forbidden pleasures are awakened.

Arnold's resolution must have been very strong if it were never shaken for an instant during those eighteen months. The English had found their man: strange to say, they trusted this traitor, and the traitor remained true to them.

The goal was near. On the 21st of September

Major André got into Westpoint in the disguise of a peasant, and made the final arrangements with Arnold. The two accomplices had examined the fortifications, agreed upon points of attack, and simulated preparations for defence, so that the American general might withdraw without giving rise to suspicion. The crime was about to be consummated, when the Unforeseen, that unknown factor which thwarts the best-laid plans, brought the criminal compact to nought.

The *coup-de-théâtre* occurred in this wise. On the conclusion of the Hartford conference, Washington and Lafayette resolved to proceed to Westpoint, and they sent two aides-de-camp in advance to give General Arnold notice of their coming. The aides-de-camp presented themselves, and found Arnold at breakfast with his wife. They were invited to partake of the meal, and while the little party were talking, a messenger came in suddenly and handed a sealed note, sent by Arnold's subordinate, Lieutenant-Colonel Jameson, to the General. Arnold opened the paper, started, bent over his wife and whispered, "Farewell for ever." He went out, proceeded to his own room, collected a few things, had a horse saddled, desired one of his aides-de-camp to tell Washington that he was obliged to go away, but would return in an hour, mounted, and rode off at a gallop.

His wife had fainted. The two officers remained with her, doing all they could to restore her to consciousness, understanding nothing of what was passing, and unable to assign any cause for Mrs. Arnold's sudden swoon.

On this scene Washington and Lafayette arrived. The mystery of the flight of the General and the emotion of his wife was speedily cleared up.

What had happened was this. On leaving the fortress, Major André had gone towards the bank of the Hudson, where an English frigate was waiting to convey him away. But, to his great surprise, the sloop which had carried him from the frigate to the land was not at the appointed place. Both the frigate and the sloop had been forced to retire by the Westpoint guns, which were turned upon them, and had proceeded two leagues lower down the river. It had been impossible to inform Major André of this unavoidable departure from the plan of action. He sought about, came and went, all in vain, and finally determined to get to New York by land. He started immediately. The road was by no means safe for him; however, he happily avoided the American posts, and might have believed that he was safe, when he encountered some peasants, who, in spite of his disguise, or perhaps in consequence of it, stopped him, and, notwithstanding his protestations, handed him over to three militiamen whom they met on their way.

Major André then showed them a passport signed by General Arnold. The militiamen, either because they doubted its authenticity, or because they thought it strange that a person like him should possess such a passport, took no notice of it, but brought him along. He felt his danger, and strove to win over the three men by promises and offers of money; but the soldiers were more honest than their chief—they resisted temptation and conducted their prisoner to the nearest post at North Castle

Lieutenant-Colonel Jameson was in command there; he hastened to apprize his superior officer of the arrest of a spy. But that superior officer was General Arnold, and it was to him that the letter which announced the capture of Major André, and consequently the discovery of his own treason, was delivered. This marvellous stroke of chance, following close upon the first, which had ruined him, afforded him the means of safety. Thanks to it, he was warned in time and could fly.

In the meantime the prisoner had been searched, and proofs of his identity, of the plot, and of his agency in it were brought to light. Various papers were found upon him, among them "the report of a very interesting council of war, the state of the garrison and the works, observations on the means of attack and defence, the whole in the handwriting of General Arnold."

Such was the intelligence that awaited Washington and Lafayette on their arrival at Westpoint. Their astonishment may be imagined. The commander-in-chief, however, quickly recovered his composure, and without loss of time he reassembled the troops that had been more or less scattered by Arnold, and took all the necessary measures for the safety of a place which "the English would respect less on better acquaintance."

Then he gave orders for the arrest of the chief culprit, and the pursuit was instantly begun. But Arnold had had a good start; no one suspected that he was a fugitive, and, of course, he had not been stopped at any post. The traitor had procured a boat and reached the English frigate *Vulture*. The wretch, being sure of escaping punishment, took pleasure in mocking his former chief.

When Colonel Hamilton, who had come closest to the fugitive without being able to reach him, appeared near the place where he had found refuge, he was met by a parliamentary who handed him two letters for General Washington. One of these was from General Arnold, who took a high tone with his former superior, and spoke of his treason as a perfectly natural thing, without even attempting the slightest justification. The other was from the English general, Robertson, who demanded the release of Major André in a very insolent style, that officer, he affirmed, having acted only "by the permission of General Arnold."

Washington made answer to these two letters in a manner which was at once worthy of his humanity, and in conformity with his duty.

Knowing that Mrs. Arnold was in a state of extreme anxiety at Westpoint, he would not have the poor woman, who was innocent of her husband's crime, punished more severely than he. He accordingly despatched one of his aides-de-camp to inform her that "he had done all in his power to arrest Arnold, but that not having succeeded, it gave him pleasure to inform her that her husband was in safety."

As for Major André, he could not give him up: he was brought before a court-martial. The case was simple, the sentence a foregone conclusion. Nevertheless, his judges did not condemn the brilliant young officer to death without being touched by his youth, his coolness, and his courage.

André was deeply moved when he saw the gallows that had been erected for his execution. This was not the death the soldier had foreseen. He understood, too late, the dishonourable nature of his action, although the fault lay with his chief, and betrayed the shame he felt. In the words he addressed to those who witnessed his death he gave expression to that shame. Those words were :—

"You are witnesses that I die like a man of honour."

As for Arnold, his treason was rewarded by his being made brigadier-general of the British forces, and subsequently second in command of the army under Lord Cornwallis; but the latter did not like the presence of this traitor at his side, so he got rid of him and sent him back to New York.

Arnold's action did not bring about any defection among the revolted population. It met with unanimous reprobation.

"If I had fallen into your hands, what would you have done with me?" said Arnold one day to an American who had been captured by the English. His fellow-countryman answered—

"We should have cut off the leg that was wounded in the service of the country, and hung the rest of your body on a gallows."

He escaped the gallows, but not the pillory of public scorn.

Lafayette records in his *Mémoires* that "General Arnold was the only American officer who ever thought of using his command as a means of gaining money." Such disinterestedness and patriotism are all the more admirable, because times of revolution are propitious to nefarious transactions of every kind, and also because American nationality was of very recent formation.

Just at this time the cause of Independence had received a serious check: General Gates had been beaten by Lord Cornwallis in South Carolina. His close intimacy with Arnold had exposed him to suspicion, which was increased by his defeat, and immediately upon that misfortune he was recalled to Philadelphia, and the Congress appointed General Green to succeed him. Gates was unjustly suspected, but his dismissal did no harm to the Americans, thanks to the merit and the military ability of his successor.

The three States of New York, Connecticut, and Massachusetts now took a step which shows how deeply the necessity of an indisputable authority in times of disturbance impresses itself upon even the most ardent lovers of liberty: they nominated Washington dictator, with the most widely extended powers. The measure was wise, for a firm and strong hand was needed to restrain the unequal and scattered elements of the great resistance, and to unite them solidly against the enemy.

This precaution was rendered all the more necessary by the approach of winter, and with it the setting in of a period of inaction, so fatal to troops composed of volunteers and soldiers "on the job," so to speak.

Rochambeau's corps remained in the same position, still stationed at Newport, still isolated, and without any communication with France.

"It was ten months since we left France," writes Lauzun, "and we had received neither news nor money." Fersen, making the same statement, adds: "This oblivion on the part of the Minister or the Ministry is unpardonable."

Their prolonged solitude affected the spirits of the entire force, and, with the addition of the annoyance which all felt at having been brought so far to fight, and then having to remain hidden behind ramparts, "like an oyster in its shell," produced a considerable abatement of enthusiasm among even the best disposed.

Fersen made a second excursion with Rochambeau, but the admiration of the earlier time is absent from his narrative. "We have seen," he writes, "neither a fine country nor good people; they are, in general, idle and grasping.

How are they, with these two characteristics, to be made useful for the war?" (7th November 1780.)

A few days afterwards he returns to this subject and dwells upon it: "The spirit of patriotism exists only in the leaders and in the principal personages of the country, who make very great sacrifices; the others, forming the majority, care for nothing but their personal interest. Money is the moving spring of all their actions, they think only of how to acquire it; every man is for himself, none are for the common weal."

Is not this generalisation rather too severe? Can poor peasants be blamed with any justice for selling the produce of their industry in order to live? However exacting patriotism may be, it cannot require patriots to starve. Fersen condemns them, with greater fairness, for selling to "their friends the French" at too high a price, especially as the resources of the French were considerably diminished after their long sojourn at Newport.

"The inhabitants of the coast, even the soundest Whigs, supply provisions of all kinds to the English fleet in Gardiner's Bay, and that because they get well paid. They fleece us mercilessly; everything is exorbitantly dear; they have treated us like enemies rather than friends in all the dealings we have had with them. Their cupidity is unequalled; money is their god; virtue, honour, all that is nothing to them compared with coin. Not that one may not find estimable persons among them, persons of noble and generous natures; there are many such; but I speak of the nation in general. I believe it is more Dutch than English."

We hardly expect to find the Dutch brought into this affair, for that nation has not the monopoly of cupidity any more than others—unless, indeed, to be a trader is to be guilty of that vice.

Fersen had to complain of matters more important than these small grievances. First, it is "a coolness between General Washington and M. de Rochambeau." The latter was unaware of the cause of this, but he did what prudence dictated; he wrote to the American general, and commissioned Fersen to be the bearer of the letter, and to inquire into the origin of Washington's dissatisfaction.

"You see, my dear father," writes the young Swede, "that I have gone into negotiation; this is my first attempt, I shall endeavour to get out of it well." He did get out of it well, and Washington's displeasure was not lasting.

Fersen does not even allude again to the incident, and no after-occurrence recalled this momentary misunderstanding, real or supposed.

Then it came to Fersen's own turn—the calm and judicious Fersen himself—to be displeased with his chief.

"I am getting tired of being with M. de Rochambeau," he writes. "He treats me with distinction, it is true, and I am very sensible of this; but he is disagreeably, and even insultingly, distrustful. He has more confidence in me than in my comrades, but even that is little; and he places no greater trust in his general officers, who are very discontented on this point, as the superior officers of the army are likewise."

A few months later Fersen said of the same general: "I do not doubt that the troops he asks for will be sent to M. de Rochambeau; he knows too well how to make use of them."

When he went away, the officers and soldiers were entirely agreed in the opposite sense:—

"M. de Rochambeau left us at Providence: the whole army regrets him, and with reason."

"We have parted with M. de Rochambeau with pain; all were glad to be commanded by him. It is to be hoped there may be the same feeling with regard to Baron de Viomesnil. The Baron has not the coolness of M. de Rochambeau. He was the only man to command us out here, and to maintain the perfect harmony that has prevailed between two nations differing so widely in manners and language, and who, in reality, do not like one another. . . . The wise, prudent, and simple bearing of M. de Rochambeau has done more to gain the friendship of America for us than four battles fought and won could have accomplished."

It was well to quote these contradictory statements in order to show, once more, how little reliance ought to be placed upon the verdicts returned by subordinates upon commanders-in-chief. The latter are more easily called to account for what they do not, than even for what they do. Besides, is it possible for them to make explanations to their subordinates? Obviously it is not; how then are the latter to form a just judgment of them in their ignorance of the necessarily secret motives which actuate them? This remark applies equally to every age.

It was more than a year since the little French army had left France, and the troops were weary of idleness at Newport; but the day was drawing nigh when it should cast off its torpor, when the courage and good-will of every man in the corps would be put to the test; when every trifling quarrel and selfish complaint were to be forgotten in the common peril of conflict; when gunpowder was to speak, and its roar was to cover every other discordant sound.

A second interview between Washington and Rochambeau took place, and again at Hartford. The end of May was near, a propitious moment for the beginning of a summer campaign. It was necessary to strike a great blow. The English were making too good use of time; on the one hand they burned and pillaged where they were resisted, on the other they lavished money, and by the two means, terror and bribery, they were gaining friends and partisans. Their progress in the South was so considerable that they were credited with the intention of putting a stop to a costly war by recognising the independence of a portion of the North, so as to secure a more solid footing in the Southern provinces.

Money, in which lay the great strength of

the English, was scarce with the Americans, and especially with the French. The latter, being reduced to their last resources, were obliged to practise a lamentable economy. They could not even learn what was going on in the enemy's camp; for they were unable to pay spies. Those who served the allied army in that capacity were poor men, who did so from motives of pure patriotism. Their obscure heroism furnished Cooper with the theme of one of his most thrilling romances, "The Spy," and Harvey Birch, "the spy of the neutral ground," is a typical figure. Volunteer-spies, however, were becoming few, for, as Fersen remarks, "Men soon tire of an unpaid business which leads to the gallows."

The decisive hour had come. The chiefs knew that it was so, and the troops were put in motion. At last the French left Newport and effected their junction with the Americans (12th June to 6th July 1781).

Washington immediately made a demonstration on New York to deceive Clinton; the trick succeeded perfectly. He then took his way to Philadelphia, rejoined Lafayette at Williamsburg, and afterwards proceeded to besiege Yorktown, where Lord Cornwallis was shut up.

On the 29th of September the investment was complete; on the 6th of October the first trench was opened. Two external redoubts were attacked by two columns, one composed of Americans, the other of French; rivalry made them perform prodigies of valour, and as they were equally brave, their success was equal: the two redoubts were carried.

On the 16th of October all was ready for the assault. Lord Cornwallis, who had resisted so long as he could, expecting the arrival of Sir Thomas Clinton, who had promised to come to his assistance, but did not appear, endeavoured to effect the escape of his army by the York River; but this daring and foolish enterprise was frustrated by a violent storm which scattered all his boats. Resistance had now become impossible, and on the 17th he proposed a capitulation. Only ten balls and one bombshell remained in his arsenal.

The vanquished army yielded up the fort and passed before the conqueror. Cornwallis pleaded illness to escape this humiliation. He was represented by General O'Hara, who advanced towards Rochambeau and presented his sword.

"I am only an auxiliary," said the Frenchman as he refused to receive it, and pointed out Washington as the chief to whom the Englishman[1] was to surrender.

This capitulation produced an immense effect. The English had now in their power only New York, Charlestown, and Savannah, and their prestige was considerably lowered. The cause of Independence was triumphant; peace rumours were already abroad.

The presence of the French was, however, still necessary to the consolidation of the success that had been achieved. Rochambeau's

[1] O'Hara was an Irishman.

forces prepared for winter quarters, and headquarters was established at Williamsburg, "a wretched little town, more like a village."
Most of the officers shrank from the doleful prospect of again passing three long months without either fun or fighting, and several asked for leave. "All our young colonels of the Court are going away to pass their winter in Paris. Some will not come back, others will, and will be much surprised that they are not made brigadiers for having been at the siege of Yorktown; they think they have done the finest thing in the world. I shall remain; I should have no other reason for going to Paris than my amusement and my pleasure: I must sacrifice these."
The Duc de Lauzun acted more adroitly; he contrived to get himself sent to France as bearer of the news of the brilliant success of the allies. He embarked on the *Surveillante*, and, after a voyage of eighty-two days, he arrived at Brest, from whence he proceeded to Versailles. There he passed the winter, and did not return to America until the following year. Fersen, on the contrary, had remained, like the brave and noble soldier that he was; for the courage of a soldier resides in the doing of his duty, whatsoever that may be, without always claiming to be paid in gold or in glory.
Nor was this time lost by him. He turned it to advantage in an intelligent and practical manner, by making himself better acquainted with the country, and with the people among whom he was detained. He visited various

parts of the new State, accompanied by the Chevalier de la Luzerne, an amiable and talented Frenchman, and described his excursions to his father in letters full of interest and vivacity, which denote remarkably sound judgment on his part.

In the first instance he relates his experiences in Virginia (25th March 1782):—

"We have had a charming journey, and the canteen which Luzerne brought with him, packed with patés, ham, wine, and bread, prevented us from noticing the poverty of the inns, where there is nothing to be had but salted meat, and no bread.

"In Virginia, only Indian-corn cakes are eaten. These cakes are heated in front of the fire, and though hardened on the outside, are merely raw dough inside. The only drink is rum, otherwise sugar-brandy, mixed with water; this they call 'grog.' Apples have failed this year, so that cider is not to be had.

"In the part of Virginia called 'The Mountains,' all is different. The soil is better; the great tobacco-culture is carried on there; the land produces wheat and every kind of fruit; but in the Plain, in the region of the coast, only Indian-corn is grown.

"The chief product of Virginia is tobacco; not because this province, the largest of the thirteen, is not suited to other kinds of cultivation, but because the laziness and the vanity of its inhabitants form an obstacle to industry.

"In fact, the Virginians seem to belong to another race; instead of occupying themselves with their farms and with commerce, every landowner wants to be a 'grand seigneur.' A white man never works; as in the West Indian Islands, all the labour is performed by negro slaves, who are superintended by white men, and there is an overseer at the head of each plantation. There are at least twenty negroes to one white man in Virginia; and this is the reason why the province sends so few soldiers to the army.

"All the traders here are regarded as inferior to the landowners, who say that the former are not 'gentlemen,' and will not associate with them. They hold aristocratic principles, and, when one sees them, one can hardly understand how they have come to join the general confederation, and accept a government founded upon conditions of absolute equality. *But the same spirit which has led them to cast off the English yoke might well urge them on to other measures, and I should not be surprised to see Virginia, when peace comes, detach itself from the other States.* I should not, indeed, be surprised to see the American government become a complete aristocracy."

Is it not curious that the young officer should already comment upon the antagonism between the North and South, which was not to break out until eighty years afterwards, and should in a measure foresee "the War of Secession"?

Fersen made an excursion to Portsmouth with Rochambeau and the Chevalier de la Luzerne. On their return they heard of the disastrous defeat of M. de Grasse, who was captured with the *Ville de Paris*, the Admiral's ship, and six other vessels; a victory which gave the superiority in the West Indian Islands to the English. "This is most vexatious," writes Fersen, "especially if we have the misfortune to be kept here (at Williamsburg). The heat is already excessive; just think what it will be in July and August" (27th May 1782).

No news came from France. Lauzun was impatiently expected, but he did not arrive. The situation again became gloomy. The Americans talked of attempting the siege of New York, but they were too weak for such an enterprise, and a check would mean the risk of very serious results.

All of a sudden, just as the forecast of events was tending to ill, a change of attitude on the part of the English took place. Peace was talked of—peace was meant. The English, victorious on the sea in America, had experienced great reverses in India, and Suffren was threatening that other colonial empire, which it would ruin them to lose.

The war had cost them one hundred millions; their trade was encountering obstacles all over the world; the nation was weary of such heavy sacrifices. The Government gave way.

On the 17th of August 1782 Fersen wrote to his father: "From the news which we have from England, for as yet we have none from France, it appears that peace is near. England is very well disposed, if only France be moderate in her demands.

"This idea causes universal joy; it gives me pleasure which I cannot express."

It was natural that he should feel thus, even apart from the consideration of those whom he hoped to rejoin in Europe, for he greatly needed rest. He had been moving about incessantly for some months, and "ill with a heavy cold." Nevertheless he had discharged all the duties of his service—a severe one, especially as the heat was great, and water was scarce in the country. Now the cold weather was setting in; his "tent and mattress" afforded him only meagre protection, for he was "not very well off for blankets, but eked them out with his cloak."

The hour of departure was drawing near. The news regarding peace was confirmed. Lauzun returned, and transports were prepared to convey the French volunteers back to France.

The troops assembled at Providence to await embarkation. Count Fersen availed himself of the opportunity to visit his friends in the little island of Newport and bid them farewell. This duty being accomplished, he rejoined his comrades and proceeded with them to Boston, where the ships awaited them. Fersen went on board the *Brave* with the Comte de Deux-Ponts and the three first companies.

The *Brave* was a ship of seventy-four guns, and would certainly not have deserved to keep her name had she been responsible for the shortcomings of her captain, the Chevalier d'Amblimont, who had already behaved very ill in the disaster of the 12th of April. Instead of obeying the signals, he fled, and on being hailed by Bougainville and asked the reason of such conduct, he replied that "as the fleet was lost, at least one ship should be saved for the King."

His foresight had apparently done him no harm, as his command had not been taken from him. And then he really was a charming man; "so amiable," says Fersen, speaking of him, "so polite. He has a good ship. I am well berthed and well fed. This is all I want. I can dispense with his courage."

Contrary winds detained the fleet at Boston until the end of December. The orders of the Government were that the ships were to proceed to the Antilles. "The voyage," wrote Fersen, "was horrible; while on board, occupation was impossible; being always in the same room with forty-five persons was odious. It is a horrid kind of life. The navy is a wretched calling, especially in France."

All the ships in the fleet were driven by the wind and dispersed; several were lost with all on board, and one of them, the *Bourgogne*, carried 400 men. A few put safely into port at Curaçoa; the *Brave* took thirteen days to make the thirty-five leagues which divide that island from Porto-Cabello, a Venezuelan port (13th February 1783).

Fersen had cause to congratulate himself upon being on board one of the best ships. He regarded it as "a miracle" that he had "reached *terra firma* safe and sound." Not that the place was attractive or agreeable by any means; there were no resources of any kind in Porto-Cabello. But, bad as this haven

A FORBIDDEN DECORATION

of refuge was, it enabled the fleet to collect its scattered numbers. Crossing the seas from thence, the returning expedition reached France in June.

By his three years' service with the expedition, Count Fersen had gained the decoration of the Order of Cincinnatus, a glorious memorial, given by General Washington himself, but the King of Sweden forbade him to wear it.

France derived an analogous advantage from her intervention. By the Treaty of Versailles (1783) she had obtained that England should recognise the independence of the United States. The latter gave her an unexpected proof of their independence: they had treated with England separately, and unknown to France, six months previously.

CHAPTER IV.

A letter from Gustavus III. to Louis XVI.—Count Fersen at the Court of France—Mdlle. Necker—An abortive project of marriage—Stedingk and Staël—Gustavus III. in Germany, in Italy, and in France—Count Fersen's return to Sweden (1784)—Political events—Preludes to the Revolution—Queen Marie Antoinette—Unpopularity—The French Court—The Comtesse Jules de Polignac—Baron de Besenval—The Duc de Lauzun—The Duc de Coigny—The diamond necklace—The louis-d'or of Strasburg—M. de Calonne—"The King has sent in his resignation"—The Assembly of the Notables—Count Fersen's impressions—Sweden in 1788—Finland expedition—Count Fersen's mission in France—Mme. de Chicogne—Valenciennes and Paris—Revolutionary agitation.

COUNT FERSEN returned to France—

"—— paré de cette gloire
Que donne aux jeunes cœurs la première victoire."

The halo of military gallantry now enhanced his personal merit, and it shone all the more brightly because his fame had been gained in a distant and popular war.

The King of Sweden was proud of his subject; he thought it a good opportunity to obtain a position in the French army for him similar to that which he held in the Swedish. Accordingly, he wrote to the King of France at the beginning of September 1783, as follows:—

"Sir, my brother and cousin,—Count Fersen, having served in the army of your Majesty with general approbation, and having thereby rendered himself worthy of your good-will, I do not think that I commit an indiscretion in asking you for a proprietary regiment for him. His birth, his fortune, the place that he occupies about my person, the prudence of his conduct, the talents and the example of his father, who formerly enjoyed the same favour in France, all authorise me to believe that his services cannot fail to be agreeable to your Majesty; and as he will remain equally attached to my service, and will divide his time between the duties of his posts in France and in Sweden, I see with pleasure that the confidence which I accord to Count Fersen and the high position which he enjoys in his own country will still further extend the relations that exist between the two nations, and will prove the constant desire which I have to cultivate more and more the friendship which unites me to you and becomes each day more dear to me." [1]

As a proof that his recommendation was the genuine expression of his esteem for the Count, the King made him "titular colonel" in his army, a knight of the Order of the Sword, and lieutenant-colonel "in service" in the King's Light Horse. This significant example was not necessary. Fersen's deserts and the services he had rendered were well known at the French Court; he did not want for interest, especially in high places; absence had not caused him to be forgotten, and on his return he was welcomed as a friend.

[1] *Gustave III. et la Cour de France*, par M. Geoffroy.

The Queen herself replied to the letter of the King of Sweden, on the 19th of September:—

"Sir, my brother and cousin,—I profit by the departure of Count Fersen to repeat anew the sentiments which attach me to your Majesty. The recommendation that you have made to the King has been received as it ought to be, coming from you, and in favour of so good a subject. His father is not forgotten here; the services which he rendered and his good reputation have been renewed by the son, who has greatly distinguished himself, in the war in America, by his character and his good qualities, and who has gained the esteem and affection of all who have had the opportunity of knowing him. I hope that without delay he will be provided with a regiment. I shall not fail to second the views of your Majesty in everything, and to give you on this occasion, as on every other, proofs of the sincere attachment with which I am, sir, your good sister and cousin."

Promise was quickly followed by performance. Fersen, who had been previously decorated with the Order of Military Merit, was made proprietary-colonel of the Royal Suédois, a regiment then in garrison at Valenciennes.

This post, these favours, the personal kindness of Louis XVI. and Marie Antoinette to Fersen, were likely to give a fresh start to the gossip which it had been his purpose to arrest by his departure for America. In fact, his return was an imprudence from one point of view; but although, being master of himself and of his passion, he had formed the most generous and difficult of resolutions in a moment of heroic courage, heroism unhappily has its limits, and perhaps he considered that, by three years of absence, he had purchased the right to see her whose image he always bore in his heart, the right to be near her and to render her devoted service.

He might have diverted, if not entirely dispelled suspicion, if he would have taken advantage of his social success, and made himself conspicuous as the lover of some fashionable frail beauty. Handsome, renowned, sought and courted everywhere, why did he not imitate his contemporaries? What prevented Fersen from becoming a Richelieu, a Lauzun, a Tilly? Nothing, if not himself; he preferred to respect his love, even as he respected its object, and to remain Fersen.

Communication of the despatch of Count Creutz had apparently been made to Fersen's father, Count Frederick; but either because he did not believe at all in a lasting mutual attachment between such young hearts, or because he thought it could not possibly survive three years of absence, the Count desired that his son should marry, with a view to the perpetuation of their illustrious family. He wrote to Count John, reminding him that it was time he should think of marriage; and as Count John was nearly twenty-eight years of age, and in a prosperous position in all respects, he had no good reason for opposing his father's wish —no reason, at least, which he would divulge.

F

The consequence was that, as he had formerly done in the instance of Mdlle. de Leijel, he allowed several schemes of marriage to be put forward in a sketchy way; but we may be certain that he did nothing towards their realisation, and that he was not altogether innocent of the successive failure of every such project.

At this period an heiress, who was already almost famous by reason of her father's name, fortune, and high position, and her own remarkable intelligence, but who was not endowed with beauty, was attracting numerous suitors. Renowned personages from almost all countries put themselves on the competitive list; it was a sort of cosmopolitan tournament. This heiress was Mdlle. Necker.

Certain political personages are treated by their contemporaries either with unlimited indulgence or with unmitigated severity. In the former case, everything is admired, even their faults; in the latter, nothing is forgiven, not even their greatest services. Many politicians have owed much to, or suffered severely from, these two currents of opinion. M. Necker was just then deriving great benefit from the rush—as blind as that of a torrent —in his direction. The extraordinary public favour that had carried him into the Ministry, accompanied him while there, and followed him to his retreat, was as fervent as ever.

In reality, this public favour was no more justified in his case than in a hundred others.

M. Necker, pretentious and self-sufficient as

a parvenu, austere and tiresome as a devout Calvinist, consoled himself for his fall by receiving assurances of regret from numerous Frenchmen, and tokens of admiration from a few foreigners. He lived at Saint-Ouen with his wife and daughter.

Baroness Oberkirch, a clever woman, had an opportunity of seeing the Necker family when she accompanied the Russian Grand-Duke and Grand-Duchess Paul (travelling under the name of Comte and Comtesse du Nord) to their house. She wrote an account of her visit in which the following remarks occur:—"As for me, I did not like M. Necker. I was struck by a resemblance in him to Cagliostro, without his brilliant glance and bewildering countenance. He is a stilted Cagliostro, stiff and disagreeable, a regular bourgeois of Geneva. There is nothing amiable about him, although he tries to make himself agreeable. Mme. Necker is still worse. In spite of the great positions she has occupied, she is a schoolmistress and nothing more, pedantic and pretentious beyond anything. She is the daughter of a country pastor of the name of Churchod; she has received a good education, but profited by it contrariwise. She is handsome and not agreeable, she does good and is not liked, her body, her mind, and her heart want grace. The Creator, before giving her form, dipped her in a tub full of starch. She will never possess the art of pleasing. In a word, she can neither weep nor laugh. Her father was poor, she set up a school for girls at Geneva;

she was taken to Paris by Mme. de Vermenoux, well known for her beauty and light conduct. This Mme. de Vermenoux associated with the Abbé Raynal, M. de Marmontel, and other philosophers, also with M. Necker. She soon tired of the latter—I readily understand that; I should have tired of him quite as soon —and she got rid of him by marrying him to Mdlle. Churchod.

"'They will bore themselves so thoroughly together,' she said, 'that it will be an occupation for them.'

"They did not bore themselves, but they bored other people, having taken to adoring, complimenting, and burning incense before each other perpetually, especially Mme. Necker, who is thurifer in permanence to her husband.

"The Grand-Duke wished to have some private conversation with the great man. The reputation of the ex-Minister justified such a desire.

"'I have come,' said His Imperial Highness, 'to add my tribute of admiration to that of the whole of Europe.'

"On leaving the great man, the Grand-Duke seemed less satisfied. He asked us in the coach whether we knew the fable of the sticks floating on the water. This from the Grand-Duke was quite sufficient comment.

"Mdlle. Necker seemed to me a totally different person from either of her parents, although she too had a little of the Genevese about her and a great deal of the thurifer. Her eyes are fine, but otherwise she is ugly; she has a good figure, a clear skin, and something rarely intelligent in her look—it is a flame."

Many were the wooers who fluttered round that flame; the fine eyes of the young lady did not prevent them from perceiving "les beaux yeux de sa cassette." Pitt, the famous English Minister, young Staël, and several others with them, tried their luck. The number of suitors enabled Fersen to put himself on the list without too much danger—that is to say, without any great chance of success.

Presently another candidate was introduced, and by the Queen herself. Human hearts are difficult to read. Was Marie Antoinette displeased by Fersen's seeking a tie which would have imposed other duties upon him; or had she no other object than to secure a good match for a gentleman who was worthy of it in every respect?

Stedingk and Fersen were friends, and had been on intimate terms for years before the war in America. Stedingk was one of the first to go out to the scene of strife, and he returned in advance of the others, having received a wound which obliged him to use crutches. But the wound being one of those which are cured in time, this visible and temporary infirmity offered an additional charm to a tender heart. It seemed as though Stedingk must succeed. Nothing of the sort! The political greatness of Pitt, the courage and the crutches of Stedingk, were eclipsed by the merits of the young diplomatist; marked preference was manifested for M. de Staël. Fersen waited no longer to renounce a project which he had not seriously entertained. He hastened to inform his father of his renunciation in very significant terms.

"You will have seen already that the idea which I had concerning Mdlle. Necker could not have come to anything, even if you would have consented to it, on account of my friend Staël, whom this (marriage) will suit perfectly, much better than it would suit me. *I never thought of it except to please you, my dear father, and I am not at all sorry that it cannot be.*"

He had his reasons for not regretting a failure which indeed he ardently and secretly desired. Whatever he had to endure for the sake of the one love of his life, the future proved to him that he had chosen the better part.

M. Necker, who had at first opposed his daughter's choice, yielded at length to her wishes, and authorised a marriage that did not give him the son-in-law he had hoped for. What was a diplomatist, even though he were on the eve of becoming Swedish Ambassador, in comparison with the "great Commoner"? He would have preferred Mr. Pitt infinitely, but the young lady preferred M. de Staël, and her wishes prevailed.

The marriage, one of inclination on the part of the wife, but of interest on that of the husband, did not make either of them happy. It was conducive in the beginning to the establishment of De Staël's political fortunes, but it soon ceased to be a real union, by reason of the quarrels of the pair, and the scandalous conduct of the wife.

Madame de Staël equally failed to find happiness in illicit relations. Her intellectual gifts did not atone for the defects of her person; she inspired esteem, she excited curiosity, but she did not awaken love. She would not, however, abandon the hope of doing this, and more than once she strove to win the happiness she dreamed of; but if she captivated the imagination, she never won a heart, although she gave her own. As an eminent author, she enjoyed the triumphs of vanity, but what were they in comparison with the tribute which she failed to win? That fine and melancholy saying, " A woman's fame is only showy mourning worn for happiness," is hers.

While M. de Staël was rising to the high position at which his ambition aimed, Count Fersen was preparing to return to Sweden and his home, after an absence of more than five years. His departure was retarded by an important event.

Gustavus III. resolved to resume the journey that had been interrupted by the death of his father, and at the end of the year 1783 he was travelling in Germany. The King desired to see Count Fersen, and summoned him. The Count had only to obey, and did so, rejoining his sovereign at Nuremberg.

The royal scheme of travel fitted in admirably with Fersen's secret inclinations; after an excursion in Italy came a sojourn in France; and so he was brought back to his beloved Paris, and his more beloved Versailles.

The King of Sweden adopted the name of Count Haga, although he did not travel incognito. He alighted at the Swedish Embassy, Rue du Bac, and made his first visit in the afternoon of the same day (17th June 1784) to the King of France at Versailles. He was not expected. Louis XVI. was engaged in his favourite occupation, hunting at Rambouillet. He was informed of the arrival of the royal visitor, and returned in haste to the château. That evening Count Haga supped with the King and Queen.

Gustavus III. was more fortunate on the second occasion of his visiting France. Marie Antoinette, who did not like him at first, got over all her prejudices against him. Perhaps he owed this alteration in her mood less to his better known and more justly appreciated qualities, than to the favour with which the Swedish nation was regarded in France, owing to the three gentlemen whose names occur, and are to recur so frequently, in this narrative—Fersen, Stedingk, and Staël. All three deserved the general esteem in which they were held, although their merits were of different kinds. The Queen purposed to give a fête in honour of Gustavus III.; it pleased her to pay a compliment to Sweden in the person of the chief representative of the nation, and she would also have an opportunity of showing off the embellishments of her favourite abode. In her hands, and by her tasteful care, Trianon had become a delightful retreat, whither, unhappily for her, she was tempted to resort too frequently, for the enjoyment of quiet and liberty, while she neglected the wearisome but imperative duties of a Queen.

Gustavus III. was astonished. "Surrounded by these young Swedish officers, who were in such favour at the French Court, he might have fancied himself in his own country. He has described this fête in one of his letters. *Le Dormeur Éveillé*, by Marmontel and Grétry, was acted with sumptuous scenery and a ballet; afterwards the company supped in the groves, while the English garden was illuminated.

"A large number of persons were admitted to the park by invitation; all the ladies were dressed in white. Gustavus describes it as 'fairy-land,' a spectacle worthy of the Champs Elysées! The Queen would not sit at the table; she was entirely occupied in doing the honours.

"She conversed of preference with the Swedes, and gave them a marked welcome. With the exception of the Princes (Monsieur and the Count d'Artois), with whom the King was displeased, the whole of the royal family and all the Court were present. The Princesse de Lamballe was charming."[1]

Up to that time, it was still possible to sup, to dance, and to act plays. But the calm and tranquillity of the reign of Louis XVI. were passing away. It must be said that the royal pair made the most of those last days, and that their life was a happy one. An incapable Minister, in the guise of the most supple and insinuating of courtiers, was gaily leading the monarchy to ruin, and France to bankruptcy, along a flower-strewn path with a precipice at the end of it.

[1] *Gustave III. et la Cour de France*, par M. Geoffroy.

Count Haga left Versailles and France, delighted with all he had seen, having renewed at its source his admiration for that royalty which to him was still the royalty of Louis XIV., and went back to his own cold and melancholy kingdom to endeavour to imitate it in a measure.

Fersen returned to Sweden at the same time. Royal favour had once more been extended to him: Gustavus III. had obtained a pension of 20,000 livres payable by the French treasury for the Count.

The time was approaching, however, when the accumulated errors of the preceding reigns, and the incapacity of the successive Ministers of Louis XVI., were to bring the situation to a point at which it would be impossible for it to remain. The nation, tired of paying dearly for mere suffering, wanted to have something else for its money; and the moment was not distant when the peasant and the working-man, aweary of their prolonged subjection, were to shake off their apathy.

The old social edifice, worm-eaten, undermined, and worn-out, was cracking on all sides, and the defenders who still stuck to it were not remarkable for either worth, courage, or intelligence. Did it deserve any other sort of champions?

Reforms were of imperative necessity. To perceive and acknowledge all that was just in the demands of the nation, a superior mind would have been required; to cause all that was just and good in those demands to pass into the laws of the country, a strong will would have been needed. And there was nobody but Louis XVI.!

Marie Antoinette was her husband's superior in courage, and in intellectual and moral worth; but she was not a woman of political ability, who, failing the King, would be capable of taking the management of affairs into her own hands. For a long time past the queens of France had been satisfied to be nobodies in the state. What place does either Marie Thérèse (the wife of Louis XIV.) or Marie Leczinska (the wife of Louis XV.) occupy in history? If Anne of Austria played a more active part, it was because her queenship and her womanhood had the same animating motive, and in defending Mazarin, her Minister, she defended her lover.

But Marie Antoinette, had she possessed the ability requisite to make up for her husband's incapacity, would have found it difficult to put herself forward. The few attempts of the kind which she made, on the suggestion of injudicious friends, served only to expose her to a fierce attack from Mirabeau: "There is but one Majesty in the kingdom, and I regard it as disrespectful to pronounce the word 'Queen' in a monarchy where queens can never be kings. Our King, whose intentions are good, whose ill-fortune is interesting, personally possesses the public confidence, and needs neither bail nor surety; *the place of Queen, his august consort, is to give him relaxation from the cares of his throne, and not to be implicated in the affairs of the State.* When she was pleased to permit the fairest of the arts to represent her, crowned with all her graces, all her rights, it was with her children about her that she was painted, not with the globe in her hand, or the map of France under her eyes."

The happy days of Marie Antoinette were nearing their close. As a matter of fact, the Queen had not been very popular at any time; it seemed as though an evil fate pursued her, and superstitious persons did not fail to attribute this mischance to the unhappy hazard of her birth upon a day of mourning throughout the whole of Christendom, the 2nd of November, "the Day of the Dead," a day that brought frightful calamity upon one of the most beautiful cities of the world by the earthquake of Lisbon.

It would be foolish to attach importance to such notions, but the historian ought to make mention of them, not in order to give them importance which they could not possess, but because they illustrate the state of the times and reveal certain tendencies of the public mind.

In fact, everything had more or less militated against her; her nationality, her family, her tastes, her beauty, her friendships.

Her nationality—she was Austrian. Choiseul, in making her Queen of France, flattered himself that he was forming a bond of union between those two hereditary enemies, the House of Austria and the House of France: his hopes were disappointed, the old distrust still subsisted, and the Queen passed for a spy in the interests of her race.

Her family—she had two brothers; one, Archbishop and Grand-Elector of Cologne, was named Maximilian, and he was stupid. On his visit to the Jardin des Plantes, Buffon offered him a copy of his works, and the prince replied:

"Many thanks, sir; I should be very sorry to deprive you of it."

The other was Leopold; he was Emperor of Germany, and had plenty of brains. He, too, visited the Jardin des Plantes, and said to Buffon:

"I have come for the book my brother forgot to take away."

By the same sort of fatality, the stupidity of the one brother and the cleverness of the other were equally ill-taken; the former was ridiculed, the latter was feared, and the most preposterous ideas took possession of the people. Even the poultry-women discussed the current rumours.

Let us pause and think of just one incident, that of Renée Millot. Having met the Comte de Coigny one day, the girl was emboldened by his kindly familiarity to ask him gravely:

"Will the Emperor go on for ever making war against the Turks? Why, if so, France will be ruined by the quantity of money the Queen sends every month to her brother; it must be at least two hundred millions by this time."

Coigny was amused by the question, and

could not resist the pleasure of amusing himself by answering it; so he said seriously:

"You are quite right! yes, it has already cost more than two hundred millions, and we have not come to the end of it yet!"

This jest, retained in the silly brain of the hearer, was repeated in the form of a solemn deposition at the trial of the Queen before the Revolutionary Tribunal.

Her tastes and her beauty—she was young, and she was welcomed with fêtes and rejoicing. Was it surprising that she resorted to amusement for relief from the troubles which came to her through etiquette, politics, and her husband, "that big ill-bred boy," as Mme. du Barry called him? No doubt, she was not to blame for liking card-playing, but she did wrong in abandoning herself to that pastime with an excessive passion, especially by playing very high, and keeping up games at lansquenet for an unreasonable time, as she did one "All-Saints," when the party broke up after thirty-six hours!

That she should like to drive out in carriages and sledges was quite reasonable, also that she should care to attend the masked balls at the opera; but did she not go beyond the limits of prudence by passing whole days in driving about and showing herself everywhere, and also by addressing strangers at the balls? Such were her pleasures, and she enjoyed them most thoroughly when they were unshared by the King—a fact which did not escape attention.

Rivarol has described in one striking sentence the impression which she produced :—

"Always belonging more to her sex than to her rank, she forgot that she was meant to live and to die upon a real throne; she longed too much for the fictitious and fleeting empire that beauty confers upon ordinary women, and which makes them the queens of a moment."

Her friendships—the mere word awakens most painful recollections, for certainly the sentiment which she entertained for one of the most enigmatical creatures who ever gravitated in the orbit of kings was among the greatest misfortunes of her life. By what chance Marie Antoinette first saw "the angelic face" of Madame de Polignac, and became infatuated with the woman to the point of summoning her to Court, heaping benefits upon her, her husband, her lover, and her sister-in-law, and appointing her to the great position of "Governess of the children of France," is not known, but only too surely that chance was fatal.

Was the Queen even repaid by devotion equal to her affection, and gratitude in proportion to her bounty? Mme. de Polignac accepted her benefits, devised some fresh pretext every day for securing others, while affecting to evade them, and, when the hour of peril came, when the Queen, forgetting herself to save her friend, urged her to fly from France, the favourite had the courage to obey her, and the cowardice to go.[1]

[1] Mme. de Polignac was true to her base nature in all vicissitudes. Mme. de Rémusat, in her celebrated *Mémoires*, gives some interesting details of her falsehood and ingratitude to the restored royal family and to the writer herself.—*Translator's Note.*

How different are the recollections attached to the friend who loved more than she was loved ; and yet, how can we regard her fidelity otherwise than as a misfortune, since it was one of the Queen's keenest sorrows to learn the awful and tragical fate of the unfortunate Princesse de Lamballe !

With regard to her men friends—Fersen excepted—was the Queen more fortunate ?

Among those who rank as her intimates, Baron de Besenval holds a prominent place ; he contrived to acquire real influence and to maintain it for several years. The Duc de Levis has defined that influence very clearly in the portrait he has drawn of the Baron.

"He was a Swiss officer who had served with distinction during the Seven Years' War. To the intrepidity which has been an invariable characteristic of his nation, he united the fiery valour that belongs to ours. He had a fine figure, an agreeable face, intelligence, courage ; what more was needed to ensure his success ? Accordingly, he was very successful with women, but his manners were too free, and his gallantry was in bad taste ; even among men his conversation was more remarkable for coarseness than for piquancy, and his good-humour was cynical rather than hearty.

'He soon succeeded in getting into the Queen's own circle ; then, by mingling flattery with the pernicious maxims that he set forth with an air of assurance well calculated to impose on an inexperienced princess, he acquired a baneful ascendency over her; this I, and other persons who had the means of judging, regard as one of the principal causes of her ruin. The Queen had a very good heart, but also an unfortunate propensity for trifling. He applauded this defect, which might almost be called a vice in her rank. The consequence was the alienation from her of all the really estimable women at Court, whose experience and good counsel would have been so valuable, and were so much needed.

"The Queen, at the age of pleasure and frivolity, and in the intoxication of supreme power, could not endure constraint; etiquette and ceremonial bored and irritated her. She was told it was ridiculous that her life should not be made as pleasant as that of her chief subjects, who also delighted in society; that, in so enlightened an age, when all prejudices were set aside, sovereigns ought to release themselves from the fetters of custom; and, finally, that it was absurd to suppose their people's obedience depended upon the number of hours more or less which the royal family passed in a circle of weary and wearisome courtiers."

Mme. Campan states that the hot-headed Baron did not confine himself to merely giving advice, but that one day he ventured, notwithstanding his age—he was then over fifty—to make a declaration of love to the Queen. There was something in this to offend the Queen of France, but not to hurt the woman; certain offences of a particular nature flatter more than they anger those who receive them. Marie

Antoinette, if we are to accept Mme. Campan's version of the matter as authentic, did not resent the conduct of Baron de Besenval for any long period, and he remained on the same terms of friendship and confidence with her. If this be true, it would tend to prove that the Queen was less strict upon the point than most of her historians.

Besenval had more than one imitator; among others, the Duc de Lauzun. We have seen how highly Fersen praises him in his letters to Count Frederick; yet the Duc de Lauzun did not altogether deserve Fersen's eulogium, if we are to believe some of his contemporaries, beginning with the Duc de Lévis.

"The Duc de Biron, known in his youth as Duc de Lauzun, had entered society with every advantage: he was handsome, clever, affable, brave, gallant, and his manners were as noble as his birth. He was successful in every way; but unfortunately judgment and good sense were not among his endowments. He began by wanton extravagance in youth, and in middle age grave faults and fatal errors led to his ruin. According to the general belief, his gallantries were inspired by his excessive vanity rather than by inclination."

It is certain that on his return from America he paraded "an insolent passion" for the Queen. An adventure bearing on this subject, which must have been very disagreeable to him, is recorded.

"In order to attract the attention of the Queen, he had the audacity to don her livery, to follow her about for a whole day wherever she went, and to remain at night like a watch-dog at the door of her apartment."

But this manœuvre failed; the Queen did not observe him.

"He was about to give up the game, when, at the moment of the Queen's alighting from her coach on returning from a drive to Trianon, it occurred to him to kneel on one knee, so that she might put her foot on the other instead of using the velvet carriage-step. Her Majesty, much surprised, looked at him for the first time, but, like the quick-witted and sensible woman she was, she did not appear to recognise him. She called a page:—

"'I beg, sir,' she said, 'you will have this person dismissed; he does not even know how to open a carriage-door.'"

It must, however, be admitted that if Lauzun displayed some vanity, even some insolence, in regard to the Queen, the latter was not altogether free from reproach. With the natural coquetry of a pretty woman, she allowed him on several occasions to perceive that she was not insensible to his attentions, and he may have considered that his boldness was authorised, or at least excused, by her undeniable affability.

A masked-ball adventure was talked of, in which "there was levity on one side and indiscretion on the other." And there was the story of the heron's plume. One day the Duc de Lauzun presented himself at a reception held by Mme. de Guéménée, in uniform, "with a helmet glittering with gems, and adorned with the most superb heron's plume that could possibly be seen."

Marie Antoinette complimented Lauzun and vehemently admired the plume. Lauzun immediately resolved to give her the beautiful feather, and begged Mme. de Guéménée to convey it to her. The Queen might have refused the gift of a subject, or, having accepted it, left it in the bottom of a drawer; but she did neither; she appeared one day with the feather in her head-dress, and took care that the Duke should remark it. In this there was nothing wrong, but it was likely to be misinterpreted, and certain not to pass unperceived.

The Queen, who had by degrees effectually got rid of the formalities of etiquette, had no notion of submitting to constraint with her own friends. Before Fersen's return it was not Lauzun who held the first place among that favoured few; it was not any of them with whom public rumour was busy: it was the Duc de Coigny.

Count Tilly writes of him at the time of his highest favour; he was then forty-five years old :—

"Coigny was not a very handsome man, nor was he very talented, but he was better than either; he had exquisite manner, perfect bearing, a fine presence, a just and simple mind, composure and politeness, a true heart which his elevation had not corrupted or favour spoiled. Coigny, who was beloved by all, had no enmity towards any."

There is no doubt that at one time he had great influence with the Queen. Lauzun gives a proof of this in his *Mémoires*. It was at Choisy. He presented himself after an absence to the Queen, who received him graciously, manifested great pleasure on seeing him again, and talked with him for a considerable time. Afterwards he heard Coigny say to her—she was sitting near the door—"You have not kept your word; you promised not to talk much with him, and to treat him like everybody else."

Lauzun knew this applied to himself, and on the Queen's approaching a few minutes later, with the intention of speaking to him, he said—

"Take care; you will get yourself scolded again."

She seemed embarrassed, but recovered herself, and jested with him about the incident.

Was it surprising that the spite and jealousy of the many found matter for comment in the favour shown to a few by Marie Antoinette? And yet, all this was nothing in comparison with "the affair of the necklace."

The story is well known; a brief recapitulation of it is all that is necessary in this place. Cardinal de Rohan was desperately anxious to win the favour of the Queen, who had treated him with marked coldness, and encouraged by a scheming adventuress, Mme. de la Motte, who was remotely and illegitimately connected with the Valois family, he imagined that a princely present, the gift of a necklace worth sixteen hundred thousand livres, would soften the heart of Marie Antoinette. Mme. de la Motte, to convince him of this, had got up the most audacious comedy that ever was acted on any stage, and, wonderful to consider, her audacity succeeded fully. She had discovered among women of a certain class one who was strikingly like the Queen. A skilful disguise completed the deception, and she took this woman one evening into a grove in the park of Versailles.

The Cardinal came there by previous arrangement with Mme. de la Motte, and he really believed that it was Marie Antoinette herself who let a rose fall from her hand at his feet, and who murmured the words,—"The past is forgotten."

This scene filled the prelate with hope and joy. He bought the famous necklace; but it was easier for him to intrust it to Mme. de la Motte to be handed over to the Queen, than to pay the price of it to the Court jewellers. The latter demanded their money, and Marie Antoinette was involved in the scandal of this dark intrigue, notwithstanding her innocence, and indeed ignorance, of the matter.

For the moment it seemed that calumny was to triumph, and the Queen to be overwhelmed by the persistent statements of the wretch, La Motte, who declared that she acted solely by her Majesty's orders. The Cardinal, as much through conviction of their truth as from prudence, confirmed the woman's story, which was fatal to the Queen.

Who was the woman, if not she, who had

spoken in the nocturnal scene in the park of Versailles?

A strange chance upset Mme. de la Motte's plan of defence, and happily disproved her statements.

The trial had already begun, when one day a friar-minor, Père Loth, sought an interview with the Procureur-Général, and asked permission to make a full avowal, no matter what disgrace it must involve to himself. Truth, and the duty and fidelity he owed to the King and Queen, constrained him to take this course. He was received and heard, and his statement was as follows:—Being desirous to preach before the Court, he had pondered how to secure the permission of the Grand Almoner of France, Cardinal de Rohan; but as he was unknown to His Eminence, he could not think of any means of approaching him; then he heard of Mme. de la Motte and the great interest she possessed. Access was more easy on this side; he hastened to make acquaintance with her, and was soon on familiar terms. Thus it happened that he had seen and heard many things which he did not understand at first, but that might have some bearing upon the case under investigation. In particular he had one evening seen the "demoiselle d'Oliva" (a name conferred for the nonce on the woman d'Essigny) dressed, or rather disguised, by Mme. de la Motte, and had been so struck by her likeness to the Queen that he had remarked upon it. He knew that Oliva had been taken to Versailles the same evening.

He also named a certain Retaux de Villette as the accomplice of Mme. de la Motte in the affair. This person had taken flight, but Père Loth put the magistrates on his track, and he was arrested in Switzerland. Oliva was also brought out of her hiding-place, and the two detected persons acknowledged their respective parts in the scheme. Oliva had personated the Queen at Versailles, and Retaux had forged the notes which the Queen was supposed to have addressed to Cardinal de Rohan. Although these notes were signed "Marie Antoinette de France," the Cardinal, who certainly ought to have had his suspicions aroused by so absurd a signature, never doubted their authenticity.

The depositions of Père Loth, Retaux, and Oliva changed the aspect of things; the trial took place, and the truth was brought to light. But the sentence acquitting the Cardinal on the ground of "good faith" and condemning Madame de la Motte, did not kill the scandal or hinder its results. So hostile, it must be admitted, was public opinion to the Queen, that it caught at any opportunity of a demonstration against that unfortunate woman. No one among the masses would admit her innocence, although it was real, and her culpability became a fixed article of popular belief.

For several years past calumny against her had taken various forms; that of pamphlets and newspapers, or gazettes, as they were then called, in particular. Some time after the affair of the necklace, a great number of louis-d'or on which the King's head was represented with a horn very skilfully and visibly stuck up in the hair, were put in circulation. These coins, which were called "Strasburg louis," because they were struck in that town, excited the strongest indignation at Versailles, all the more because the Comte de Provence was believed to be the author of this dastardly manœuvre.

The thing was not at all impossible, and seemed very like his ordinary conduct. Nay, so mean an infamy was not even unlikely on the part of the King's younger brother. He had not forgiven his sister-in-law for becoming a mother, and he had actually cast a doubt, on the occasion of the baptism of Marie Thérèse (Madame Royale), upon the parentage of the children who were to bar him from the throne. He vehemently denied the allegation, and perhaps he was not guilty. In this single instance it is possible that he was wrongfully accused of a crime against his own kin.

On the other hand, it was he who gave to his brother's wife, to the Queen of France, the nickname of *Madame Déficit*. This terrible nickname spread rapidly, and was eagerly adopted by the populace, who hated her, so that in the affair of the deficit, as in so many other matters, she bore the responsibility of acts in which she had taken only the very slightest part.

No doubt, the Queen had incurred great expense in the embellishment of the Petit-Trianon; no doubt she had been unwise in her generosity in several cases, heaping money and lucrative posts upon her creatures, the

Polignacs and others; but the deficit, which had long existed in the finances of the kingdom, and had survived the first Necker Ministry, was in no wise of her making. To clear her from that accusation it needs only to mention the name of Calonne.

M. de Calonne was chosen for the post of Comptroller-General in 1783, for one of those strong reasons which Figaro put so neatly—

"Il fallait un calculateur."

We know the rest. Calonne himself was quite frank on the point.

"The finances of France are in a deplorable condition," he said to M. de Machault; "you may be sure that I should never have taken charge of them but for the bad state of my own." M. de Machault, in recording this speech, adds, with his usual gravity and *finesse*—" And yet I had done nothing to merit so extraordinary a confidence."

At his first interview with the new Comptroller-General, Louis XVI. received a similar avowal.

"Sire," said Calonne, "I have just debts to the amount of two hundred and twenty thousand livres. A Comptroller-General might readily find means to pay that sum, but I prefer to confess the whole truth to your Majesty, and to owe everything to your goodness."

The King, taken by surprise, had nothing to say, and all he could do was to take out of his cash-box shares in the Compagnie des Eaux to the value of two hundred and thirty thousand livres, and hand them to Calonne.

This incident supplies the measure of the audacity of the one man, and the stupid good-nature of the other. We can judge what that administration was bound to be. Calonne, who had the generosity of a ruined man, and the prodigality of a Minister who desires to secure partisans, held by the axiom that one can only get money if one is rich, and that one can only pass for being rich by a lavish expenditure. The worst of it was that this axiom verified itself practically, at least for a certain time. Calonne passed for a great Minister, a model Comptroller-General.

"When I see everybody holding out their hands," said a certain prince, who suited the action to the word, " I hold out my hat."

Louis XVI. continued to admire his Minister. It would have been interesting for an observer to have been present at the interviews between the two, when we think that in one single year Calonne made cash payments to the amount of one hundred and thirty-six millions, twenty-one millions being paid on orders to bearer, while the King, true to habits of petty economy, continued to note his expenses, without omitting the smallest item, just as, when he was Dauphin, he put down in the account-books which still exist—

"At Epinay, for a basin, six sous;
"For six sheets of paper, four sous;
"For some cotton, six sous;
"At Epinay, for expense, four sous three deniers. . . .[1]

---

[1] An obsolete coin, the twelfth part of a sou.

The wonder was that the bringing forth of coin out of empty coffers lasted for three whole years. But the hour came at last when the model Comptroller had to acknowledge the state of the Treasury (as it was still called by force of habit) to the King. His usual adroitness did not fail him on this occasion; while admitting the deficit, he took care to put forward a plan for supplying it, and restoring order to the finances of the kingdom.

"But it is Necker that you are giving me, nothing but Necker!" exclaimed the poor King, who was equally embarrassed and distressed by the position of affairs.

"Sire, in the actual state of things," replied Calonne with imperturbable coolness, "nobody can offer you anything better."

There was but one thing for Louis to do: to dismiss the incapable Minister who had deceived and led him to the brink of the precipice. He did not do this; he had been blind for three years, he now allowed himself to be blinded afresh by the promises of Calonne, and consented to inaugurate the execution of his plan by convoking an Assembly of the Notables.

This had an ill sound in the ears of the nobles. What! royalty, which was absolute, to have recourse to the advice of any Assembly whatsoever! What was happening? The effect was deplorable, as d'Allonville testifies.

"I supped with Count Berchini," he says, "towards the end of December 1786. The Vicomte de Ségur arrived from Versailles, and was immediately surrounded and asked for news.

He put on an air of mystery, and said in a half-whisper—

"'The news is very great and very important; you will hardly believe it.'

"'What is it, then?'

"'The King has just sent in his resignation.' Everybody laughed, and wanted to know the meaning of this joke.

"'It is not a joke,' said Ségur, and then told them of the decree of the Council convoking an Assembly of the Notables."

The people were too wise to rejoice. What could "Notables,"—that is to say, persons privileged by birth or by fortune—do to meet so enormous a deficit? They could make sacrifices. The small fry knew that it would be proposed to the Notables to do this, but that they themselves would have to pay in the end.

Calonne's new plans excited ridicule instead of inspiring confidence. Here is a specimen of the criticism they received, in the form of a theatrical announcement:—

"Notice is hereby given, that the Comptroller-General has formed a new Company of Actors, whose first performance will take place before the Court on Monday, the 29th of this month; the chief piece will be *Les Fausses Confidences*, to be followed by *Le Consentement Forcé*; after which an allegorical ballet-pantomime, composed by M. de Calonne, entitled *Le Tonneau des Danaïdes*, will be given."

This arrow hit the blot; the programme was carried out from point to point. But although the Notables were unable to find any remedy for the state of affairs, their meeting was so far useful that it revived the remembrance of the States-General in the minds of the people.

Certain things which made an impression were said during the sittings, especially the following weighty sentence :—

"The States-General only have power to decree the land-tax, such as is proposed."

Count Fersen, whose double service obliged him to divide his time between Sweden and France, had returned about this time, and was then at Versailles. He was present at the last sitting of the Assembly of Notables, and he writes on the 25th of May 1787—"I am very glad to have witnessed this ceremony; it is very imposing, and probably will not take place again in our time.

"The results of the Assembly of Notables are great reforms in the households of the princes; but the most of these apply only to old customs, whose pompous ostentation escaped notice, and which served no purpose except that of absorbing an enormous sum of money. The Comte d'Artois has already returned 400,000 livres to the King out of the allowance for his household. The reduction in the Queen's stables amounts to 100,000 crowns; in short, it seems that a firm resolution to correct abuses so far as possible has been taken.

"The King has already reformed his hunting establishment—the wild-boar and wolf-hounds, the hawks, all that is called *le vol*, and the salary of the Grand Falconer are to be suppressed, it is said. There are other reductions that I do not remember. A diminution by two-fifths of all pensions above 10,000 livres is much talked of, but this is not certain."

No, that was not certain, any more than other reforms, demanded not so much by the Notables as by necessity, were certain.

In a few cases only reductions were carried out, to the displeasure of all those who feared that their own turn for revision might come. Baron de Besenval promptly made himself the mouthpiece of the malcontents.

"It is really dreadful," said he to the Queen, who could do nothing at all in the matter, "to live in a country where one is not sure of having to-morrow what is one's own to-day. Formerly it was only in Turkey that such a thing could happen."

That a man who was not devoid of intelligence and good sense should utter such words, is an indication of an intellectual condition in revolt against the lessons which events were already indicating. When we recognise this we are less surprised that Louis XVI., being forced to dismiss Calonne, because it was impossible to hold out any longer against the attacks made upon him, should have replaced him by M. Loménie de Brienne, Archbishop of Toulouse, an ambitious prelate, who hid his insignificance under his dignity, just as he concealed a skin disease beneath his purple robe. Everything went from bad to worse.

While these events, big with consequences and danger for the future, were occurring in France, things were becoming complicated in the North. His sojourn in France had completely intoxicated Gustavus III., who no longer thought of anything but grandeur of every description,

palaces, theatres, singers, and actors. In order
to realise his visions he had taken to spending
money which he did not possess, and, being
obliged to face the problem of ever-growing
debts, he resorted to deplorable measures. He
displeased the clergy by selling benefices, the
nobility by curtailing some of their privileges,
the middle classes by rescinding a portion of
their liberties, and the people by raising the
price of brandy.

The manifestation of opposition to his Government was too strong for the King to disregard
it; he had to endeavour either to disarm or
to satisfy the general feeling. Yielding to his
adventurous nature, he endeavoured to get rid
of his difficulties by engaging in a war with
Russia. The least of the defects of this war
was its uselessness, and so convinced of the
fact were his troops, both the chiefs and the
soldiers, that they refused to obey his orders.
Gustavus was obliged to fly from his mutinous
army, and hastily returned to his kingdom,
where his position was seriously compromised,
when an invasion by the Danes, who threatened
Gothenburg, gave him an opportunity of recovering his prestige and his authority.

Without loss of time he mustered six thousand
of his faithful Dalecarlians, marched upon the
Danes, and forced them to retreat. The intervention of Prussia and England did the rest,
and Gustavus III., more lucky than wise, got
happily out of the scrape which he had created
for himself. Count Fersen, who shortly before
had been made captain-lieutenant of the body-

guard, followed him in this double campaign, but the services he rendered the King were insignificant in comparison with those expected of him.

The position of Gustavus III. respecting the Court of France was very difficult. The chivalrous and arbitrary King of Sweden did not favour the new ideas which were dawning on Europe at the end of the eighteenth century, and he considered the maintenance of the cause of the monarchs always and everywhere one of his most imperative duties. Now, it was easy to perceive, from symptoms only too significant, that the throne of Louis XVI. was already tottering; and Gustavus, who was more than ever desirous of obtaining exact information upon the state of things in Paris, felt that it was essential to have a man placed there on whose fidelity, zeal, and discretion he might absolutely reckon.

He might have employed his own ambassador, M. de Staël, for this purpose; but M. de Staël, the first victim of his new family relations, had been won over to liberal if not revolutionary ideas; he leant towards the parties who were hostile to the royal family. To remove the ambassador was out of the question. On the occasion of his marriage, M. de Staël had obtained a promise from the King that his ambassadorship should last for six years at least, and that, in case unforeseen circumstances should lead to his being deprived of it, he was to receive an equivalent place, or an annual pension of 20,000 livres. This was certainly

H

paying very dearly for the honour of having Mdlle. Necker's husband for his ambassador, but Gustavus had committed the imprudence, and he had only indirect means of repairing its unpleasant or harmful results.

He therefore directed Baron Taube to form a sort of secret Ministry of Foreign Affairs for things appertaining to France, and he constituted Count John Fersen his secret representative at Paris, a sort of ambassador *in partibus*.

This organisation began its work in 1788, and the two Swedes did their best to annihilate the influence of Mme. de Chicogne (their nickname for Mme. de Staël). The curious situation led to a double and necessarily contradictory correspondence, and the King and Queen of France were apprised of this, so that the documents might not become a source of endless confusion.

"The King commands me also to inform you," wrote Baron Taube to Count Fersen, "that all the despatches to Staël are written in the sense of the Revolution; he means to feign that he pays attention to what he (Staël) says, but this is only to ascertain their real projects and their views. The King commands you to inform the King and Queen, so that they may make no mistakes. You will assure them that the King will never vary in his sentiments and in his attachment to them, and this he will endeavour to prove to them under all circumstances."

Gustavus III. could not have chosen a more safe ambassador, or one more agreeable to those to whom he was accredited. Louis was charmed to see the Swedish gentleman, who was famous for his military exploits, and faithful to the old ideas and the old races. As for Marie Antoinette, the hour of danger had come; many wavering friendships had forced her to see that the powerful err by ceasing to be or to appear powerful, and she could not fail to rejoice in knowing that a man was near her whose heart she possessed, and who—so different from many others—would be all the more devoted with her increasing need of his devotion, as the moment for putting it to the proof approached.

The presence of Count Fersen was naturally explained by the functions which he had accepted. Was he not colonel of the Royal Suédois? His regiment was in garrison at Maubeuge, Valenciennes, and neighbouring towns; he visited these from time to time, returning frequently to Paris, according to custom at that period.

Paris was not so far from Versailles but that he also found his way to Trianon. Those were happy days for him, passed in that sweet and already old companionship; and Marie Antoinette also was happy in the society of her faithful friend.

It was during one of his visits to Trianon that she gave him her portrait, a miniature by Roquet, and a pocket-book, with the following lines written on the first leaf:—

> " Qu'écrirez-vous sur ces tablettes ?
> Quels secrets leur confierez-vous ?
> Ah ! sans doute elles furent faites
> Pour les souvenirs les plus doux !
> En attendant qu'à cet usage
> Le souvenir soit employé,
> Qu'il soit permis à l'amité
> D'en remplir la première page."

Although Lafont d'Aussonne remarks that "French poetry had a thousand charms for the heart of Marie Antoinette, and she cultivated it with success," the question whether these lines are really the Queen's has not been settled. But what does it matter? By the care with which she wrote them out herself, she made them hers, and the evidence of her affection was equally precious to him who was honoured by it.

Count Fersen passed in France the year that preceded the outbreak of the greatest events which have yet taken place in the internal history of a nation. His intellect, thoughtful and sagacious as it was in the ordinary course of life, was not sufficiently lofty to forecast, however imperfectly, the great work that was about to be accomplished; but the agitation of men's minds did not escape him, and it made him fear another, and far more dangerous, kind of agitation—that of appetites let loose, and an era of violence opening upon France.

"All men's minds are in a ferment; nothing is talked of but a 'constitution;' the women especially are joining in the hubbub, and you know as well as I what influence they have in this country. It is a mania, everybody is an administrator and can talk only of progress; the lackeys in the antechambers are occupied in reading the pamphlets that come out, ten or twelve in a day, and I do not know how the printing-presses can do the work." (Paris, 10th December 1788.)

The secret ambassador of Gustavus III. found it difficult to understand how the French people could take so much pleasure in reading "those

THE MISERY OF THE PEOPLE

pamphlets." He was imbued with all the ideas of the past, with all the prejudices of the old social order; he was one of the privileged caste; he did not see what the philosophers of the age had accomplished; the destruction of the old society, hunted down by the wit of Voltaire, and the reconstruction of a new society elaborated by the genius of Rousseau.

He felt nothing of what the people felt. But the people—like the blind who are conscious of obstacles which they do not see, who scent danger and find the right way by a marvellous instinct—the people felt that something great was in preparation for them.

A man of genius might have given it to them; an intelligent prince might have helped them to take it; the weak and narrow-minded descendant of the Bourbons tried to snatch it from them; and so he let loose the storm.

And no matter what has been or may be said, the people were the chief victims of that awful time. Everything seemed to combine to exasperate them. In the months prior to the assembling of the States-General, the already serious distress was increased, and a winter of unexampled severity added to its gravity. The cold was so intense that infants were frozen in their cradles, the rivers were frozen, the roads were frozen: how was wheat sufficient for the food of millions to be provided? Dearth set in, and famine was impending.

Those dark days were but forerunners of darker days to come.

CHAPTER V.

The 5th of May at the door of the Menus-Plaisirs—The States-General—The taking of the Bastille—Count Fersen's impressions — October days — The mob at Versailles — The Queen in danger—The Royal Family returns to Paris—The Journal of Louis XVI. — Count Fersen at Aix-la-Chapelle—Baron Taube—The Fête of the Federation—Political news — Incidents of the 18th of April 1791—Preparations for departure—Uneasiness among the people—Vigilance of Citizens Busebi and Hucher—The 21st of June—M. Lemoine enters the King's bedchamber—It is empty—Disappearance of the Royal Family—Commotion in Paris—*Au bœuf couronné.*

"WHAT more is wanted?" replies Figaro in *La Folle Journée,* when Count Almaviva bids him arrange the salon for the public audience: "The big arm-chair for you, a stool for the clerk, good chairs for the plain honest people, two benches for the lawyers, the floor for the fine folk, and the riff-raff at the back. The floor-polishers (*frotteurs*) may go now." Figaro's sally raised a laugh, but that it had not corrected anybody became only too evident in the early days of the Revolution.

On the 5th of May 1789, a considerable crowd assembled before a small side-door of the great hall known as the Salle des Menus-Plaisirs at Versailles. Those who composed this crowd were dressed in a sort of uniform, or rather in a sort of livery, for their costume was extremely simple,—black coat, breeches, and stockings, a short cloak of some woollen stuff, a cambric collar, and a three-cornered hat, such as the inferior clergy wore. They talked in groups, some coolly, others with animation; all were grave and stern. At length the door was opened, and through that modest portal they slowly passed into an immense hall, magnificently decorated, and lighted from the roof—which was supported on pillars—by three skylights, a very large one in the centre, and two smaller ones at either end. White silk blinds placed before these apertures rendered the light soft and pleasant. Behind the pillars were graduated rows of benches filled with spectators.

In the centre of the hall, within a space twenty feet long and fifty feet wide, arrangements had been made on a plan exactly corresponding with that of Figaro.

At the far end was the throne, under a rich gold-fringed canopy, beside it an arm-chair for the Queen, court-stools (*tabourets*) for the princesses, and folding-seats (*pliants*) for the princes; on the right were the seats reserved for the clergy; on the left those for the representatives of the nobility.

In the lower part of the hall were rows of forms; these were intended for the deputies of the Third Estate.

The men dressed in black who had entered by the small side-door were the six hundred deputies of that order, and they had been purposely snubbed beforehand by being obliged to don a costume symbolical of their so-called inferior position, according to an old and ridiculous usage.

Thus did the people make their entry into the Assembly of the States-General. Relegated to the lower end of the hall, they confronted from thence the heir of all their kings, the successors of those who, by their virtues and their learning, had made the Church of France, and the descendants of the warriors and statesmen who had served king and country.

The spectacle they contemplated was very different from that which they presented; the bishops were arrayed in purple robes with lace rochets, the curés in large cloaks and square caps, the nobles wore cloth of gold and silken mantles, Henri IV. hats, and had swords by their side.

What effect could the sombre array of the Third Estate produce in the presence of all this brilliancy and magnificence of costume? It must surely be eclipsed by such a show. This was not so, however. Already, in the procession through the streets of Versailles the day before, it was the men in black to whom the sympathy and the acclamations of the crowd were given; and again the people were for the men in black, with whom the hopes of all those who toil, pay, and suffer, had entered through that small side-door. Only a few years were to pass before the men on whom it was intended to play a good trick by forcing them to wear the garb of mutes, would justify that expedient by "conducting" the funeral of the monarchy, the clergy, and the nobility.

Count Fersen, still in France, divided his time between Paris and Valenciennes. He had been affected by the course of events to the extent of having his pension of 20,000 livres reduced to 13,000, in consequence of the diminishing resources of the Treasury.

He augured nothing good from the state of things. He did not comprehend the great movement that was upheaving the French nation; he recognised only the disorder and confusion accompanying the emission of ideas, new and absurd to him and to those of his caste. He wrote to his father (26th June 1789) :—

"The ferment is extreme; you know what French heads are, and you can easily picture to yourself to what turbulence they may be roused, but you could never have imagined the indecency of all this, and God knows how it will end!"

He takes note of a few instances in which the King was inclined to resist, but he is chiefly anxious because "they are not sure of the French soldiery, and are obliged to employ foreigners as much as possible."

Not all foreigners, however, for Louis XVI. had just dismissed his Genevese Minister, Necker, and replaced him by "men of his own." The dismissal of Necker was not a bad move; "the great man infected with popularity" was no better able to cope with events than another. The misfortune was that the King should have replaced Necker as President of the Council by Baron de Breteuil, of whom the Marquise de Fleury said, not without justice, "The Baron is not merely stupid; he is a fool."

The old Marshal de Broglie was made Minister of War.

The result of these appointments came with promptitude. Fersen writes on the 22nd of July.:—"The populace have seized upon the Bastille and massacred M. de Launay, the governor, in a horrible manner. They took 36,000 muskets from the Invalides; all vehicles were stopped in Paris; every one had to go on foot, and the mob reviled the nobility."

These violent acts of the populace led to a fresh concession by the King, who had said, "I will not have one single man perish in my quarrel." Necker was recalled.

This was a good opportunity for the princes to come forward and prove their courage and resolution. Much was expected of the young Comte d'Artois, who posed everywhere as a defender of the rights of the monarchy, and was the first to condemn his brother's weakness; but that expectation was soon dispelled. The Comte d'Artois, more prudent than valiant, bent upon taking care of himself rather than the royal authority for which he professed so much solicitude, thought proper to get away immediately with his children, thus setting the example of emigration and giving the signal for the exodus.

The three princes, Condé, Conti, and Bourbon, followed him, and Baron de Breteuil, that he might not be taken for a fool this time, promptly put the frontier between himself and his fellow-countrymen.

These successive departures augmented the

evils of the time by increasing the popular suspicion. What was it all those princes, all those nobles, had gone abroad to seek? Safe shelter for themselves in the first place, but also enemies for France. The effect of the emigration was, therefore, to diminish the number of the champions of royalty, and to create fresh enemies for it.

The popular fear grew apace, and found utterance in violence. A disturbance that took place at Valenciennes was easily put down, but tumults arose constantly in Paris, and at the same time desertion was largely increased. Fersen writes on the 15th of August:—" It is said that, according to the reports made by the regiments to the War Office, *there have been, since the 13th of July, twelve thousand seven hundred and fifty deserters*, not reckoning the Gardes Françaises. . . . There is no longer law or order, justice, discipline, or religion in the kingdom : all bonds are broken, and how are they to be reconstituted? I cannot tell; but such is the effect of the progress of learning, of Anglo-mania, and philosophy. France is ruined for a long time."

On the 3rd of September he writes :—

"All bonds are broken, the authority of the King is gone, and Paris is trembling before forty or fifty thousand ruffians (*bandits*) or vagabonds. *In the provinces the people are full of the notion that the philosophers have been disseminating for so long, that all men are equal; and the abolition of feudal and other rights, upon which the Assembly decided*

*in three hours, and after supper, has persuaded
them that they need not pay anything.* . . .
The nobles are in despair, the clergy are like
men suddenly gone mad, and the Third Estate
is very ill-content. Several regiments have revolted ; some have even struck their superior
officers. In our garrison it has not yet come
to this, but the soldiers, having forced the gates
of the quarters and the town, and gone out to
drink in the country, committed terrible outrages there for three days together. The third
day they would have pillaged and set fire to
the town had not the drums beat to arms ;
then, with the assistance of the town militia,
we restored quiet and order.

"If I were writing from Paris, I could not
venture to tell you all this ; the epistolary
inquisition has been very active there ; even
the letters of the King and Queen have not
escaped it."

At this particular moment Count Fersen
left his garrison at Valenciennes and came to
Versailles, in obedience either to a suggestion of
his own heart or to a request. Events speedily
proved to him that his presence was likely to
be useful.

The ferment, which was increasing in Paris,
gave rise to well-founded fears for the safety
of the royal family, and also for that of the
National Assembly. At Versailles there was
no longer any force capable of resisting the
slightest popular movement : since the deser-
tions and the decomposition of the regular army,
the means of defence was reduced to a small body

of militia. Now Versailles was beginning to be directly threatened by Paris. This was openly stated; the plans of the rioters were no secret to any one, and the fact was known to Mirabeau, who spoke freely of it to one Blaisot, a bookseller at Versailles.

"My dear Blaisot," said he, "out of regard for you I wish to give you notice that in a few days you will see great troubles, and even horrors: blood will be shed at Versailles. I warn you of this, so as to keep you from any personal uneasiness: good citizens like you have nothing to fear."

Loustalot wrote in his Journal: "There must be another fit of revolution; everything points to this."

The Comte de Saint-Priest, the only brave and active Minister, resolved to resist the pre-announced attack, and summoned the Flandre regiment, one of the few that could still be trusted.

But even precautions became dangers in those disastrous days. The arrival of the soldiers aroused the anger of the patriots, and that anger rose to fury when the events of the 1st and 2nd of October became known.

The body-guards had invited their comrades of the Flandre regiment to a banquet, which was given by permission of their Majesties in the theatre of the château. The officers and soldiers were excited by the generous wines, and by the presence of all the distinguished personages still remaining at the Court, by whom the tiers of boxes were crowded; their enthusiasm was fired by the entry of the King followed by the Queen, carrying the Dauphin in her arms, and when the orchestra greeted the royal visitors with the well-known strains of "*O Richard! ô mon roi! l'univers t'abandonne,*" they were carried away beyond all restraint, and madly cheered their Majesties. Then followed an extraordinary scene. They tore off their tri-coloured cockades, replaced them by white ones hastily made up with ribbons which the women who were present detached from their dresses, and then, forming an escort to the royal personages, they left the scene of the banquet and went out into the great courtyard, frantically renewing their expressions of loyalty.

Louis XVI. had not sufficient firmness to stop these dangerous manifestations at once; the Queen enjoyed the acclamations, to which she was no longer accustomed; everybody was carried away by the enthusiasm of their faithful champions, which they took for a forecast of victory.

The awakening was terrible. Paris thrilled with rage when these occurrences, amplified and distorted by rumour, were related. "Was *patrouillotisme* to get the better of patriotism?" according to a caricature of the day. What disgrace for the conquerors of the Bastille! But no, no! that should not be. Out of their lairs came the frantic populace; Maillart was there; the hags and shrews followed him; the Faubourgs rose in tumult: the starving mob was roused to fury against the feasting soldiery.

THE MOB AT THE CHATEAU

All the scoundrels and beggars of Paris marched upon Versailles.

It was the 5th of October. The old capital of the kings was quiet, and the royal family, reassured by the joyous shouts that still echoed in their ears, had dispersed to follow their respective inclinations in the employment of that peaceful day. Louis XVI. was stag-hunting in the neighbourhood of Rambouillet, Marie Antoinette had sought the quiet of Trianon, Madame Elizabeth had gone to Montreuil, and Mesdames, the King's aunts, were at Bellevue.

The news of the approach of the mob spread quickly; the King returned in haste to the palace, and received a deputation of women, who clamoured for bread. Then came parleying, in the attempt to gain time. Marie Antoinette had left Trianon; the family, collected together, were conjecturing whether she would take advantage of the still-remaining possibility of flight, and so escape from the threatening populace, when Lafayette appeared. Lafayette had endeavoured to stop, and then to moderate, the tumult. Finding either impossible, he assembled a few battalions of the National Guard and followed the mob, in the hope of preventing any great calamity. His presence certainly moderated the popular violence.

Night fell, and redoubled the fear, if not the danger, of the unhappy persons shut up in the château. Fersen was with the Queen, and, if we are to believe a statement made by

Mme. Campan, reported by Lord Holland to Talleyrand, and embodied in the *Mémoires* of the latter, he did not leave her for a moment, even following her into her bedroom, and when the tumult was revived by one of the body-guards firing a shot, he escaped in disguise from that room, which anybody might invade.

He did not go away, however; the danger was too great and the defenders were too few. The night passed in terror for the royal family, their attendants, and the body-guard. At length, the dawn came; the crowd, with ever-increasing numbers, was still there, howling under the windows, and ever above the uproar rose the shout, "Down with the Austrian woman!"

Lafayette was in the château; he was unable to quell the tumult, and equally unable to induce the King and Queen to submit to the will of the crowd, who desired to bring them back to Paris. The cries and threats were redoubled. What was to be done?

Time was passing, and the popular fury was increasing with every moment. Lafayette had an inspiration.

"Madame," he ventured to say to the Queen, "what is your personal intention?"

In the hour of peril the daughter of Maria Theresa showed all the courage of her race.

"I know the fate that awaits me," she replied firmly, "but my duty is to die at the feet of the King, and in the arms of my children."

"Then, Madame, come with me!" said

Lafayette; and he moved as though to lead her to the balcony facing the crowd.

Brave as she was, Marie Antoinette hesitated.

"What! alone upon the balcony? Have you not seen the signs that have been made to me?"

In truth, those signs were equally terrible and expressive.

"Yes, Madame, let us go there," insisted Lafayette, who risked his own life by this act.

Fersen was present. By a look the Swedish gentleman gave fresh courage to the Queen of France. She decided instantly, and valiantly walked forward into the view of the people. Lafayette could not speak; his voice would not have been heard. He resorted to a "hazardous but decisive sign:" he took the Queen's hand and kissed it.

This action worked an instantaneous change. Courage, daring, produced their usual effect; the conquered crowd passed from rage to admiration; a great clamour arose, carrying to the astonished ears of the actors in this scene, cries of "Long live the General!" "Long live the Queen!"

But, whether it found voice in shouts or in howls, the will of the crowd had to be obeyed.

They intended to bring back "the baker, the baker's wife, and the little baker's boy," to Paris. They believed that they would be safe from court-plots when they should have the royal family in their possession. No resistance could be offered, and preparations were made for the return. At half-past two the carriages were ready, and the royal prisoners set out for Paris. Count Fersen followed with the members of the King's household.

Paris was not reached until evening; it was dark, and the long-disused Tuileries, sombre and silent as a tomb, received the unfortunate royal family. There were scarcely enough dismantled beds and rickety chairs for their use. Some articles of furniture were hastily procured; it seemed as though the new-comers were but temporary lodgers in that ancient dwelling of the kings.

Count Fersen settled himself in Paris, in the Rue du Bac; he would not leave those to whom he was bound, not so much by his diplomatic mission, as by his affection for them.

On the 9th of October he informs his father of these sad events.

"I witnessed everything, and I returned to Paris in one of the King's carriages; we were six hours and a half on the road. May God preserve me from again beholding so afflicting a spectacle as that of those two days! The people seemed enchanted to see the King and his family. The Queen was warmly applauded, and she cannot fail to be when she is known, and justice is done to her desire for good and the kindness of her heart. The States-General are about to come to Paris, and will begin their sittings, but I do not yet know the day."

After the storm came the calm that ensued

on all the violent crises of the time. Louis XVI. indicates this in his journal :—

"*October* 5.—Killed twenty-one head at the Châtillon gate; interrupted by events; went and returned on horseback.
"6.—Departure for Paris at half-past two; visit to the Hôtel de Ville; supped and slept at the Tuileries.
"7.—Nothing. My aunts came to dinner.
"8.—Nothing."

The winter was a dismal time for the royal family. The people of Paris, excited by the increasing poverty and the stormy discussions of the National Assembly, which reached them in an exaggerated and envenomed form through the gazettes or the speeches of the club orators, had ceased to regard the King and Queen with either affection or respect. The Queen continued to be the object of terrible threats. The situation grew worse day by day, and it was very difficult to hope for a revulsion in public opinion.

Count Fersen was alive to the danger of prolonged inaction, although his ardent devotion to Marie Antoinette and his great admiration of her had led him into certain delusions. Thus, although he writes to Gustavus III., on the 7th of January 1790, that "the King's party was already much strengthened in the Assembly and in the provinces," that "the courage, the firmness, and the good conduct of the Queen had brought many people back to her," he did not persuade himself into false security. He had gone to Valenciennes to meet Baron Taube, and had passed a week with him there.

Baron Evert Taube, lieutenant-general and first gentleman of the King's chamber at the Court of Sweden, possessed the entire confidence of Gustavus III., and as he was a most intimate friend of Fersen, the two had been chosen, as we have seen, as the safest and most active intermediaries for the secret negotiations to be carried on between the Tuileries and Stockholm. All the correspondence passed through their hands, and never were more faithful agents employed in the service of the royal prisoners. After they had conferred together and agreed upon the course to be taken, they parted; Taube went back to Sweden, and Fersen set out on his return to France. He proceeded so far as Aix-la-Chapelle, from whence he wrote a long letter to his King, thanking him anew for the mission he had confided to him. He did not reach Paris until the 17th or 18th of January.

From that moment he carried on an active correspondence with Sweden. It was of two sorts, the one, addressed to Gustavus III., being entirely political, the other, addressed to his father, containing the narrative of his impressions according to the progress of events under his observation.

His comments possess deep interest and are very curious, for they are those of a witness as impartial as it was possible for him with his old monarchical creed to be. His severe judgment of Necker is justified.

"M. Necker," he writes, "as ignorant in administration as he is said to be learned in finance, and imbued with the philosophic ideas, never bethought him that it was necessary to make friends for the King. He regarded the means of persuasion as hardly honest; he wanted to count as an honest man among rogues, and he merely to be reckoned their dupe. His unbounded self-esteem made him believe that he could persuade them; but English money had stronger and more irresistible arguments to offer. M. Necker is not guilty of ignorance only, he is also guilty of treason. He desired to be the people's Minister, to reign through the people, and to force the King into being unable to do without him; he has sacrificed the King and the State to his ambition. It is true that he has been punished for this, for his influence is now gone; but his punishment is no remedy for anything, *and the King has been wrong in not reigning through him, seeing that he cannot reign without him.*

"Among the Ministers, only M. de la Luzerne and M. de Saint-Priest mean well to the King; the others are all fools or rascals, in whom no confidence can be placed. M. de Saint-Priest combines character and firmness with ability, and if occasion arise he is the only one on whom the King can lean. I get on very well with him; his house is mine; he showers kindness, politeness, and confidence upon me. Through him I know everything that takes place; he even consults me frequently. Notwithstanding all this, I only tell him what I think fit; prudence is more than ever necessary" (1st February 1790).

"You will see by the public papers what a state the army is in; there is no longer either order or discipline. Everything is turned upside down. The soldiers form committees, break, try, and often execute their officers" (28th of June 1790).

In the midst of this disorder a great fête was organised. The idea of this fête was fine, and its effect could not fail to be imposing. The *Constituante* decreed that on the 14th of July, in order to celebrate the taking of the Bastille, an immense assembly, composed of envoys from all the departments, should take the oath of fidelity and obedience to the new Constitution. The idea was novel as well as patriotic, and it was admirably carried out. The people were delighted with the place selected; it was the Champ-de-Mars, surrounded by raised sod seats; in the centre an altar was erected. The people had not yet learned to dispense with the forms of religion. The ceremony began with a Mass. One individual who had the honour to officiate would have passed unnamed, had he not afterwards won universal renown, although he ultimately discarded his sacred calling. The celebrant was the Bishop of Autun, M. de Talleyrand-Périgord, who owed solely to his episcopal dignity a favour from which the faults of his youth, the scandals of his private life, and his well-known unbelief ought to have debarred him. His evil reputation had inspired Chénier with the following epigram:—

"Roquette dans son temps, Périgord dans le nôtre
Furent deux évêques d'Autun ;
Tartufe est le portrait de l'une,
Ah ! si Molière eût connu l'autre ! "

But individuals were effaced by the majesty of the place and the grandeur of the idea in this great manifestation of France as a whole : the vast federated multitude marching past with their banners before the King, the Assembly, and the Municipality formed so impressive a sight that all the spectators were enthralled by it. The Queen herself, sharing the general emotion, held up her son in her arms and showed him to the people, as though she would commend him to their love.

The people, enraptured in their turn, forgot their wrath, their resentment, and their suspicions for a brief space, and responded by prolonged acclamations.

Count Fersen was present at this spectacle, but the cool spirit of the North is not readily inflamed, and the Swede was alive only to the minor points of that federation, or at least he dwelt upon these only. In the account which he sends to his father, he describes the people of the lower class who were present as making the tour of the amphitheatre, singing and "dancing as savages do before devouring a Christian."

It is evident that he shared the impressions which these revolutionary festivals made upon the partisans of the old régime, who condescended to mock at them, after the fashion of the opposition in every country and at all times. In a *dossier* of the Revolutionary Tribunal there is a song which was seized at the abode of Mme. Quatresols de Marolles; it seems amusing enough to be reproduced here.

SONG.

To the air: *Ah! le bel oiseau, vraiment!*

Oh! queu superbe serment!
Comm'ça t'on n'en verra guère.
Oh! queu superbe serment,
S'il n'y eût ni pluie ni vent.

Figurez-vous le Champ-de-Mars,
Qu'est bien plus grand qu' not' cimetière;
Il était tout plein d'soudarts
Qu'avaient quasi l'air de guerre.
Oh! le superbe serment, &c.

Malgré c'te pluie et le vent,
On fit défiler l's armées.
Je m'disais en les regardant:
Ah! bon Dieu! que d'poules mouillées!
Oh! le superbe serment, &c.

Fallait voir nos députés
Dont queuques-uns faisaient la moue,
C'étaient de vrais culs crottés
Qui se traînaient dans la boue.
Oh! le superbe serment, &c.

Il y a t'un' chos' sapendant
Qui m'afflige et qui m'oppresse.
Ça fait du tort au serment:
C'est l'boiteux qu'a dit la messe.
Oh! le superbe serment!
Comme ça t'on n'en verra guère,
De ce superbe serment
Qu'était si beau, qu'était si grand!

Ils disaient que ce jur'ment
N'était pas de bonne trempe,
Ce s'rait dommage vraiment
Si c'nétait que d'la détrempe.
Oh! queu superbe serment!
Comm' ça s'ra biau en estampe!
Oh! le superbe serment!
Là n'y aura ni pluie ni vent!

The harmless song quoted above caused Mme. de Marolles to be sentenced to death and executed.

Returning to the impressions of Count Fersen, it is but fair to note that in his letter to Baron Taube he does not omit what may pass for a favourable symptom, but relates with satisfaction that there was a good deal of "Long live the King," "Long live the Queen," "Long live the Dauphin," but no other "vivats."

He is careful to record the impression which Marie Antoinette produced upon the deputies from the provinces. "They were enchanted with the Queen," he writes; "she bestowed upon them all the kindness and graciousness of which she can be so lavish."

Is he not too partial when he sums up his impressions in these words: "The ceremony was ridiculous, indecorous, and consequently unimportant, notwithstanding the stage on which it was performed, which was superb"?

The Fête of the Federation, by the happy hazard of events, afforded an opportunity which would have enabled a spirited and energetic prince to regain his wavering rule over subjects still inclined by ancient custom towards the object of their former veneration. Paris, still quiet enough and safe enough for individuals, was not satisfied with the Assembly, which was not fulfilling its promises to the city quickly enough. Therefore, Count Fersen hopes that "when once the discontent has risen to its height, the new order of things will be overturned as quickly as the old; this will be effected by the vivacity and the levity of the French." The King got finally rid of Necker, of whom it was said that "he gargled his throat with all the virtues, but did not swallow one drop of any of them." Mirabeau was making approaches to the Court party, and thus it was believed that M. de Lafayette, "that poor rascal," whose sworn enemy the great orator was, might be successfully opposed.

Unfortunately nothing availed to change the character of Louis XVI. "He feels his position keenly," writes Fersen to Baron Taube on the 7th of March 1791, "but he has not the gift of expressing himself, or saying pleasant things." The Queen only was equal to the occasion: "her courage never fails, and it is impossible to admire her sufficiently."

Such was the state of things when fresh incidents again altered the situation and precipitated events.

The King, who never paltered with anything that touched his religious principles, objected to the ministrations of a priest who had taken the oath to the Constitution. He had, therefore, decided upon fulfilling his Easter duties at Saint-Cloud. On the 18th of April 1791 he gave his orders accordingly. The carriages were drawn up in the courtyard, the King, the Queen, the Children of France, and Mme. de Tourzel came down and took their places; but they were hardly seated before the National Guards surrounded the carriages and refused to allow them to start. In vain did Lafayette press forward and try to speak to these madmen. They would not listen to him, and declared that they would prevent the departure of the King, whom they called "*an aristocrat, and a fat pig.*" "*He is paid twenty-five millions,*" they cried; "*the least he can do is our will.*"

The Queen ventured to interpose.

"There's a nice b—— to give orders!" they shouted. Lafayette, indignant at this disgraceful and ridiculous scene, asked the King whether it was his pleasure that force should be used to set him free and to cause the law to be respected; but Louis would only repeat the same sentence, "I will not have blood shed for me; when I am gone you may employ any means you please to cause the law to be respected."

In the meantime, the postilion was threatened with death if he stirred, and the outrider narrowly escaped hanging. If the King had not decided upon closing the discussion by re-entering the château, blood would have been shed, and the law would have been broken without waiting for his departure.

It was impossible to prove more clearly to the royal family that they were captives in Paris, or to make a plainer suggestion of flight, since a resolution to offer open resistance to the rapid advance of the Revolution could not be put into the mind or the heart of the King.

The mass of the people understood this instinctively, and a vague uneasiness got abroad. Not that they cared for the King—not that they considered his presence useful to the working of the Constitution; but they knew very well that the King, free, in a frontier town or in a foreign country, could not fail to unite the enemies of France and inspire the adversaries of the Revolution with ardour that would be dangerous to the whole nation.

Thus every one dreaded to learn that Louis XVI. had eluded the vigilance of his keepers, and with the passage of time this fear grew. Simple citizens turned themselves into spies and sentinels. Camille Desmoulins relates an incident which occurred on the night of the 20th of June 1791, as follows :—

"That night, one Busebi, a wigmaker in the Rue de Bourbon, called on one Hucher, a baker, and sapper in the battalion of the Theatines, in order to impart to the latter his fears founded on what he had just learned concerning the King's arrangements for flight. They hastened on the instant to arouse their neighbours, and, some thirty persons being assembled, they went immediately to the abode of M. de Lafayette, and informed him that the King was about to fly; they then demanded that he (Lafayette) should take immediate measures to prevent this. M. de Lafayette laughed, and advised them to return quietly to their homes. They asked him for the password, so that they might not be stopped, and he gave it to them. When they had procured the password, they directed their steps towards the Tuileries where they could perceive no movement; a number of hackney-coachman were, however, drinking at the little moveable booths close by the gate of the Carrousel. They then proceeded to inspect the courts up to the gate of the Riding-School, in which the sittings of the Assembly were held, but perceived nothing suspicious. On their return, they were surprised to find only one hackney-coach on the stand. All the others had disappeared."

A few hours afterwards a rumour spread through the city. It was said that at seven o'clock in the morning, M. Lemoine, the King's valet-de-chambre, having entered his master's room according to custom, heard no sound, and drew back the curtains of the bed. No one was there; the bed was empty!

He gave the alarm, and a search for the King was instituted. The attendants rushed into the rooms occupied by the Queen, the children, and Madame Elizabeth—all were empty! There was no doubt about it; the royal family had fled! The news spread from the Tuileries to every quarter of the city. The department of the municipality was informed of the event, and upon their order three cannon-shots were fired.

At this alarm-signal, the crowd flocked to the Tuileries. Everybody inquired, all wanted to know. The news was speedily confirmed; and the consternation was great at first, but the people soon recovered themselves, and proceeded to the Assembly: "Our King is there," they said: "Louis XVI. can go whither he pleases."

They tried to make out how he had fled.

False reports were already in circulation; it was said that the King had escaped by a canal attainable from the Pavillon de Flore, and that Bouillé had taken him and conveyed him to Metz.

Then, according to the difference of temperament, the people were filled either with anger or with fear. Some there were who rejoiced, and as every event lends itself to comic treatment, a facetious citizen pasted up the following notice on a wall of the Tuileries:—

"Notice is hereby given to the citizens, that a fat pig has run away from the Tuileries: those who may meet with him are requested to bring him back to his sty; they will receive a moderate reward."

This was not all: the popular fury vented itself in smashing things; all the royal emblems and memorials were attacked; escutcheons and fleur-de-lys were torn down. Insult was added to injury, and some wags, inspired by a happy thought which would have become the Comte de Provence, actually forced a humble tavern-keeper to take down his signboard, which bore these words: "*Au bœuf couronné.*"

CHAPTER VI.

Flight contemplated—The plan of M. de Breteuil—The Marquis de Bouillé—Count Fersen is charged with the negotiations—Intervention of the Emperor of Germany—Movements of troops on the frontier—Baron de Goguelat—Forces at the disposal of M. de Bouillé—Plan of journey—Reims to be avoided—Stages so far as Montmédy—Goguelat reconnoitres the route—The King's commands transmitted to Bouillé—Preparations in Paris—Baroness Korff—The berline—Meeting of Count Fersen and the Duc d'Orléans at Vincennes—The Tuileries watched—Doors made in the wood panelling—Persons associated with the projected flight: Count Fersen, Mme. Sullivan, Colonel Crawford—Lafayette—Mesdames de Tourzel, Brunier, and de Neuville—The body-guards, Messieurs de Valory, du Moustier, and de Maldent—The 20th of June in Paris—The final preparations—Count Fersen at the Tuileries—A chest of pistols and bullet-casting—Leaving the Tuileries—Incidents—Count Fersen disguised as a hackney-coachman—At Bondy—Separation—First relay—*Pourboires* too liberal—The royal family think they are out of danger—A saying of Louis XVI.—His imprudence—He is recognised by various persons—Pont Sommevesle—Commotion caused by the presence of the detachment commanded by Choiseul and Goguelat—Sainte-Menehould—M. d'Andoins—He warns the King to hasten onward—Drouet the postmaster and Guillaume—A quartermaster escapes and pursues, but does not come up with them—Clermont—M. de Damas—Drouet arrives at Varennes at a quarter to twelve o'clock—The Procureur of the commune is warned—The bridge barred—The berline arrives and cannot pass—Arrest of the travellers—The alarm-bell—The National Guard in arms—M. Destez—The King makes himself known—The night at Varennes—Goguelat attempts to deliver the King—Louis XVI. tries to gain time—M. de Bouillé does not appear—Arrival of Messieurs Romeuf, aide-de-camp to Lafayette, and Baillon—Departure from Varennes for Paris—Incidents—Murder of M. de Dampierre—Meeting at Epernay with the three commissaries sent by the National Assembly — Barnave, Latour - Maubourg, and Pétion—Pétion's narrative—Paris re-entered—The attitude of the population—The King's Journal.

SINCE the October "days" and the return to Paris, no doubt could exist that the royal family were in danger, not only from the decisions of the National Assembly, but also from the angry passions of the multitude. Over these the representatives of the nation had no influence, and the King could not control them by force, the army having in reality ceased to exist.

Louis XVI. and Marie Antoinette had looked around them for the means of safety, or rather for saviours. Those who presented themselves were not inconsiderable persons. The greatest in renown, and by right of his genius, was Mirabeau. In his capacity of agitator, Mirabeau could estimate the force of the storm, since it was he who had let loose the winds; but since he had passed over to the side of the Court he required a force to count upon, and did not want the royal authority to be completely annihilated. Accordingly, ever since October he had been advising the King to withdraw himself from the demagogic influences of Paris. By this he did not mean flight; on the contrary, it was his idea that Louis XVI. ought to depart quite openly, in the noonday, to the knowledge and in the sight of everybody, as a constitutional monarch making use of his prerogative, and to retire either to Fontainebleau or to some other royal residence, near enough to Paris to keep up the feeling that royalty was still present, far enough off to afford protection against a surprise like that of October, and where the nucleus of a faithful army, capable of resisting the National Guards of "*Gilles César*," as he called Lafayette, might be formed.

Marie Antoinette would readily have adopted this course, but Louis XVI., with his usual indecision and apathy of mind, could not arrive at a decision, but said Yes one day and No the next. Precious time was lost by his indecision, and the project, which might have been easily realised in 1789, and was still possible in 1790, became utterly visionary in 1791; this was proved by the incidents of the 18th of April.

In fact, the King and Queen distrusted Mirabeau; what he proposed seemed suspicious as emanating from him, and while the execution of his plan was indefinitely postponed, they lent an ear to more trustworthy friends (as it was believed) of the monarchy. The Marquis de Bouillé, who was in command at Metz, entreated the King to make a pretext of war-threats for seeking refuge in his army. The Emperor Leopold could easily be induced to mass some troops upon the frontiers, so as to frighten France and render the departure of the King from Paris legitimate. A device of M. de Breteuil, which was not very different from that of M. de Bouillé, was adopted. The idea was to fly from Paris to a place on the frontier, from whence the royal family might either reach a

K

foreign country if their lives were in danger, or return to Paris if events were favourable to the King's cause.

This project was neither the bold expedient proposed by Mirabeau, nor the plain and open line of action proposed by Bouillé; it was adopted, nevertheless, because Breteuil, more than any other adviser, had the King's ear, and also because the King was unlucky, and always chose the wrong instead of the right alternative.

From November 1790 the idea of flight became rooted in his mind. Yet he could neither face it without perturbation nor prepare to carry it out with firmness. He read the history of England assiduously, and particularly the reigns that seemed to him to be most analogous to his own, those of Charles the First and James the Second. He was frequently heard to remark that the sentence of death pronounced upon Charles the First was due to the fact that he had entered into a war with his subjects, and that if James the Second lost his crown, it was because he fled from his kingdom. These examples, which were constantly in his mind, shook his already faltering resolution. It required all the persistent efforts of those who were about the King to drag him out of his prolonged inaction.

Early in November 1790 the Marquis de Bouillé had written a long letter to the King in cipher, requesting that a decision to put the plan of retiring to a frontier town into execution, should be arrived at without delay. In taking this step, the Marquis de Bouillé was actuated by motives which it will be useful to state. He was not one of those irreconcilable royalists who hated the Revolution by instinct, and recognised only two courses to be taken in regard to it—either forcible resistance or emigration. On the contrary, indeed, he had received the new ideas with favour, in so far as they remained compatible with the preservation of royalty. Constitutional monarchy was his ideal, therefore a king was necessary to him, and his staunch adherence to Louis XVI. was more political than chivalrous.

When he found that the King was a prisoner in Paris, he immediately resolved to offer him the means of safeguarding the prerogatives which the Constitution granted him.

Bouillé, commanding the troops in Alsace, Lorraine, Champagne, and Franche-Comté, was the only general who had preserved his authority over his soldiers; he alone had not yielded before tumult. In the preceding summer, the garrison of Nancy having mutinied, he forced the troops to return to their duty by prompt and stern repression; this had procured him the thanks of the National Assembly.

His firm conduct, added to the prestige which he had acquired by his campaigns in India, in the Colonies, and in America, had preserved some remains of discipline among his troops. He believed he could count upon a few faithful battalions, and this conviction, which was shared by the King and Queen, made them accept his overtures. From the time they received his letter, the royal couple, agreed upon the goal of the enterprise, began to prepare the details of its execution.

They were so closely watched that it was out of their power to take an active and personal part in the arrangements; it was for them now to find a man who would become the soul of the plot. This man must have full liberty to communicate with the persons whose aid would be necessary in preparing for the projected escape, without arousing attention, without exciting suspicion.

It would have been easy to find, among the gentlemen loyal to the monarchical cause who had remained in France, some who would have welcomed such an appeal to their fidelity. The King's choice, guided by the Queen, fell upon a foreigner, if, indeed, under the circumstances, the term can be applied to the friend whom she selected. That friend was Count Fersen.

Although the Queen's selection gave rise to dissatisfaction among the French when it became known afterwards—the Duc de Lévis made himself the echo of this sentiment, declaring her choice to be "unbecoming in more than one respect"—it is no less true that it was a foregone conclusion, and it is readily explained now that we know the relations of the Swedish gentleman with the Court of France, and his passionate attachment to Marie Antoinette.

Count Fersen, to whom the plan was imparted from the first, left nothing undone to ensure its success, and although he may be accused of some mistakes, neither his activity nor his zeal can be questioned.

In February 1791 he made an allusion to the probable flight of the King in writing to Baron Taube : " If the King of France left Paris, *which will probably happen,*" &c. . . . He was already endeavouring to prepare the minds of the sovereigns for this event, so that he might have recourse at need to their moral and material support.

Although the project was in course of fulfilment, "*Festina lente*" was the order of the day. But the slow hastening was accelerated by the death of Mirabeau, which occurred unexpectedly on the 2nd of April 1791, and dispelled every lingering hesitation by removing, if not the last chance, at least the last illusion of safety. The Marquis de Bouillé was informed that the plan of flight was finally adopted. Louis XVI. and his family would escape from Paris, and would place himself under the protection of the troops at Montmédy, not far from the frontier of Luxembourg. On receipt of this news the General set to work at once. Convinced of the necessity of accounting for the movements of troops by the appearance of a danger from without, he applied for the support and complicity of "the foreigner."

"The movement of the Austrian troops on the frontier is necessary," he wrote to Fersen. "It is indispensable that a body of troops should arrive from Luxembourg, and some squadrons be placed at Verton and Arlon, and that some other points should be garrisoned ;

without this I might not be able to get out of Metz, and to send out four German and Swiss battalions, which form the only garrison at present, and I could not make the mounted troops distributed about the flat country march on the frontier. If the Emperor sincerely desires to serve the King, he must lend himself to this plan and hasten the march of the troops upon Luxembourg."

The Emperor was quite sincerely disposed to serve the King, his brother-in-law, and the negotiation with him, carried on by means of Fersen and Mercy Argenteau, did not meet with any difficulty.

In April, Bouillé had sent Baron de Goguelat, a half-pay officer on the staff, and famous for having grossly insulted the Duc d'Orléans, to Paris. Early in May Louis XVI. sent him back to Bouillé with a letter in cipher, announcing that, in accordance with the wishes of the latter, the Austrian troops would be sent back to Arlon about the 12th of June, and that the King himself would set out on the 15th.

The date seemed far off, but this could not be helped, for two reasons. The first was that, as we have seen, the Austrians would not be ready sooner; the second was that a large sum of money was necessary, and the King desired, before he set out, to get possession of the two millions of his Civil List, which were paid to him within the first fortnight of each month.

The forces of the Marquis de Bouillé, supposing them to be faithful, were sufficiently strong to secure the safety of the royal family. They were composed of twelve battalions, twenty-three squadrons, and an artillery train of sixteen guns. Bouillé received 993,000 livres in assignats, hidden in a white silk cover. This sum was ample for the defraying of the necessary expenses. The King kept four millions for himself, and, anticipating the case of his attempting something after his escape, he had charged M. de Bombelles to request the Emperor to give him "his credit for a loan of fifteen millions," in default of the loan itself.

The route adopted at first was "Meaux, Châlons, Reims, Ile-Béthel, Pauvre," as Fersen informed Bouillé. The Marquis did not approve of this.

"On reflection," he wrote, "the shortest, safest, and plainest route is by Meaux, Montmirail—bear in mind that the road to Montmirail must be taken at La Ferté-sous-Jouarre—Châlons, Sainte-Menehould, Varennes, Dun, and Stenay, not passing through Reims." Then he added, "Here is the route in detail: from Paris to Meaux, ten posting-leagues; from Meaux to La Ferté-sous-Jouarre, five; from La Ferté to Montmirail, nine; from Montmirail to Châlons-sur-Marne, fourteen; from Châlons to Sainte-Menehould, ten; from Sainte-Menehould to Varennes, five; from Varennes to Dun, five; from Dun to Stenay, three; from Stenay to Montmédy, two. You can see this route on the map of the Departments. It comes altogether to sixty-one posting leagues.[1] By setting out at night and travelling the following, they will arrive within the second day."

[1] The figures are not correct: it comes to sixty-three leagues.

The plan of avoiding Reims was readily adopted, in that the town was larger, and besides, Louis XVI. had been crowned there, and would consequently run a greater risk of being recognised.

The route being fixed, there remained the question of the precautions to be observed. From Paris to Châlons, it was impossible to think of taking a single officer of a military post into confidence—not one was safe. Even to Châlons body-guards could not be sent: "the town had demanded to have no more of them;" but after Pont-Sommevesle, a little village situated between Châlons and Sainte-Menehould, the route lay within Bouillé's command; it was possible to place detachments here and there.

A certain incoherence in the mind of the organisers of the enterprise makes itself manifest on this point. Count Fersen wrote at first: "The most essential point of all is the security of the flight; an escort dispersed along the route must be had; one shudders to think of the horrors that might occur if they were betrayed and arrested" (9th May).

A few days later his view is somewhat changed. He writes: "There will be no need of precautions from here to Châlons; *the best of all is to take none;* everything must depend upon celerity and secrecy, and if you are not sure of your detachments, *it would be better not to place any, or at least not to place them until after Varennes, so as not to excite attention in the country. The King will then pass quite simply.*"

These almost prophetic fears were realised only too fully, to the misfortune of the fugitives.

Bouillé took no account of them, thinking himself " sure of his detachments." He kept the Royal Allemand regiment at Stenay, and sent a squadron of hussars to Dun; two squadrons of dragoons were to be at Clermont on the day when the King should pass. These squadrons, commanded by the Comte Charles de Damas, would bring a detachment to Sainte-Menehould, while fifty hussars of the Varennes troop were to proceed to Pont-Sommevesle, under the conduct of young Choiseul and Goguelat.

A rumour was to be spread that these unusual movements of troops were for the purpose of escorting a treasure.

On the 27th of May the King writes to Bouillé that the departure is fixed for Sunday evening, the 19th of June, that he will leave Paris in a hackney-coach, and have himself conveyed to Bondy, where he will take the berline prepared for the journey. A body-guard will be at Bondy, and will go on alone to apprise the General, in case of the failure of the attempt to escape.

So that there might be no surprise, and that the detachments should not be stationed too long beforehand in localities fermenting with revolutionary ideas and full of the disturbance that was spreading all over the kingdom, Bouillé gave Goguelat a final charge to reconnoitre the route stage by stage, ascertaining precisely the number of leagues between the different relays, and the number of hours necessary to accomplish the distances.

Goguelat acquitted himself of this duty with the greatest care, and returned to Bouillé, from whom Fersen received the following little note, dated the 7th of June :—" Goguelat will have told you all. Nothing is altered, the departure is fixed for the 19th; if this is changed, I will inform you by the courier of the 11th. If you receive nothing by him, it will mean that there is no change." A few days afterwards, Fersen, still using his cipher, which, as he believed, could not be detected, begged the General to send Goguelat again to Paris, instead of the Duc de Choiseul, as the King wished to see him. " No one is more staunch," wrote Fersen, " but he is a young man and flighty; I dread some indiscretion; he has too many friends, relations, and perhaps a mistress, to save."

The letter arrived too late; the Duc de Choiseul had already set out. He reached Paris at five o'clock in the morning on the 11th of June. His conduct did not in any respect justify Fersen's fears; but the injunction which he renewed at the close of his letter was only too well justified. " Make yourself very sure of the detachments, or place them from Varennes only."

Everything was arranged, the Marquis de Bouillé left Metz on the 13th of June, on pretext of an inspection. On the 15th he was at Longwy, where he received the following communication from Fersen :—

"13th June 1791.

"The departure is positively fixed for the 20th, at midnight. An ill-conditioned woman in attendance on the Dauphin, who cannot be got rid of, and whose turn of service lasts until Monday, is the cause of the put-off until Monday evening, but you may reckon upon that time. .... The King will have a red coat, and will make himself known according to Choiseul's report of the spirit of the troops. ... I am well content with the Duc de Choiseul. If all should fail, he will be at Metz on Friday morning, but if not, you may set out on Sunday morning, and reckon upon the departure from hence at midnight on Monday. There was no means of getting rid of this woman without risking discovery. If, by chance, your marching orders for the detachments have been sent off already, you might delay their departure for one day on the pretext that the quarters are not ready."

At the same time Bouillé received a letter from the King confirming the delay of twenty-four hours, and informing him that the Marquis d'Agoust, whom he had been particularly recommended to take with him, was not to be of the party. There was, in fact, no room for the Marquis, Mme. de Tourzel, as Governess of the Children of France, having claimed her right to be with them. Let us observe here respecting this statement, which was contained in the King's letter, and repeated by Bouillé, that it discredits the protestations of Mme.

de Tourzel, who defended herself against the charge of having made any such claim. It was clearly the interest of Mme. de Tourzel to deny that she had taken the place of a man like the Marquis d'Agoust, who possessed both head and heart; and it is impossible to assign a motive for the King's writing such a thing to Bouillé, or for the latter's inventing it. On behalf of Mme. de Tourzel, who was apparently very glad to make her escape with the royal family, it may be urged that she could not have foreseen the incidents which caused the fugitives to regret so bitterly, not her presence, but the absence of the Marquis d'Agoust.

Louis XVI. had appended the following order to his letter:—

"By the King.

"My intention being to proceed to Montmédy on the approaching 20th of June, the Sieur Bouillé, lieutenant-general of my armies, is ordered to place troops, according as he shall think proper for the safety of my person and that of my family, along the route from Châlons-sur-Marne to Montmédy; it is my will that the troops employed for this purpose execute all that shall be prescribed by the said Sieur Bouillé, who is hereby rendered responsible for the orders which he shall give them.

"Given at Paris the 15th of June 1791.

"Louis."

Furnished with this paper, Bouillé proceeded

to Stenay on the 20th of June; then on the 21st he informed the general officers that the King was about to pass, and remitted the King's order to them, with the addition of the usual formula :—

"M. de Mandell, the officers, sub-officers and troopers of Royal Allemand are enjoined to execute and cause to be executed the present order.

"BOUILLÉ.
"*Stenay, 21st of June* 1791."

The Duc de Choiseul, and Goguelat, were sent to Pont Sommevesle, the most distant post from Stenay, and consequently the nearest to Châlons. Their instructions were to let the King pass unnoticed if he were not recognised, and not to mount until some hours afterwards; but, if he was recognised, to make every effort to deliver him, taking care to inform the General immediately.

M. de Choiseul had received 17,000 livres on leaving Metz for Paris on the 9th of June; a second sum of 80,000 livres was now remitted to him and to M. de Damas, for the purpose of sustaining or stimulating the fidelity of their men.

The day was wearing through on the 21st, and M. de Bouillé, who was exceedingly anxious, received no news. At last his impatience got the better of him; his fears grew with the darkness. He mounted his horse, rode away from Stenay accompanied by a few officers, and advanced to the gates of Dun, but did not venture to enter, fearing to agitate the people by his presence. There he waited, perplexed and uneasy : the safety of the royal family was not his only care; he well knew all that he was personally risking in an adventure which must compromise him terribly if it should fail. Every sound made him start; was it the berline arriving, and bringing, with the King, the certainty that he (Bouillé) had really won the marshal's bâton which had been sent to him some days previously by the hands of Leonard, the Queen's hairdresser—a singular messenger? Or was it Choiseul, or the body-guard who was to be sent to announce to him that the flight had failed, and that he would have barely time to secure his personal safety?

Meanwhile, the carriages which contained the royal family and their suite were advancing towards Varennes; but the end of the journey had yet to be reached, and although the danger seemed to lessen as the distance between the fugitives and Paris was increased, it still existed.

It was a miracle that the carriages had ever travelled so far, for it must be owned that never had flight been arranged with more devoted zeal and less judgment. Since the details of these events have become known, our wonder is how the fugitives were able to get out of the Tuileries, to pass the gates of Paris, and so nearly to gain the frontier.

The preparations made in Paris ought to have attracted the attention of the Municipality, the National Guard, and the police. It was like an escape in a comic opera.

In the first place, there was the singular idea of having a special carriage, a huge berline, built for the occasion. That such a vehicle was in course of construction could not be kept secret, and its imposing and uncommon bulk could not fail to attract the attention of all who saw it in motion. Bouillé had proposed that two small English post-chaises, of a light and convenient kind, frequently used for posting-journeys, should be employed; but his advice was not taken, and a certain Mrs. Sullivan, who was friendly to the royal family, had been employed to procure the desired vehicle. Representing herself to be Baroness Korff, a Russian lady of rank, she ordered a berline, to accommodate nine persons easily, six inside and three upon the box, from Jean Louis, a coach-builder. It was no light matter to build such a vehicle; it took time, and as it was important to have this unwieldy means of flight always at hand, Baroness Korff was perpetually at the coach-builder's yard, pressing him with entreaties to hurry on his workmen.

At last, the berline was ready for the road on the 12th of March. On the 26th, Jean Louis, who had been at heavy expense, sent in his bill, which amounted to 5944 livres. The King immediately sent him 2600 livres on account, by the pretended Baroness Korff.

The final touches were given, and the machine was worth the price, if we are to believe the description of it, compiled from the bill, by

Eugène Bimbenet, formerly Clerk of the Court of Orleans:—

"This must have been a handsome travelling-carriage, for 5944 livres represented a very important sum in 1791; it was a combination of the solid and the rich. In the interior, luxurious decorations and skilful devices hid the provision made for the material necessities of life. The net of the imperial was adorned with silken cords and tassels; portable pockets were hung on the carriage doors, to contain the articles usually required in travelling; small bolsters covered with taffety and morocco leather supported the travellers on either side; the cushions on which they sat covered the indispensable utensils, which were made of varnished leather. A cooking apparatus had been contrived; lamps with reflectors shone in front, although the nights were so short that there was hardly any darkness at all; two stout tarpaulins covered the imperial; the carriage was also provided with a skid, an axle-strap, and two iron-shod forks to steady it on the hill-sides.

"At the back was a canteen, in leather, to hold eight bottles of wine. Underneath the coachman's seat, which had a knee-covering and leathern pockets, there was a tool-bag containing all the implements that might be required in case of accidents."

The berline was delivered by the coachmaker early in June, and taken to Count Fersen's private residence in the Rue du Bac. The Count, thinking it well to make sure of the strength of the heavy machine, on which the safety of so many persons was to depend, had six strong horses harnessed to it, and drove along the Vincennes road at their full speed. As luck would have it, he met the Duc d'Orléans driving with Mme. de Buffon; he recognised Fersen, and called out—

"Are you mad, my dear Count? You are likely to break your neck at that game."

"I don't want my carriage to break down on the road," answered Fersen, stopping his horses.

"Why have you got such a big one? Is it to carry away a whole opera chorus?"

"No, Monseigneur, I leave you the chorus."

"Adieu, a good journey to you."

And they parted.

Fersen was well aware of the Duke's enmity to his cousin. At the first news of the departure of the royal family, the Duke would recall his meeting with Fersen, and knowing the relations between the Count and the Court, he might instantly give a description of the carriage in which the fugitives had escaped. The Duc d'Orléans did nothing of the kind, but that fact did not palliate Fersen's imprudence in showing himself in public after such a fashion.

Nor was this his only rash proceeding. The berline remained in the courtyard of Count Fersen's hotel, where every passer-by could see it, although the coach-builder, who feared that it would be injured, urged that it ought to be placed under shelter. Not until some days later was it removed, ostensibly to the abode of the persons about to start for Russia, but in reality to the abode of Colonel Crawford, an Englishman, who lived in the Rue de Clichy at the other end of Paris.

Fersen kept the Queen informed of all that he was doing; he had found means of getting into the Tuileries without being seen by the National Guards. This was not an easy thing to do, for the château was already strictly watched.

In the daytime there was some disguise about the precautions; for instance, so soon as the King, the Queen, or Madame Elizabeth came out, the National Guards would surround them, as though to form an escort and do them honour; but at night the escort was changed into a squad of gaolers. The doors of the bed-chambers were carefully secured, the soldiers placed their pallets across the threshold and slept there. Most of the persons attached to the King's household were subjected to similar treatment, and it would not do to make any effort to avoid it.

M. de Duras, first gentleman of the bed-chamber to the King, having asked Lafayette one day whether it was by his orders that ten or twelve men were stationed before his (Duras') door, received the following stern reply:—

"Yes, sir, and if it were necessary I should put one in your bed."

Measures had now to be taken for the outwitting of this watch, so that the attempt to escape might not be frustrated at the outset.

For the first time Louis XVI. found an opportunity of turning his mechanical skill to good use. In the month of January, with the assistance of trustworthy persons, he had constructed "in the wood panelling of Madame Elizabeth's apartment a door artistically made, so that it was difficult to perceive its existence, unless a close search were made for it.

"There was also another~door, difficult to discover, at one end of Madame Elizabeth's bed. The first of these doors had been prepared for secret interviews."

The means of getting out of the palace being secured, and the berline being ready, the next thing was to procure a passport. Here again the pretended Baroness Korff, otherwise Mrs. Sullivan, intervened. She solicited a passport for herself, her two children, their governess, and a confidential servant, and then, as she did not intend to remain in Paris, where she would not be safe if her share in the flight of the King were discovered, she pretended that the passport which she had procured had been burned by accident, and M. de Montmorin, Minister of Foreign Affairs, sent her a second, by order of the King. Mrs. Sullivan left Paris on the 17th June with Colonel Crawford, whose mistress she was.

This "sentimental Englishwoman" and the foreign colonel, in addition to Count Fersen, the ladies of the palace, and the body-guards chosen to accompany the royal family, were the only persons in the secret of the contemplated flight; at least they were the only persons concerning whom we can be certain. The question was put, and is still put, as to whether Lafayette did not know of it. Various little incidents lead to the belief that he did. Mrs. Elliott says in her Memoirs:—"Every one knows that in the summer of 1791 the King and the royal family made an attempt at flight. I do not doubt that Lafayette was in the secret, but he betrayed it afterwards through fear."

This solution is not admissible. If Lafayette had been "in the secret," the avowal of the fact would probably have been found either in Bouillé's *Mémoires* or in Count Fersen's papers, as those persons who were cognisant of the project are named in both. Besides, it is hard to believe that Bouillé, who did not like his cousin, and Fersen, who detested the Commandant of the National Guard, would have consented to his being intrusted with so formidable a secret.

Without being an accomplice, Lafayette might merely have discovered the secret and "let it alone." That he did so is a second theory, more plausible than the first, but also very unlikely. What interest could Lafayette have had in the departure of the King? The presence of the unhappy sovereign confined in the Tuileries did not interfere with his ambition. Did his pity for the royal family constitute an interest? We must not forget that the safe-keeping of that royal family was committed to him, that his life would have been risked by such an act, and that the popular fury took him quite unawares on the morning of the 21st of June. To accept either of these hypotheses would be to do too much honour to the person of whom the Comte d'Allonville said, not unjustly, that he was "a great booby, as white-livered as he was pale-faced." Lafayette was not capable of either so much heroism or so much subtlety.

Although he was in a way the soul of the scheme, Count Fersen was not to have a place in the famous berline. "I shall not accompany the King, he does not wish it," he wrote to Bouillé on the 29th of May. Then Mme. de Tourzel was substituted at the last moment for the Marquis d'Agoust, a gentleman whom Bouillé had most particularly recommended to Louis XVI. Mme. de Tourzel was to occupy a seat in the berline with the King, the Queen, the Children of France, and Madame Elizabeth. On the box-seat were to be M. de Valory, M. du Moustier, and M. de Maldent, all carrying arms, which Count Fersen had actually had marked with his initials. Two waiting-maids, Mme. Brunier and Mme. de Neuville, were to follow in a cabriolet.

The body-guards were not apprised of the facts until the last moment; not late enough, however, to prevent them from talking. M. du Moustier could not refrain from telling his mistress, Mdlle. Préville, who talked about the matter with her servant. The latter, proud of the important news thus brought to her knowledge, carried it to the hall-porter of the Hôtel Poyen. Mdlle. Préville also apprised her sister,

Mme. Théogat. M. de Valory had been equally indiscreet. After all this, is it surprising that rumours of the intended flight of the King were in circulation? Fortunately they became vague in travelling from mouth to mouth, and had not time to go very far.

A more serious danger was the presence of Mdlle. Rocherette, the Dauphin's waiting-woman, at the château. She was suspected of being a demagogue; but was she really of the "demagogie"? She was the mistress of Gouvion, Lafayette's aide-de-camp, and "she told him everything." This was quite enough to make her an object of distrust, and as it was impossible to conceal anything from her while she was on duty, the departure had to be postponed for twenty-four hours.

During the last days, Count Fersen, availing himself of the means he had discovered for evading the vigilance of the patriots of the National Guard, had a great number of interviews with the King or the Queen.

On Thursday, the 16th of June, at half-past nine, he went to the palace, and took to Marie Antoinette the plain and humble garments which were to form the disguise of the royal family. This matter was effected in the greatest secrecy. "They suspect nothing here or in town," he writes in his journal. On the 17th he went so far as Bondy, in order to reconnoitre the route, and came back by Bourget. On Saturday, the 18th, he returned, and was with Marie Antoinette from two o'clock until half-past six. The Queen informed him that she had received a letter from her brother, which confirmed all the orders given for the manifestation on the frontier. On the 19th, Sunday, Fersen went again to the château, and remained from eleven o'clock until midnight. The King handed over to him eight hundred livres and the seals.

On the following day, at half-past seven in the morning, he went to the coach-builder's to see about the post-chaise which was to be occupied by Mme. Brunier and Mme. de Neuville. He returned to his hotel in that vehicle, and dismissed the coachman who had driven it, with instructions to return at noon precisely. At that hour he had horses put to his carriage, and drove to the Swedish Embassy. His visit, of only a quarter of an hour's duration, was a precaution taken against M. de Staël, to dispel his suspicions, if he had any.

Having returned home, he waited a few hours, then ordered his carriage to take him to the sitting of the National Assembly. He had no intention of going there, for he alighted at the Pont-Royal, and entered the garden of the Tuileries. Thus he had contrived the means of seeing the King and Queen once more.

They were expecting him, and in that last interview the respective characters of the three personages were revealed. Marie Antoinette, full of trouble and emotion at the approach of the hour of departure, full of fear for her children, her friends, herself, was in a state of nervous excitement and wept profusely. Louis XVI., as passiv as usual, listened to Count Fersen, who was cool and resolute.

The Count reminded the royal couple of the dangers which they were about to incur; but the King and Queen with one accord answered him that "there could be no hesitation, and that they must go."

For the last time the place of meeting, the hour, and the order of departure were discussed and settled; and as the success of the flight still remained doubtful, notwithstanding the precautions that had been taken, it was decided that Count Fersen should proceed to Brussels, and that should they be stopped, he was at once to act for them with the other sovereigns.

Time was flying. It was necessary that the Queen should go to the promenade with her children, according to custom, so that she might be seen there. At about six o'clock Fersen took leave and withdrew.

"Monsieur de Fersen," said the King earnestly, "whatsoever may happen to me, I will not forget what you are doing for me."

The Queen's tears spoke no less plainly to Fersen's heart. He regained his carriage and proceeded to the Rue de Clichy to inspect the berline and make sure that it was in readiness.

At eight he wrote a few words to the Queen on the subject of an alteration in the place of meeting first appointed for the waiting-women. He took the note to the palace himself, and remarked with satisfaction that everything was quiet as usual. He then returned home. At this same hour an incident had occurred at his hôtel which might have had most serious consequences. He had directed his valet-de-chambre to take three cases to the Rue de Clichy, and a hackney-coach was engaged for the purpose. The driver witnessed a spectacle on entering the courtyard of the hôtel which naturally astonished him. Two servants were engaged in loading seven pairs of double-barrelled pistols, and were casting the bullets themselves. They asked the driver to provide himself with a ladle, and to come and help them. At that moment one of the pistols unaccountably went off; the bullet passed through a pane of glass, and narrowly escaped killing a person in the street. The hackney-coachman, wondering at these preparations, asked for what purpose so many pistols were required. Count Fersen's footman explained that his master, who was in the service of Russia, was about to return to that insecure country, and the pistols would be necessary on his journey. The man was satisfied with this reply.

Meanwhile the valet-de-chambre brought various parcels down from the upper rooms, and among others an English saddle and bridle; all these things were placed in the hackney-coach, and transferred to the berline by the valet on arriving at the Rue de Clichy. He requested the driver to open one of the cases, which were made of sheet iron, and about ten inches square. The case that was opened contained plate; a silver goblet was added to the contents, and all three were placed in the huge carriage. Another box was shaped like a dressing-case; and as the smallest details of the royal flight are interesting, it may be added that it contained eatables, and especially a large piece of *bœuf à la mode*. Count Fersen's forethought extended to the smallest things.

Towards evening two body-guards, dressed as couriers, went to his hôtel. He directed them to proceed with his coachman, Balthazar Sapel, to the Rue de Clichy, and to take the berline from thence to the new Barrière du Faubourg Saint-Martin. The coachman being struck with the appearance of the carriage, remarked upon it, and taking his two companions for persons of his own condition, he said, "Who are your comrades, mates? They seem to be very rich!" "Comrade, you will learn that," they replied. This was all he could get out of them.

The three arrived at the Porte Saint-Martin a little after midnight. During this time Count Fersen, who was not recognisable in the costume of a hackney-coachman, placed the post-chaise intended for the attendants on the quay, opposite to the Poitevin Baths. At a quarter-past ten he proceeded with another carriage to the Cour des Princes, and there he waited for the fugitives, who ought to have been leaving the palace at that moment.

Nothing unusual had occurred at the château during the evening. The children had been put to bed at the customary hour. The King and Queen had retired afterwards, but no sooner had their personal attendants been dismissed than all arose. The King put on a plain coat, so as to bear out the character of a valet-de-chambre assigned to him in the passport of Baroness Korff. The Queen and Madame Elizabeth also put on the attire of waiting-women. Madame Royale was quickly dressed, but the little Dauphin, being aroused out of his first sleep, did not understand what was happening, and why he should have to wear a girl's frock. "Are we going to act a play?" he asked. Madame Brunier and Madame de Neuville were there. All except the King and Madame Elizabeth assembled in a dressing-closet, where Madame de Tourzel joined them. Then the Queen herself opened the door, and, taking her two children by the hand, she preceded the three women down a staircase and along a corridor which communicated with one of the doors of the unoccupied apartment of M. de Villequier, situated on the entresol. While waiting for the opening of this door, Madame de Neuville sat down on the ground and rested the head of the poor little Dauphin, who was sound asleep, on her knees.

It had been decided that the party should enter the Cour des Princes in separate groups, so as to avoid attention. The door being opened, the children were sent on in front with Madame de Tourzel. They reached the carriage without any difficulty; it was then a quarter-past eleven. At that moment Lafayette passed twice through the court, vehemently but unnecessarily alarming the fugitives, for he saw nothing, and so the flight was actually accomplished under his eyes. At a quarter to twelve Madame

Elizabeth arrived; the King followed her closely; the Queen only lingered. The small party began to get frightened—time was passing. At length she appeared. She also had met Lafayette's carriage, and had shrunk into a recess to avoid being seen. This incident had somewhat disturbed her; and the body-guard who accompanied her being unable to find his way—the quarter was at that time encumbered with houses and traversed by narrow dark streets—they had gone astray. Midnight struck before Madame Brunier and Madame de Neuville, who were on foot, reached the carriage intended for them.

The King, the Queen, Madame Elizabeth, the children, Madame de Tourzel and the body-guard got into the carriage, Fersen driving, and they started at speed. They reached the Pont-Saint-Martin just as day began to break. The berline was there; Fersen drew up so that the doors of the two carriages were side by side, and the travellers passed from one to the other without alighting. He returned to the first carriage, took the horses by their bits and forced them back into the ditch, throwing one of them down; so that the abandonment of the vehicle might appear to have been caused by an accident. He then got up on the coach-box of the berline, while M. de Maldent took his seat behind, said to the coachman, Balthazar Sapel, who held the reins, "Go on! quick! drive quick!" and taking the whip, he cracked it incessantly to excite the horses.

The time that had been lost in waiting for the Queen, and the increasing light, augmented the danger; they were still so near Paris. Fersen was frantically anxious to get his precious charge into safety. He reproached his coachman, " Come, come, Balthazar, your horses are no good; get on, get on; they will have time to rest when we get to the regiment." Balthazar Sapel, who believed that his master was returning to Varennes to rejoin his regiment (Royal Suédois), obeyed him as best he could, and in less than half-an-hour they reached Bondy.

A relay of six horses was in readiness. Count Fersen and his coachman alighted from the carriage; M. de Maldent took the front seat with Valory and Du Moustier; the postilions started their horses and cracked their whips, the berline rolled away, carrying the royal family towards the unknown.

Count Fersen watched them out of sight. The King did not wish that he should accompany them, because he would not endanger a foreigner in the service of France, and also because the Count's presence might be compromising to Louis himself.

At any rate, the separation was not to last long. At that moment the chance of success seemed great. In two days they would meet, far from their enemies, far from the populace of Paris, in safety. The Count desired this too strongly to believe in it completely; and the compulsory ignorance in which he was left, the mere absence of news, was extremely trying to him.

Immediately on his arrival at Mons, on the Tuesday morning, he wrote a note to his father, in which he betrays his anxiety :—

"MONS, *June 22nd,*
six in the morning.

"I have this instant arrived here, my dear father. The King and all the family got out of Paris safely on the 20th at midnight. I drove them to the first post: may God grant that the rest of their journey may be equally fortunate. I shall now continue my route along the frontier to join the King at Montmédy, if he be happy enough to arrive there."

In these dubious words we read the presentiment of a loving heart for her he loved; for although his hand wrote "the King," his heart named the Queen. Neither one nor the other had been so happy as to arrive at the goal of their journey, and at the very hour when Count Fersen was still trying to hope, all was lost. His next meeting with the victim whom he had attempted to tear from the grasp of the Revolution was to take place under terrible circumstances.

While he was advancing towards Mons by the nearer route, the berline had taken that of Châlons. At Claye the royal party was joined by Madame Brunier and Madame de Neuville, and the two carriages proceeded at a fair pace. The zeal of the postilions was stimulated by excessive gratuities. M. de Valory, slipping his arm under the glass beneath the box-seat, took handfuls of money out of a bag which hung inside the vehicle. This generosity had the desired effect, but it also had a second, which was dangerous. "Who can this great personage be, who pays so well?" said the postilions. "They have given us four livres and ten sous pour-boire!" It was dangerous to excite any kind of curiosity, but they did not think of this. The travellers were so delighted that they had not been stopped, and that they had escaped from Paris, their dreadful prison, that they were too confident. The King talked in what for him was a jesting fashion. "You may be very sure that once I get into the saddle, I shall be very different from what you have seen me up to the present! Lafayette does not know what to do with himself just now."

Nevertheless, a man driving a cart in a little village through which they passed recognised him. "That is the King," said he to the body-guards, who were passing for couriers. The latter denied the fact. "But it is the King and the Queen," the man insisted; "I have seen them several times at Versailles," he repeated.

They started again very quickly. This incident ought to have convinced the King that the greatest prudence was still necessary, but it had no effect. When the road was hilly, he got out and followed the berline. At the posts he mixed with the people who were standing about and looking at the fine berline; he talked to the peasants, conversing with them on the state of the crops, and was glad to keep out of the carriage, giving way to his dislike of any kind of physical restraint.

An accident to the carriage occurred; the travellers had to stay for more than an hour at Montmirail, between Meaux and Châlons. This circumstance, added to the King's obstinacy in insisting on walking up the hills, prolonged the journey for three hours more than had been calculated, and it also led to confusion in the instructions which had been given to the officers in command of the detachments, and left time for the presence of the troops to create a ferment among the people.

At Châlons the fugitives incurred a great risk. The King was again recognised. His persistence in showing himself, and in alighting during the change of horses, exposed him seriously, and on these occasions it was doubly to be regretted that the Marquis d'Agoust did not occupy the place of Madame de Tourzel. He alone would have had sufficient authority to restrain the imprudence of the unfortunate monarch.

One of the members of the municipality of Châlons, who was standing close to the carriage, entertained no doubt whatever that its occupants were the royal family, but, moved by respect for such illustrious misfortune, he did not think of betraying them; on the contrary, he was helping to harness the horses in order to abridge the delay, when a workman approached him and said in a low voice, "But that is the King; I recognise him." He tried to deny the fact, the other maintained it more emphatically. He then risked all, for all. "Yes," he answered; "it is the King; but if you say so, the greatest misfortunes may occur, and upon you the responsibility will fall." The tone in which these words were pronounced so impressed the workman, that he withdrew without having revealed his discovery. This incident shows how slight was the thread on which the safety of the travellers depended; and yet at that moment they had almost ceased to fear!

They were nearing that portion of their journey which was under the command of M. de Bouillé, and were soon to meet the detachment at the place arranged. As they approached this spot, the confidence of the royal family became complete; they felt that the sight of the first dragoon would be the signal of their deliverance.

Great was their delusion, and happy would it have been for the fugitives if action had been taken upon the wise and prudent counsel of Count Fersen, that "the best protection was to take none," and that "the King should pass quite simply."

The occurrences at Pont-Sommevesle were a warning, but it came too late. Bouillé had sent fifty hussars, under the joint command of the young Duc de Choiseul and Baron de Goguelat, a brave and daring Nivernois, who was devoted to their Majesties, and fully informed of the details of the contemplated flight.

M

The presence of these soldiers would at any time have caused some commotion among the inhabitants, but it was most unfortunate under the particular circumstances. The people in the villages had refused to pay taxes, and were threatened with compulsory measures. They thought that the hussars had been sent for this purpose, and immediately assembled and rung the alarm-bell to apprise their neighbours and call them to their help. Curiosity also being roused, the little troop was surrounded; the men and their officers were placed in a difficult position. In vain did they say that they were sent to Pont-Sommevesle to wait for and escort a treasure; they were only half-believed or not believed at all. In these troublous times, when suspicion was sown broadcast in the ignorant masses by demagogues, and the hardly emancipated population dreaded everything at the hands of their former masters, the slightest event produced a tumult.

What could the little troop do against the hundreds of peasants swarming round them, some armed with muskets, others with stones, and others with sticks, and becoming more inimical every moment? It was useless to think of dispersing the crowd by force. This could not have been done even supposing the fifty hussars would have implicitly obeyed their officers. On the other hand, the latter were extremely anxious; they had been told that the berline would pass at about two o'clock; it was now half-past five, and there was no appearance of the carriage. No doubt there had been a counter-order on the part of the King, or else the fugitives had been stopped on their way What was occurring at Pont-Sommevesle rendered the latter conjecture very probable. The Duc de Choiseul and Goguelat consulted together. If they remained, they could not be useful in any way to the security of the royal family in case they should arrive at this place. But would they arrive? The thing was becoming more and more doubtful. The officers resolved to withdraw, and as they had been very ill received at Saint-Menehould, they decided upon returning to Varennes, and proceeding to Stenay by the cross-roads.

They have been much blamed for this decision, and the majority of those who had reason to reproach themselves for some negligence or some fault in the course of the adventure were the first to condemn them; but in this they were wrong; from every point of view, the conduct of Choiseul and Goguelat was correct. In the first place, as for disregard of the orders they had received, the officers were exculpated by the fact that after three hours and a half of waiting the royal carriage did not appear. In the second place, being incapable, on account of their small number, of resisting the opposition which was evidently intended, they constituted a danger to the fugitives, and not a resource. Finally, they may claim in their justification that events proved them in the right. No sooner had the little troop disappeared than the tumult subsided.

The peasants, content with having intimidated the soldiers who had come to molest them, dispersed, and quiet was so completely re-established, that when the berline arrived, an hour later, only a few curious loiterers noticed it, and, to use Fersen's phrase, "the King passed quite simply."

Although this point had been happily cleared, the travellers were exceedingly puzzled by not seeing either Choiseul or Goguelat, and by receiving no explanation of their absence. At the following relay at Orbeval, all passed off quietly, and they recovered a little of the serenity and confidence which had been temporarily disturbed. At last they were approaching Saint-Menehould; there they hoped they should see the detachment sent by Bouillé. They saw nobody. The King was very uneasy, put his head several times out of the window, without reflecting that the movement might attract attention, and that some eyes in the crowd might be too sharp-sighted.

At that moment, the son of the postmaster, who had not lost sight of the travellers, although he was superintending the harnessing of the horses, whispered a few words in the ear of a soldierly-looking man, who was there as a spectator; then taking his postilions apart, he desired them, assigning various reasons, "not to hurry themselves." After this he quickly disappeared.

During this time an officer drew near the carriage, and managing so as not to be heard by the crowd, he rapidly uttered a few words to Mme. de Tourzel. "Your measures are ill taken. Set out, hurry; you are lost if you do not hasten. I am going away to avoid arousing suspicion." This was M. d'Andoins, who commanded the thirty dragoons sent by Count Damas.

The incidents of Pont-Sommevesle were to some extent repeated at Saint-Menehould. No sooner did the people see the soldiers coming than they rose in arms to meet them, and, amidst increasing tumult, insisted that each dragoon should place the six cartridges with which he was supplied in the hands of the municipal officers. This was immediately done, and the people being emboldened by the concession, then proceeded to demand the disarmament of the little troop. M. d'Andoins was indignant at this fresh exaction, which, however, was a strictly logical one, since he had yielded to the first, and he resolutely refused to submit to it. The crowd, now in its turn illogical, did not insist, but actually applauded the refusal of the commandant. They surrounded the soldiers, however, and finally succeeded in making them dismount and retire into a sort of barrack, where they were shut up without protest on their part.

Notwithstanding these unfavourable circumstances, the horses were changed and the carriage started without any difficulty. The royal family was already far on the road to Varennes, when at about eleven o'clock official information of the flight of the King arrived.

The anger of the people of Saint-Menehould at finding themselves thus tricked broke out with violence; the patriots were indignant; everybody wanted to rush after the fugitives and arrest them.

Unnecessary zeal! Two of their compatriots had undertaken that task. These were Drouet, the son of the postmaster, and his companion, Guillaume, formerly a soldier in the Queen's Dragoons. While the postilions, mindful of their master's orders, were proceeding leisurely, Drouet and Guillaume were riding at full speed to Varennes through the fields and the woods, and by short cuts well known to them, with the intention of outstripping the travellers and arriving before them.

And, as though all things were to combine against the royal family on that fatal day, and to neutralise the fidelity and devotion that had been lavished upon them, Drouet and Guillaume escaped a death which would have secured the safety of their illustrious prey. Among the imprisoned dragoons was a quartermaster who was still loyal to the King. Finding that something of a grave nature was happening, he had jumped over the wall, mixed with the crowd, arrived at a vague notion of the state of the case, found his horse, and galloped off upon the Varennes road. He soon perceived two horsemen ahead of him and pursued them. Who were they? He did not know. If these men should be enemies of the King! At that thought he drew his pistols out of the holsters, but a doubt checked his hand. Suppose these men were faithful servants like himself, and were pushing on to warn the King! He replaced his pistols. Ten times over he did the same thing. At length, at a turn of the road, he lost sight of the two men, and his courageous action was of no avail.

The travellers had been made very uneasy by the warning given to Madame de Tourzel. It was, however, too late to recede; besides, M. de Bouillé must be now approaching with a strong force; let them but join him and they would be in safety. At half-past nine the berline passed through Clermont. M. de Damas, who was in command there, had not been more fortunate than the other officers and their detachments, and the hostile attitude of the population had been too much for the courage or the fidelity of his soldiers. He passed alongside the carriage and carelessly asked one of the body-guard to whom it belonged, then rode away, having hardly heard the answer. Montmédy was from thirteen to fourteen leagues off; this thought revived the hopes of the travellers, the more so that, after all, notwithstanding delays and perils, the most difficult part had been cleared. The three leagues which divided Clermont from Varennes were got over slowly, and it was nearly a quarter to twelve when the travellers arrived at the latter place.

The town of Varennes, on the little river Aire, is divided into two distinct quarters, one on each bank, united by a bridge. At the entry to the bridge is a tower built over an archway, which forms a dark narrow passage. Baron de

Goguelat, knowing the configuration of the place, had taken care to establish his relay at the far end of the town, on the other side of the Aire. By this arrangement the carriage would go at once through this dangerous passage, and not be obliged to stop for a change of horses until it had reached the far end of the town. This was a very prudent measure; but either the travellers had not been informed of it, or they had forgotten it, for they stopped at the entrance to the town. No relays; everything was silent and quiet. The travellers alighted, endeavoured to make inquiry, roused some of the inhabitants, who naturally could give them no information, got into the berline again and ordered the postilions to start; but the latter obeyed reluctantly. They drew near to the river, the carriage was about to pass under the archway, when all of a sudden the horses were stopped. An overturned cart barred the way, and several men sprang out of the darkness and surrounded the carriage. One of them, coming forward and announcing himself as the Procureur of the Commune, demanded their passports. The body-guards stood up on their seats and took up their arms, but the King ordered his defenders not to defend him. Madame de Tourzel exhibited the false passport of " Baroness Korff, proceeding to Frankfort with her two children, one woman, a valet-de-chambre, and three men-servants."

The demand was only a pretext; the Procureur took the passport, but said it could not be *visé* at that hour; in the morning he would see. The travellers, who knew the danger of this delay, urged that they should be allowed to pursue their journey. They were not listened to, but were forced to alight, and taken into the house of the Procureur of the Commune, one Sauce, a grocer. Everything had turned against them; the chances were all on the side of their enemies. Drouet and Guillaume had arrived at Varennes at a quarter past eleven, long before the fugitives; they had gone immediately to Sauce and informed him that two carriages were about to pass containing the King, his family, and some persons of his suite. It concerned the safety of France to prevent them from reaching a foreign country, from whence they would immediately raise monarchical Europe against her. Sauce, who was a man of the new ideas, roused his children and desired them to dress themselves promptly and give an alarm by running through the town shouting "Fire!" He himself lighted a lantern, and, followed by a neighbour, one Régnier, a lawyer, also by Drouet and Guillaume, he proceeded to the bridge. Finding a laden cart there, he placed it across the archway. The four men were joined by some of the National Guards, whose names have been preserved—the two brothers Le Blanc, Coquillard, Justin George, Ponsin, and two travellers named Thenevin des Islettes and Delion de Montfaucon, who lodged at the Auberge du Bras-d'or, and they all posted themselves in the darkness. We have seen how their plan succeeded.

Meanwhile the Sauce children, the accomplices of Drouet, reached the town; the alarm-bell was rung, and the suddenly-awakened inhabitants flocked to the house of the Procureur, whither the travellers had been taken. The latter, to their great astonishment, saw no military force except the National Guard, which was hostile to them. What had become of the squadron sent to Varennes? There, as all along the route, fatality had been active. The younger Bouillé, who commanded the detachment, finding that no carriage came at the appointed hour, waited for some time, then went off to bed; his men were disbanded; some of them returned to their quarters, where they were sleeping soundly; the others repaired to the taverns in the town, where they got helplessly drunk.

At the sound of the alarm-bell Bouillé awoke, hastily dressed himself, and ran to collect the hussars; but so great was the disorder that his efforts were vain, and it was impossible for him to muster even the semblance of a troop.

Meanwhile the travellers were taken by Sauce into a top room at the back of the house, which was already surrounded. It was midnight. Sauce entreated Louis to make himself known, but the King continued to maintain, in a tone which gave the lie to his words, that he was only a valet-de-chambre. This contradiction irritated the patriots, and they replied to him angrily. "If you think that he is your King," said Marie Antoinette, whose pride revolted from this ridiculous scene, "speak to him with more respect."

Sauce had gone to seek a certain M. Destez, a judge, who had several times seen the King at Paris and at Versailles, and brought him to the house. Immediately on his arrival Destez recognised him. Louis then saw that it was time to put an end to an undignified scene, and suddenly giving way to emotion as puerile as it was untimely, he threw himself into the arms of the Procureur. "Yes," he cried, "I am your King. In the capital I was in the midst of daggers and bayonets, so I have come to the country to seek among my faithful subjects the liberty and the peace which you all enjoy;" and then he began to embrace the bystanders, the very men who had just arrested him.

Marie Antoinette, broken down by prolonged suspense, by the fatigue of the journey, and by her consciousness of their danger, made a last effort. She addressed herself to Madame Sauce, invoked her compassion, and entreated her to induce her husband to let them depart. "Save the King," said she. "Bon Dieu, Madame," replied the grocer's wife, "they would kill M. Sauce. True, I love my King, but then I love my husband also; he is responsible, you see."

There is something to be said for the poor woman. Other persons who were witnesses of the scene were strongly moved; some shed tears, but nothing could shake the resolution of all to detain the King. It seemed as though they obeyed a superior will, invoked by none, but imposed on all.

At this moment Goguelat and Choiseul arrived; with them was M. de Damas; he had endeavoured to carry off his dragoons from Clermont and to bring them to the aid of the King, but he was abandoned by them and had escaped with only two sub-officers. They were taken into the house, where they saw the Queen, Madame Elizabeth, Madame Royale, and Madame de Tourzel seated on forms. The Dauphin was asleep in his clothes on an unmade bed. The King only was standing. On perceiving Goguelat he came to him and said, "Well, Goguelat, when do we start?" "Sire, when it shall please your Majesty; I wait your orders." But the King was not either morally or physically in a state to give orders. Surrounded by the members of the municipality and the officers of the National Guard, he repeated to them that he wished to go to Montmédy, and that he had never entertained any intention of quitting France.

During this time numerous emissaries were scouring the country. The National Guards from the neighbouring villages were coming in on all sides. The excitement was rising to a dangerous pitch; every moment of delay increased the risk and rendered the possibility of departure more and more uncertain. Goguelat, who was the only, or almost the only, one who had preserved coolness, and who comprehended the full peril of the circumstances, was out of patience. He was a man of action, and he could not bear to witness the King's apathy. He approached Marie Antoinette, put her in possession in a few words of what was happening on the outside, and entreated her to use all her influence to induce the King to set out at once. But the Queen herself yielded to despondency; perhaps she did not believe in the efficacy of the intervention which Goguelat expected from her. "I will not take anything upon myself," she said. "It is the King who decided upon this step; it is for him to command, and my duty is to follow him. Besides, M. de Bouillé must soon be here."

But M. de Bouillé did not arrive. Would it be too late when he came? and would he be firm enough to overcome the opposition that had been allowed to gain such strength? Goguelat thought not, he made up his mind to dispense with orders which nobody was in a state to give him, and listening only to the promptings of his courage and zeal, he left the house, and mounting his horse, rode into the town in order to procure the berline, and also to muster the hussars.

He encountered Drouet, the postmaster, who came up to him in a threatening manner. "I see that you want to take away the King," he cried, "but you can only have him dead." The Baron made no reply, so fearful was he of provoking a rising, but continued on his way. He was coming up to the place where the berline stood surrounded by a curious crowd, when one Roland, major of the National Guard of Varennes, planted himself before him and exclaimed, "If you make one step forward I will kill you." Goguelat rode at him sword in hand; the major fired his pistol point-blank at Goguelat, hitting him in the chest. A second bullet grazed his head. He fell from his horse, and was immediately seized and carried to a neighbouring house, where his wounds, which were fortunately slight, were dressed. But he was a prisoner. With him vanished the last chance of resistance. The hussars whom he had collected, being deprived of their officer, obeyed the orders of the populace, shouted "Long live the nation," and again dispersed.

The royal captives passed the night in terrible suspense. Extreme fatigue alone brought slumber to the unhappy travellers, and the three body-guards, whose courage and fidelity had been unavailing, slept with their hats on, while the King, always irresolute, went up and down the narrow wooden stairs leading to the two little rooms in which the Queen had installed herself with her children, her sister-in-law, and the ladies of her suite.

Fatigue, anxiety, and humiliation had subdued her physical strength, if not her great heart. She fell down exhausted by the side of the two poor little partakers of her misery, and it was in that night of terrible anguish that her "locks of the red red gold," once so much admired, turned white like the hair of a woman of seventy!

The dawn came. The position was unchanged. M. de Bouillé had not arrived.

Great was the perplexity of the patriots;

they did not know what to do with their prisoners. They would willingly have sent them back to Paris, but they dared not, and their dilemma encouraged the hopes of the King and Queen. They resorted to every pretext for delay they could imagine. Mme. de Neuville pretended to faint, and Marie Antoinette declared that she would not go without her.

Suddenly, between five and six o'clock in the morning, a stir was observed among the crowd around the house. Had Bouillé come at last? No; but M. Romeuf, aide-de-camp to Lafayette, and M. Baillon, an officer of the Parisian National Guard, sent in pursuit of the King, had arrived. This event was a last blow to the hopes of the fugitives, and a fresh incentive to their enemies.

M. Baillon entered the room where the travellers were assembled, and there, using exaggerated language, he described the horrors to which the capital was given over, the murders which were being committed — an imaginary detail, since nothing of the sort had occurred—and declared that the one only means of putting an end to fratricidal strife was the King's return to Paris.

M. Romeuf, who was more sincerely affected and better behaved, was satisfied with reading a former decree of the National Assembly, by which the King was prohibited from removing himself to a distance exceeding twenty leagues from the National Assembly.

Louis XVI., confused by this reminder, stammered out—

"I never sanctioned that."

He placed the paper on the bed where the Dauphin and Madame Royale lay.

Marie Antoinette snatched it up and threw it on the ground, exclaiming—

"It would soil my children's bed!"

M. Romeuf endeavoured to soothe her anger, but she responded only by reproaching him severely for having accepted an odious mission, in which she plainly recognised the hand of Lafayette.

The King, clinging to his delusive hope to the last, took M. Baillon aside and strove to move him to pity. "Yet an instant," he urged. "Is it not possible to wait until eleven o'clock?"

"Eleven o'clock" meant succour, meant the Royal Allemand led by the General, and this was just what Romeuf and Baillon did not mean to wait for. Every effort was ineffectual; it was impossible to bend those inflexible functionaries, backed by the clamour of the multitude who now filled Varennes. The prisoners were reduced to despair; how could they contend with the adverse fortune which had betrayed them and delivered them over to their enemies?

And yet one more chance, a last chance, was afforded them—but in vain; they were incapable of profiting by it. M. Deslon, a brave officer, who had commanded the squadron posted at Dun, being surprised and uneasy at the non-arrival of the royal family, had marched to Varennes during the night, and obtained admittance to the city, though only for himself. He gained access to the King, explained that he had been obliged to leave his men at the gates of Varennes by order of the municipal authorities, but that he could go and inform his general; in short, he, like Goguelat, asked the King for orders.

"You may tell M. de Bouillé that I am a prisoner, that I am much afraid he can do nothing for me, but that I beg him to do what he can."

On hearing these desponding words, M. Deslon turned to the Queen, and, as he was an Alsatian, he muttered a few words in German. Marie Antoinette stopped him abruptly. "They are listening; do not speak to me," said she. M. Deslon withdrew in despair. What could he attempt on behalf of princes who gave up their own cause? It was finished. They had to go. At any rate, his emotions did not act upon the physical wants of the King; he ate his breakfast and slept for a short time.

The carriages were soon brought up, the travellers resumed their places, and at half-past seven the big berline was once more put in motion in the midst of a crowd of National Guards, and the cortège set out on the return to Paris.

An hour and a half later a cloud of dust, visible from the town, announced the arrival of a strong body of troops; it was Bouillé. He had re-entered Stenay at three o'clock in the morning, and being joined there by two officers, learned from them that the King had been stopped at midnight. He had his horses saddled immediately, called the Royal Allemand together, distributed four hundred louis among his troopers to stimulate their zeal and strengthen their fidelity, and put them in motion, riding down the few National Guards who made an attempt to check his advance here and there. But he met Deslon with his squadron at the gates of the city, and was informed by him that the travellers had started an hour and a half previously.

Bouillé states in his *Mémoires* that he resolved on the instant to pass round Varennes and pursue the cortège in order to deliver the King by main force, and was about to give orders accordingly, when it was announced to him that the garrisons of Metz and Verdun had just sided with the National Guards and the excited populace. The attempt which he was meditating lost its best chances of success, especially as he could no longer reckon confidently on his troops in the face of so much opposition. And so Bouillé " shook his bridle-rein," abandoned the remains of his force, passed the frontier into Luxemburg, and eluded the warrant that was immediately issued for his arrest.

The heavy berline, which had travelled slowly enough on the first journey, went more slowly still on the second; it was forbidden to advance faster than the body of National Guards which escorted it on foot. This was a terrible ordeal for the travellers, and it was rendered more painful by the burning rays of the dazzling sun, for the jealous watchfulness of the people forbade the lowering of the blinds.

Presently a dreadful spectacle struck the unfortunate captives with terror, and showed what cruelty and savagery there was in these newly-emancipated citizens, who had such strange notions of liberty. A gentleman, one M. de Dampierre, conceived it his duty to salute the fallen Majesties of France when they passed before his château. He was allowed to approach and pay his loyal homage to the King and Queen; but no sooner had he withdrawn to about fifty paces than some wretches shot him "like a rabbit." He fell, they flung themselves upon his corpse, and greater wretches still cut his head off and carried the bleeding trophy to the doors of the berline.

A little farther on the Queen was grossly insulted. She had observed that among the people surrounding the carriage some looked hungry, and in her pity she offered to the nearest a slice of the piece of *bœuf à la mode* which Fersen's valet had placed in the carriage.

"Don't eat it," exclaimed a furious voice. "Do you not see that she wants to poison you?"

Tears of indignation came into the Queen's eyes. With a gesture both dignified and wrathful she withdrew the slice of meat, and immediately ate some of it herself; she also made her son do the same.

At Châlons the route had been changed, and they were returning by Epernay, when at a league and a half above that town, near the little village of Pont-à-Binson, a great clamour arose, as the crowd caught sight of the three commissaries delegated by the National Assembly—Barnave, Latour-Maubourg, and Pétion.

The cortège halted. Pétion came forward to read the decree of the Assembly. But it would be doing that illustrious personage a wrong to tell a story which he has taken the trouble to narrate. If Buffon be right, and "the style is the man," we may judge what Pétion was by reading him.

Pétion's account of the return to Paris was published for the first time by M. Mortimer-Ternaux in his *Histoire de la Terreur*. It is long and rather diffuse; some extracts from it will suffice.[1]

"On perceiving us, a cry of 'There are the deputies of the National Assembly,' was raised. They made way for us everywhere, and gave *signals* for order and silence. The cortège was superb: National Guards on horseback, on foot, in uniform, out of uniform, arms of every kind; the sun on its decline reflected light on this fine scene, in the midst of a peaceful landscape, the great circumstance, everything, I know not what, was imposing, and gave birth *to ideas which cannot be calculated, but how diversified and exaggerated was the feeling!* I cannot depict the respect with which we were surrounded.

---

[1] M. Paul Gaulot preserves the bad spelling and punctuation of this remarkable document, which can only be appreciated through a literal translation.

"In the midst of the horses, the clash of arms, the applause of the crowd, whose eagerness impelled them forward, while the fear of pressing upon us held them back, we reached the side of the carriage. The door was instantly opened. Confused sounds issued from within. The Queen and Madame Elizabeth seemed strongly agitated, distressed. 'Oh, sirs!' they said with precipitation, with oppression, the tears in their eyes—'Oh, sirs! Ah! Monsieur Maubourg,' appealingly taking his hand. 'Ah! Monsieur,' also taking Barnave's hand. Ah! Monsieur,' said Madame Elizabeth, placing her hand on mine only, 'let no misfortune happen; let not the people who have accompanied us be victims; let not their lives be taken. The King did not wish to leave France.'

"'No, gentlemen,' said the King, speaking with volubility, 'I was not going out of the country, that is true.' This scene was rapid; it lasted only a minute, but how that minute struck me! Maubourg answered; I answered by *Ahs!* by insignificant words and *some signs of dignity without harshness*, of mildness without affectation, and, cutting this colloquy short, assuming the character of our mission, I announced it to the King in a few words, and read to him the decree of which I was the bearer. The greatest silence reigned at this moment.

"Passing to the other side of the carriage, I called for silence. I obtained it, and I read aloud the decree to the citizens; it was applauded.

"We said to the King that it was fitting we should take our places in his carriage. Barnave and I stepped in, but we had hardly done so when we said to the King—

"'But, Sire, we shall inconvenience, crowd you. It is impossible for us to find room here.'

"The King replied—

"'I desire that none of the persons who have accompanied me shall get out. I beg you to seat yourselves. We can sit closer; you will find room.'

"The King, the Queen, the Prince Royal, were on the back seats; Madame Elizabeth, Mme. de Tourzel, and Madame Royale were on the front. The Queen took the Prince on her lap, Barnave placed himself between the King and the Queen, Mme. de Tourzel put Madame between her knees, and I sat between Mme. Elizabeth and Mme. de Tourzel. After the first small-talk was over, I perceived a family air of simplicity which pleased me. There was no longer any royal representation; there existed an ease and *a domestic good-nature.* The Queen called Madame Elizabeth my little sister; Madame Elizabeth answered her the same; Madame Elizabeth called the King my brother; the Queen danced the little Prince on her knees; Madame, although more reserved, played with her brother. The King regarded all this with a pretty well-satisfied air, although little moved and not sensitive.

"I also examined the dress of the travellers. It was impossible for it to be more mean. The King had a brown plush coat, very dirty linen; the women very common morning-gowns.

"The Queen and Madame Elizabeth turned again and again to the body-guards, who were on the box-seat, and manifested the greatest anxiety.

"The King spoke little, and the conversation became more particular; the Queen spoke to Barnave, and Madame Elizabeth to me, as though they had distributed their rôles, saying to each other, 'Do you take charge of your neighbour; I will take charge of mine.'"

Starting from this idea, Pétion's narrative, in which the matter is on a par with the style, shows what havoc may be made of a narrow intellect and a common mind by a too sudden rise in position, and the ill-understood teaching of Jean Jacques Rousseau. He proceeds:—

"Madame Elizabeth gazed at me with soft eyes, with that air of languor which misfortune gives, and which inspires a lively interest. Our eyes met sometimes with a kind of intelligence and attraction; *the night was closing in;* the moon began to shed that gentle light. Madame Elizabeth took Madame on her lap; she then placed her, half on her knee, half on mine; her head was supported by my hand, then by hers. Madame fell asleep; I stretched out my arm. Madame Elizabeth stretched hers upon mine. Our arms were entwined; mine passed under her armpit.[1] I felt quickened

[1] *Aisselle*, spelled *'eselle* by Pétion.

movements, heat which came through the garments; the glances of Madame Elizabeth seemed to me more touching. I perceived a certain unrestraint in her bearing, her eyes were moist, a kind of pleasure was mingled with melancholy. I may deceive myself—it is easy to confound the sensibility of misfortune with the sensibility of pleasure—but *I think if we had been alone, if, as by enchantment, everybody had disappeared, she would have fallen into my arms and yielded to the impulses of nature.*"

His sagacious mind is, however, invaded by a doubt. What if that sensibility which he analyses so ably were neither "that of misfortune nor that of pleasure"? He knows what abominations princesses are capable of, with the object of doing harm to an honest man, and he becomes suspicious. "May not Madame Elizabeth have consented to sacrifice her own honour in order to make me lose mine?"

But no, this is unlikely. "Considering that natural air, my self-esteem also insinuating to me that I might please her; that she was at the age when the passions make themselves felt, I persuaded myself, and found pleasure in doing so, that she herself wished we could have been without witnesses, so that I might have made those soft advances to her, offered those delicate caresses which vanquish modesty without offending it, and, without alarming delicacy, bring about defeat, in which only confusion and nature are accomplices."

But they were not alone, and, moreover,

Pétion was not the man to take advantage of such an opportunity. In vain, therefore, was there "something flattering" in the voice of the Princess. He answered "with a kind of austerity in which there was nothing morose," and he took good care "not to compromise his character."

"I gave all that was necessary to the position in which I believed her to be, without, however, giving enough to enable her to think, even to suspect, that anything *could ever alter my opinion.*"

The result of this noble reserve may be foreseen, or rather, Pétion's imagination, which had provided his vanity with a 'very flattering little romance, supplies the appropriate fitting ending. Madame Elizabeth "saw that the most enticing temptations would be unavailing." He then observed in her bearing " a certain coolness, a certain severity, which often arises in women from mortified vanity."

The virtuous young lady to whom Pétion imputes such feelings would assuredly have been astonished to learn what restraint he put upon himself in abstaining from "*those soft advances and delicate caresses which vanquish modesty without offending it,*" and she would have pardoned the culprit in consideration of his folly. History ought not to be more severe.

At length they arrived at Dormans, and alighted at a mean-looking tavern. "I own," writes Pétion, "that I was not sorry the Court should know what an ordinary inn is."

There was, indeed, something in this to gratify the representative of the people, the enemy of the great, who notes with satisfaction that there were occasional shouts of "Long live Barnave! Long live Pétion!" but that none cried, "Long live the King."

The next day he seated himself in the berline between the King and Queen. His purpose was to test the intelligence of Louis, and he proceeded to do this with great adroitness, in his own opinion.

"I said to him from time to time, 'See how beautiful the country is! What a fine country France is! No kingdom in the world can be compared with it!'

"I threw out these ideas with a purpose; I wanted to judge by the King's countenance what impression they made; but his face is always cold, most provokingly inanimate; to tell the truth, that mass of flesh is without feeling."

Louis XVI. certainly did not possess a superior intellect, but his remaining unmoved by the exclamations of Pétion cannot fairly be quoted against him as a grievance.

Marie Antoinette did not impress Pétion much more favourably, although she talked with him "in an easy and familiar manner." It did not take him long to perceive that all she said was "extremely superficial," and "that she did not give utterance to any strong or marked idea; she had not in any sense either the air or the attitude of her position.

At La Ferté-sous-Jouarre there was another halt, and the King was entertained by the Mayor, who owned a very handsome house on the banks of the Marne. While waiting for dinner, Pétion took advantage of the opportunity to join Madame Elizabeth in a walk on the terrace.

"There," says he, "I spoke to her with all the frankness and veracity of my nature; I represented to her how ill-surrounded, ill-advised the King was; I spoke to her of all the Court manœuvres *with the dignity of a free man and the disdain of a wise man.* . . . *She took pleasure in my conversation, and I took pleasure in conversing with her.* I should be much surprised if she has not a good and high mind, although much imbued with the prejudices of birth, and spoiled by the vices of a Court education."

The foregoing remark does not display any great perspicacity; but it appears singularly intelligent in comparison with the following :—

"Barnave talked for a while with the Queen, but it appeared to me in rather an indifferent manner."

He had already observed that their conversation in the carriage "did not seem mysterious."

Considering the change that took place from that moment in the opinions and conduct of Barnave, we may conclude that Pétion was more ingenious in imputing to persons opinions which they did not hold, than in discerning those they did.

The following morning at five o'clock the journey was resumed.

"We jogged along quietly. I was seated next to the Queen, and she addressed me frequently. I had the opportunity of telling her, with entire frankness, all that was thought of the Court, and what was said of the schemers who frequented the Château. . . . I put no constraint of any kind upon myself."

His reflections had more sense in them when he came to speak of the King's flight.

"The Queen and Madame Elizabeth often repeated that the King was free to travel in his kingdom, and that he had never had any intention of leaving it.

"Allow me," said I to the Queen, "not to go into the matter of that intention. I will suppose that the King had at first stopped at the frontier; he would have been in a position to pass over into foreign territory at any moment; he might perhaps have found himself forced to do so, and then, besides, the King cannot have disguised from himself that his absence might give rise to most serious disorder. The least evil caused by his departure was the sudden stoppage of the business of the National Assembly."

They reached Meaux early, and alighted at the palace of the Bishop, a "Constitutionel"—"this could not be very pleasing to the King; but he gave no sign of annoyance."

At six o'clock in the morning they set out

again, and Pétion resumed his former place between Madame Elizabeth and Madame de Tourzel. "Never was there a longer and more fatiguing day. The heat was extreme, and we were wrapped in whirlwinds of dust. The King offered me something to drink, and poured it out for me several times. We remained for twelve hours in the carriage, without leaving it for a moment."

As they approached Paris, the popular spirit became worse, or at least it was more openly manifested. At Pantin there was a scuffle, and in the tumult the vilest epithets were applied to the Queen.

"The ——" cried some angry men. "It is no use for her to show us her son; we know he is none of his!"

"The King heard this very distinctly. The young Prince, terrified by the noise and the clash of arms, uttered cries of alarm; the Queen checked him; the tears were rolling in her eyes."

Poor woman! poor mother! how well we understand the immense pity that seized upon Barnave at the sight of such great misery: it could not but touch a man with a heart. Pétion was safe from any such emotion.

Instead of passing through Saint-Denis, the cortège went round Paris, and entered by the Porte de la Conférence, above the Champs-Elysées.

Thousands of posters, put up by unknown hands, and reflecting the general feeling, prescribed the aspect which the people were to assume on the return of their sovereign : "Any one who shall applaud the King will be beaten. Any one who shall insult him will be hanged."

Troops were stationed from the Barrière de l'Etoile to the Tuileries, and formed a line, with reversed arms. An immense crowd had assembled, without noise or violence, and looked angrily on as the cortège passed, but "were perfectly orderly." "Every man had his hat on his head; the most majestic silence reigned."

The berline crossed the swing-bridge and entered the gardens of the Tuileries. The bridge was immediately shut; but this precaution was useless, for a crowd of National Guards in arms had been allowed to invade the garden, and these soldier-citizens were in a state of vehement excitement. They loudly threatened the three body-guards, who sat impassive on the box-seat of the berline, overwhelmed them with abuse, and at one moment seemed about to proceed to violence. The three brave fellows, powerless to defend themselves against such a number of assailants, and thinking their last hour was come, sprang off the carriage, with the chivalrous intention of at least sparing the royal family the pain of seeing them massacred before their eyes.

"Monsieur de Lafayette, save the body-guards!" cried the Queen wildly; she still retained sufficient self-command to enable her to think of others besides herself, notwithstanding the threats directed against all.

Several deputies interposed courageously, and

took the three gentlemen under their protection; thus were their lives saved.

M. de Lafayette, on horseback, presided at the arrival. The carriage doors were opened; the King stepped out — silence. The Queen appeared—murmurs arose. M. de Noailles, a Liberal deputy, advanced to offer her his arm. The haughty daughter of Maria Theresa, vanquished but not subdued, declined it, and took the arm of a deputy of the Right. The children came next, then Madame Elizabeth, Madame de Tourzel, and the two commissaries. A grotesque little incident then occurred. Although the crowd were shouting, "Long live Pétion"—it is he who says so—they evidently did not recognise the object of their acclamations, for, Pétion being mixed up with the King's servants, was taken by the collar by a zealous patriot, who was about to treat him to a good kicking, when some of his colleagues came to the spot, apprised the enthusiastic citizen of his mistake, and Pétion, being released, repaired to the royal apartments.

The royal family were in the room preceding the King's bed-chamber. Anybody might come in who liked to do so. One Coroller, a deputy from the province of Brittany, a good sort of fellow, approached the King and began to address him in a half-kindly, half-lecturing tone, as if he were reprimanding a schoolboy.

"Now, have you not made a nice mess of it? This is what comes of having such bad people about you! You are good, you are beloved; just see what you have done!"

And then he became quite tender. The King did not know how to put an end to this ridiculous scene, which was succeeded by a more respectful but perhaps more painful one, at least for Marie Antoinette, who had not the inexhaustible resignation of her apathetic spouse.

General Lafayette presented himself and said to the King—

"Sire, your Majesty knows my attachment to you; but I have not concealed from you that if you separated your cause from that of the people, I should remain on the side of the people."

"That is true," replied the King; "you have acted on your principles; it is an affair of party. Now I am here, I will tell you frankly that until lately I have believed that you surrounded me with a crowd of people of your own way of thinking, but who did not represent the mind of France. This journey has plainly shown me my mistake, and that such *is* the general mind."

"Has your Majesty any commands to give me?"

"It seems to me," said the King, laughing, "that I am more at your command than you at mine."

No one could be more good-natured, and he took his hard lot as well as man could take it. The Queen had not that virtue, or rather that weakness. Treating Lafayette as a gaoler, she wanted to force him to receive the keys of the cash-boxes which had been left in the carriage, and as he refused, she threw them upon his hat.

"Your Majesty will have the trouble of taking

them back again," he said, "for I will not touch them."

"Very well," she replied; "I shall find persons less scrupulous than you."

She did not find any such; but although the appearance of captivity was spared to the royal couple, who had been brought back to Paris for the second time, that captivity had begun in earnest, and it was close and unremitting.

As for Louis XVI., he resumed the ordinary course of his life, and his journal does not indicate any recollection of very keen emotions. We can judge, for here it is :—

"*June* 1791, *Monday* 20.—Nothing.
"*Tuesday* 21.—Departure from Paris at midnight. Arrived and stopped at Varennes in Argonne at eleven o'clock at night.
"*Wednesday* 22.—Departure from Varennes at five or six o'clock in the morning. Breakfast at Sainte-Menehould. Arrived at Châlons at ten o'clock; supped there, and slept at the former Intendance.
"*Thursday* 23.—At half-past eleven Mass was interrupted to hasten the departure. Breakfast at Châlons. Dined at Epernay. Found the Commissaries of the Assembly near the bridge at Binson. Arrived at Dormans at eleven o'clock; supped there. Slept three hours in an arm-chair.
"*Friday* 24.—Left Dormans at half-past seven; dined at La Ferté-sous-Jouarre. Arrived at Meaux at ten o'clock. Supped and slept at the Bishop's palace.
"*Saturday* 25.—Left Meaux at half-past six. Arrived at Paris at eight o'clock without stopping.
"*Sunday* 26.—Nothing at all. Mass in the gallery. Meeting of the Commissaries of the Assembly.
"*Monday* 27.—Nothing at all.
"*Tuesday* 28.—Nothing at all.
"*Wednesday* 29.—Nothing at all.
"*Thursday* 30.—Nothing at all."

CHAPTER VII.

Count Fersen at Mons—False news—"The King is saved!"—Count Fersen meets Bouillé at Arlon—"All is lost!"—M. de Mercy-Argenteau at Brussels—"He takes the gloomiest view"—Notes from Marie Antoinette—The Princesse de Lamballe—Mme. de Polignac—News from Paris—Dejection of the King—The King and Queen are interrogated by Tronchet, Duport, and d'André—Indictment of the authors of the "Abduction of the King" and their accomplices—Count Fersen's sojourn in France interdicted—M. de Damas, M. d'Audoins, M. de Choiseul, and M. de Goguelat—Courageous bearing of the three body-guards—Letter from the Marquis de Bouillé to the National Assembly—Displeasure of the Royalists remaining in France—The King of Sweden at Spa—Count Fersen at Coblentz—The princes: Monsieur and the Comte d'Artois—M. de Calonne—Count Fersen at Vienna—Interview with the Emperor Leopold—"The accursed Florentine"—The political interest of the House of Austria in the degradation of the House of France—A contemplated landing in Normandy—Louis XVI. accepts the Constitution—The Queen accused of allowing herself to be led by Barnave—Her double game—Letters to Fersen—Political and private communications.

COUNT FERSEN arrived at Mons on the 22nd of June at six o'clock in the morning. He did not yet venture to feel certain that the attempted escape of the royal family had succeeded. His anxiety was great, and many things concurred to render it painful: his love for the Queen, his own share in the flight, his dread of the frightful evils which must inevitably be the result of failure, and lastly, the thought that possibly he might never see her again.

Up to the present, however, appearances had been favourable. Mrs. Sullivan had arrived safely at Mons, and also the Comte de Provence, who had left Paris at the same time as the King, and had been fortunate enough to rejoin his mistress, Mme. de Balbi, without having encountered any obstacle. Several French people who had recently emigrated received the first announcement of the departure of the royal family with great pleasure, and went about accosting one another, and interchanging their impressions and hopes.

A monk had met Count Fersen in the street, and asked him whether the King was saved. The rumour soon got abroad, none knew how, and the false intelligence, spreading on the instant with extraordinary rapidity, was hailed with joy by all the emigrants.

But the Count did not linger at Mons; at eleven o'clock he set out again for the Belgian Luxemburg, being anxious to get near to Montmédy. After a whole day's journey in fine but rather cold weather, very different from the sultry heat to which the captives were exposed on their forced return to Paris, he arrived at Arlon at eleven o'clock at night.

He was passing through the town on his way to learn the news, when he accidentally met the Marquis de Bouillé face to face. The mere sight of the General instantly revealed the terrible truth. All was over then—the flight had failed. Bouillé told him how the King had been stopped, and related some of the deplorable incidents which had ruined everything within a few leagues of the goal; but the General could not give him all the details of the disaster; he was ignorant of most of them himself. However, he knew enough to inform Count Fersen that the detachments had not done their duty, as Count Fersen had only too clearly foreseen, and that the King had "failed in firmness and sense," as he might easily have foretold.

Fersen, who was overwhelmed by the news, sent a hasty despatch to the King of Sweden, informing him of the fatal result of the enterprise, and immediately afterwards wrote to his father in the following words, which reveal all his grief:—

"ARLON, 23d of June 1791, at midnight.

"All is lost, my dear father, and I am in despair. The King was stopped at Varennes, within sixteen leagues of the frontier. Judge what my grief is, and feel for me. M. de Bouillé, who is here, has told me this news. I am starting at once for Brussels, to convey to Count de Mercy the letters which the King intrusted to me. I have time only to assure you of my respect and my love.

"AXEL FERSEN."

By this we see that he bore in mind the injunction of the King and Queen at his last interview with them at the Tuileries, only three days previously, that he should go to Brussels, if they were stopped, and have action taken for them. This was a formidable mission, for he

would have to appeal to foreign sympathies,
and might find that where good-will existed
power did not, and that in some cases there was
neither good-will nor power.

But the Swede heeded nothing of that kind;
difficulties, of whatever nature, could not deter
him. At half-past four in the morning of
the 24th he left Arlon. At Namur he met
Monsieur, who was more elated by his own
good-luck than troubled by his brother's ill-
fortune. On the following day, at two o'clock
in the afternoon, he re-entered Brussels, and
proceeded at once to the Bellevue Hôtel, where
the Comte de Mercy-Argenteau had resided since
his departure from France.

He did not find the Comte de Mercy, but left
the King's letter for him, and made his escape
with difficulty from the eager questioning of
all the people who were in the hotel. In the
evening he succeeded in seeing the Austrian
Ambassador. The impression which he derived
from his conversation with him was not favourable. "He takes the gloomiest view" (*il voit
noir*) is the entry in the Count's journal. How
should it have been otherwise? Mercy was an
old politician; for two years he had been in close
contact with the European sovereigns and the
emigrants; only a large amount of confidence
and self-delusion could have led him to hope
much from the former, and to expect much from
the latter. In spite of everything, the young
Swede was of a different mind. He was not
a politician, but a man with a heart, and his
determination to act had other and stronger

stimulants than those which would have affected the old Ambassador.

If his zeal had required to be reanimated, two little notes which reached him from Paris would have stirred it up. But was there any need? What must have been his joy on receiving these few lines, written by Marie Antoinette on the 28th of June :—

"Be at ease about us; we are alive. The heads of the Assembly seem inclined to behave with some kindness. Speak to my relations about taking steps from the outside; if they are afraid, terms must be made with them."

The following day a second note, more touching and affectionate, brought him a repetition of the assurances which made him happy.

"I exist . . . . how anxious I have been about you, and how I grieve for all you are suffering from having no news of us. May Heaven permit this to reach you. Do not write to me; it would endanger you, and above all, do not come back here under any pretext. It is known that it was you who got us out of this place; all would be lost if you appeared. We are closely watched night and day. I do not mind that. . . . Be tranquil; nothing will happen to me. The Assembly wishes to treat us gently. Adieu . . . I shall no longer be able to write to you. . . ."

This note was written in cipher like the first, and was transcribed from the cipher by Fersen, who wrote on the margin, "The 4th of July 1791, probably the day of reception." It is reproduced here exactly as it is given in the work entitled *Le Comte de Fersen et la Cour de France*. Were the suppressed passages, marked by dots, left out by Fersen himself—that he did use suppression sometimes we shall see hereafter—or by those persons who undertook the publication of his papers? The latter supposition seems in this instance most likely, as we do not find the footnote which the editors have been careful to attach to another letter written by Marie Antoinette to Count Fersen on the 26th of September 1791.

Why then are these passages suppressed? Here we are reminded of a note inserted by Feuillet de Conches in the preface to the third volume of his *Louis XVI., Marie Antoinette et Madame Elisabeth:* "Nearly three years ago I had the honour to meet Count Fersen's grand-daughter, the Countess Gyldenstole, and I inquired of her whether there were any letters from Queen Marie Antoinette addressed to Count Fersen, among her family papers. She assured me that the collection did not include even the merest note in the handwriting of the Queen, and also that all her kin cherished a profound respect, indeed a sort of traditional reverence, for that supreme sufferer.

"Since then, a grand-nephew of the same Swedish nobleman (Count Fersen), M. de Klinckowström, recently secretary to the Swedish Legation in Austria, and now settled at Stockholm, has had the statement that neither in the Gyldenstole branch of the family nor in his own did they possess any written memorial of the Queen confirmed to me by the French Minister to the Court of Sweden, M. Fournier. *A presumption stronger than truth will have it that such memorials do exist.* Can it be that this presumption is supported by any exception?" The above note was written in 1865. Twelve years later, a grand-nephew of Count Fersen, Baron Klinckowström—is he the same of whom Feuillet de Conches speaks?—published in the extracts from his grand-uncle's papers eleven unquestionably authentic letters written by Count Fersen in 1791, and seventeen written in 1792.

Were these letters known to the family in 1865? had it been agreed that they were to be kept secret, and was the resolution rescinded afterwards? Is the discovery of them recent? These are idle questions, impossible of solution by us. What it imports us to observe is that "presumption" is stronger in the case than denial, and that it only outstripped the truth.

All this would perhaps authorise us to supply the missing passages, and would guide us in our suppositions, but to what end? Silence is sometimes very eloquent; let those understand who will.

In the Queen's note as we have it, mutilated though it be, we can discern a sentiment which is not gratitude only, and how delicately is that sentiment expressed! That friend who grieves "for all he suffers in having no news of them," well knows the heart to which she speaks! How anxiously she assures him concerning her fate!

"Be tranquil; nothing will happen to me." And how sad is that "Adieu," and her intimation that she "will no longer be able to write" to him whose love consoles and sustains her!

Of a surety that friend "without reproach," that confidant, and accomplice "without fear," well deserved that she should treat him thus. The comparison which the unfortunate Marie Antoinette was forced to draw between him and others can only have endeared the noble Swedish gentleman to her.

A few weeks later Count Fersen met Mme. de Polignac. "I felt both pleasure and pain on seeing her," he says. It might be supposed that her feelings would be similar on finding herself once more with the friend of her friend, talking of her whom she ought not to have forgotten, her whose fate should have touched her the more deeply in that the excessive favours which Marie Antoinette had lavished upon her had cost the unfortunate Queen her popularity.

Mme. de Polignac did not even resort to a pretence of gratitude. If she wept on seeing Fersen, her tears were very transient.

"She talked more about affairs than of the Queen," says Fersen; "she said a thousand things." And of those things some were not favourable to the royal family. The situation, between the King detained in Paris and the Princes free in a foreign land, was naturally strained; the latter were glad to forget their brother's peril in their own safety, and ready to put themselves forward while incurring no risk, caring not at all how much they might endanger the King. The ardour of the Comte d'Artois was particularly formidable. Mme. de Polignac was for the Princes, and "disapproved the suspicion with which they were regarded by certain persons." His first interview inspired Fersen with a poor opinion of the favourite; he met her again in the apartment of the Comte d'Artois, where M. de Calonne appeared in his nightcap, whereat they were mightily amused. A third meeting failed to alter his impression:—"I have seen the Duchesse de Polignac; she constantly talks of affairs, but seldom of her friend."

Very different was the sweet and noble Princesse de Lamballe, whom Marie Antoinette had sacrificed to the Polignac. While the latter cheerfully consented to place herself and her goods in safety, the former, who was travelling abroad, conceived that the duty of a friend, even though neglected, and even though forsaken, was to adhere to those whom she had loved in their evil fortune, and she returned to France prepared to confront the perils from which the other had fled.

Doubtless she had not a very bright intellect, and her presence was not likely to be of much use. Fersen saw her at Brussels, and met her at a dinner given by Mrs. Sullivan. Her conversation did not please him; he passes a rather harsh judgment upon it, summing it up as "silly gossip." But the woman had a heart, and, as she obeyed its impulses, her conduct was noble and generous; she resumed that place with the Queen which Mme. de Polignac had usurped, only to suffer, to weep, and to die.

It would be a mistake to suppose that all the emigrants were thinking only of a return of good fortune for the King, the Queen, and the cause of legitimate monarchy, to which they were supposed to be devoted. It would appear to us that in the face of the great events then taking place, and the growing danger that threatened the old social order, they should all have united in order to secure a triumph. This was surely imperative! Nothing, however, is more sad to record than the mean and base jealousy of those expatriated Frenchmen. Many of them openly desired that the Comte d'Artois should assume the leadership of the party, and for this reason the captivity of the King and Queen, which left them a free hand, was far from displeasing to them. They even ventured to rejoice openly in it, as we learn from Fersen, who writes, "There is an indecent joy here among our party at the arrest of the King."

He did not conceal his indignation, and when certain persons, with the importunate eagerness of mere curiosity, tried to elicit from him the details of the event which had overwhelmed him with grief, he describes himself as "disgusted by the sight of them."

Sad news came to him from Paris! "The King and Queen of France are closely watched; all the doors are open; guards are placed in the room next to the bed-chamber. The doors are shut for a moment only while the King's shirt is put on; when she (the Queen) is in bed, the guards come several times during the night to make sure. Never alone. They must not speak low. No one can enter the château without tickets from Lafayette and the Mayor."

It was not known at Brussels that the King was in a state of physical prostration. This had set in immediately upon his return to Paris. The repeated entry in his journal, "Nothing at all," during the last days of June, was the exact definition of what the King of France himself had become. He was even more inert than indifferent; he was only the shadow of his former self, and remained for days together without uttering a word.

What a spectacle for the Queen! What were her sufferings as a mother? As a wife, her misery was aggravated by the conduct of him who ought to have consoled, supported, and protected her. But no; her husband was no longer a King; he was no longer even a man; and an hour was drawing near in which the Queen, in her indignation and shame at his weakness, was to make one supreme effort to rouse him out of his torpor, throwing herself at his feet in an agonised appeal to his affection and his courage, and using those memorable words: "If we must perish, at least let it be with honour; let us not wait for them to come and strangle us both on the floor of our room!"

But although she succeeded in restoring a temporary appearance of courage to the unfortunate King by her strength of will, she was powerless to inspire him with the dignity which their terrible position demanded.

The National Assembly had appointed three of its members, Tronchet, Duport, and d'André, to receive explanations concerning his abduction (*enlèvement*) from Louis himself; for, by a fiction which did not deceive anybody, but still permitted Louis to preserve the character and the place which he held under the Constitution, it was pretended that he had only yielded to the will of his enemies in leaving Paris. His reply was as pitiful as it was impolitic.

In this document he assigns the outrages to which he and his family were subjected on the 18th of April, and the impunity of the various publications which had afterwards led to the violence done to his person, as the causes of his departure from Paris. He had no intention of leaving France; he had not planned his journey with the foreign Powers, or with his relations, or with any of the French emigrants; one of his chief motives was to refute the statement that he was not free; he had never made any protest except that which he had left for the National Assembly on the day of his departure. . . . He had not thought it possible to ascertain the public mind with certainty in the middle of Paris; but on his journey he had ascertained that it was favourable to the Constitution. . . . So soon as he learned what the public feeling really was, he had sacrificed his personal interests without hesitation to the welfare of the people, and he would gladly forget all the annoyances (*désagréments*) that he had undergone if he could secure the peace and happiness of the nation.

Marie Antoinette was also interrogated, and she made the following declaration:—

"The King being desirous to go away with his children, nothing in nature could have prevented me from accompanying him. I have sufficiently proved for two years past that I would never leave him. That which made me still more determined was the positive assurance that the King did not intend to go out of the kingdom; if he had desired to do so, I would have done all in my power to prevent him."

That these declarations did not carry conviction of their truth to anybody was their least defect. If the King had no intention of going abroad, should need arise, why had he selected a place so near the frontier as Montmédy? If he wanted to ascertain the public mind, why a secret departure by night, and why the hurried rate of travelling? Objections very difficult to refute cropped up in crowds.

The statements of the King and Queen were not believed, and their declaration that all of the persons who accompanied them were unaware of the goal of the journey went for nothing. This was inevitable; when it was decided that the principals were not to be brought to judgment, the subordinates had to be arraigned as culprits.

Warrants were immediately issued against MM. de Bouillé, Heyman, Klinglin, Desoteux, d'Andoins, Bouillé the younger, Goguelat, Choiseul-Stainville, Mandell, Fersen, "Colonel of Royal-Suédois," de Valory, de Maldent, and Du Moustier, body-guards. These persons were sent to the prison at Orleans, and afterwards brought before the tribunal of that city.

M. de Damas, and Mesdames de Tourzel, Brunier, and de Neuville were simply ordered to be arrested " as a provisional measure."

Not all the persons named in the indictment fell into the hands of justice, and among those who were arrested there was considerable diversity of action. All the officers asserted their innocence, declaring that "they knew nothing, and had done nothing but obey." Goguelat, who had displayed so much courage and daring in the hour of danger, endeavoured, like the others, to exculpate himself. "He pleaded the orders of M. de Bouillé; he said that he had no knowledge of what was taking place; that he had only heard the drum-call to arms and the ringing of the alarm-bell, and *heard tell* that the King had been stopped at Varennes. He owned that being afraid lest he might be assailed and maltreated by the people as an officer, he had laid aside his uniform, and was preparing to cross the frontier at the moment of his arrest."

Only the three body-guards, who had shown

such unflinching courage during the terrible return from Varennes and the scene at the Tuileries, still stood firm, preserving their lofty and valiant bearing. Far from shielding themselves under the pretext of the King's commands, they boldly laid claim to the peril and the honour of their action.

The Marquis de Bouillé, who had saved nothing but himself in this fatal adventure, conceived the unlucky idea of writing a furious and ridiculous letter to the National Assembly from Luxemburg, where he had found a safe refuge.

He assumed the entire responsibility of the King's flight, thinking to attract anger and vengeance to himself, who was beyond the reach of either, without taking into account that by doing so he made Louis out a puppet, without either mind or will of his own.

In vain did he assume the Bombastes vein—
"I desired to save my country, I desired to save my King, I desired to save his family: such are my crimes. You will answer for their lives—I do not say to me, but to all the kings! I tell you that if a hair of their heads be hurt, there will shortly be left not one stone of Paris upon another; you yourselves shall answer for it with your heads!

"I know the roads; I will lead the foreign armies!..."

The Assembly laughed uproariously at threats uttered by a general whose plans had been easily frustrated by a postmaster and a few willing citizens. Still, however, Bouillé took a correct view of the situation in appealing for the rescue of the King to foreign armies and to the community of interests of the European sovereigns; for royalty could only be saved from the outside now. The most effective of the monarchical powers had quitted France. "The nobility and the clergy were on the frontier." Those faithful adherents of the monarchy who remained in the country were profoundly depressed; and worse than this, they were seriously displeased with the feeble King.

All those valiant and devoted men who had declined to follow the prompt example of the Comte d'Artois by flying from France, had been deeply hurt by the withholding from them of the royal confidence. They understood, of course, that it was impossible to divulge the plan to everybody, but each one thought an exception might have been made in his own favour. They had not forsaken the King, but here was the King forsaking them! The King was among the emigrants!

His action restored their liberty, and set them free from the last tie that bound them to the now dangerous soil of France. The bearing of the King, when he was brought back foiled and repentant, was not likely to efface these painful impressions.

A similar feeling existed among the Constitutionalists; there was no mistake at all about it, the King had broken his compact with the nation. What power could they wield henceforth against the current which was driving

P

the Assembly, even against its own will, into the assumption of supreme authority? A few deputies of the Right resigned their seats. Three hundred and fifteen declared that they would cease to take part in all deliberations whose object was not "the interests of the King's person and of the royal family." This was a direct and unwise acknowledgment of powerlessness, couched in a phrase which deceived nobody.

Louis, who was incapable of the manly resoluteness of a Henri Quatre, and did not dream of regaining his authority over his rebellious subjects, had but one resource—abdication. He never thought of such a thing! He did not understand anything about the great movement that was extending to the entire people; he thought he could fence with it and trick it, and he condescended to assume the appearance of acquiescence in that which he meant to defeat to the utmost of his power by underhand means. These were perilous and disloyal tactics, which exposed him to the disgrace of receiving a humiliating pardon from his worst enemies, and led to the loss of his life after the loss of his dignity.

From the hour of his arrival at Brussels, Count Fersen's mind was set upon obtaining the support of all the united sovereigns for the royal family of France, and he set to work without delay.

"The dreadful misfortune that has happened must entirely change the progress of affairs," he wrote to Marie Antoinette on the

27th of June; "and if the resolution to employ the agency of others, being no longer able to act in person, still holds good, it is necessary to recommence negotiations, and to give a warrant (*plein pouvoir*) to that effect. The bulk of the Powers who are to act must be great enough to defy resistance, and thus to save precious lives. Answers must be given to the following questions :—

"1. Is it desired that action should be taken, notwithstanding all intimations forbidding it?

"2. Will full powers be given to Monsieur or to the Comte d'Artois?

"3. Is it desired that Baron de Breteuil should be employed under either prince, or would consent be given to the employment of M. de Calonne, or would the choice be left to him?"

In a postscript, dated Aix-la-Chapelle, he says that he has seen the King of Sweden, who is entirely "well-disposed." He adds, "I am well, and I live only to serve you. Tell me whether you wish action to be taken for you."

Of all the princes then reigning, Gustavus III. was undeniably the warmest advocate of this plan for the defence of the royal family of France. He had embraced the cause of monarchy with chivalrous zeal, and his great project was to put himself at the head of a crusade against the rebellious French, those rash promoters of new ideas, and subversive theories fraught with danger to the rights of kings.

Gustavus, being apprised of the projected flight, had gone to Spa, in order to be nearer to the news and also to the fugitives, if happily they should succeed in crossing the frontier; but he had returned to Aix-la-Chapelle when Fersen joined him, and had the satisfaction of finding him warmly interested in the project for the liberation of the prisoners of the Tuileries. The King, wishing to make sure of the co-operation of the British Government, proposed to send Fersen to England, but the Count declined that mission, and proposed Colonel Crawford in his stead. It was then agreed that he was to be sent to Vienna, and that he should endeavour to induce the Emperor to enter into the coalition for his sister's rescue.

Count Fersen set out on the 21st of July, and passed through Coblentz, where he saw Monsieur and the Comte d'Artois.

Monsieur was reasonable, listening seriously to what was said to him, making shrewd remarks, without compromising himself, and showing proper feeling for the misfortunes of his kinsfolk. The Comte d'Artois, on the contrary, assumed the heroic tone, would not hearken to diplomatic measures, insisted on the rebels being put down by force, and displayed a fine disdain of danger that was to be incurred by others. Fersen disposes of him in a sentence: "D'Artois talks incessantly, never listens, is cocksure of everything, and will hear of nothing but force. No negotiations for him." The impetuous Prince found an auxiliary in

M. de Calonne, who arrived just then from England. He was "all damp," says Fersen, for his carriage had been overturned into the Rhine, and he had swam ashore. "Why did he not stay there?" adds the Count. And, indeed, what was there to be hoped from this man, who had been so exasperated by his dismissal that he had become the accomplice of Madame de la Motte, whose *Mémoires*, abounding in infamous accusations against the Queen, were inspired, and probably dictated, by him.

Like the Comte d'Artois, Calonne had seen everything, knew everything, and spoke like a man who was perfectly sure of himself and other people. According to him, England "would respond at once if the other Powers took any steps." What was to be expected from a man who perpetually interrupted the other speakers by exclaiming, "Ah! I have a sublime idea," and then made some absolutely preposterous proposal?

Count Fersen left Coblentz for Vienna on the 27th. On his arrival he learned that the Emperor had caused it to be intimated to the French Ambassador, M. de Noailles, that he must not appear at Court, "his master being a prisoner." The pretext was worthy of the prohibition—both were equally wise and politic.

On the 4th of August he obtained audience of Leopold II. He might have supposed himself with the Comte d'Artois. "The Emperor speaks much and listens little," he writes in

his journal. At first there was a profusion
of protestations, fervent assurances of the
Emperor's devotion to the cause of his unfortunate sister; no effort of his to come to her
aid should be wanting. Count Fersen was
enchanted, but he soon perceived that these
fine words were not followed by deeds to
match—in fact, that nothing at all was done.
Nevertheless, he was not disheartened, and
on the removal of the Court to Prague, he
followed. There again he was received in
the most charming and gracious way, just
at first; after a while there was a decided
change of tone. Leopold protested that his
feelings were still the same, but he had to
contend with the views of his Council; he was
only the echo of the objections which he was
obliged to urge. . . . Presently he avoided
receiving the envoy of Gustavus III., and
the latter had to acknowledge that Baron
Taube was right when he called Leopold "the
accursed Florentine," and to own that he had
been tricked by him. Some time afterwards
Taube wrote to him as follows:—"I have told
you several times, my friend, that we were
duped by the Emperor. . . . *He wants to
mediate between the King, Queen, and the
Assembly, to rule France through the former
or the latter, to dismember it, and to keep
up anarchy in that unhappy country. His
own sister should be the first victim of this
accursed Florentine if he saw any advantage
to be gained by it.*"

Baron Taube put his finger boldly on the

sore spot. It is only too true, and the course of this narrative will afford convincing proof of the fact, that the Emperor Leopold, like most of the other European sovereigns, had no clear vision of what was happening in France. M. de Tocqueville has ably defined the state of mind of the Princes and their Ministers: "If by chance they tell the truth about it (the French Revolution) it is unconsciously. The principal sovereigns of Germany, being met together at Pilnitz in 1791, proclaim that the peril is common to all the old Powers; . . . but in reality they do not believe this. The private documents of the time make it evident that they meant it only as a colourable pretext under which they hid their own designs from the public. As for them, they entirely believed that the French Revolution was but a local and transient accident, and they had only to take all the advantage they could out of it."

The struggle between the "House of France" and the "House of Austria" still subsisted, and the latter regarded the events of the time as a means of defeating the former, or at least of humbling it for a long time.

The Emperor Leopold could not be a sincere supporter of the famous plan of Gustavus III., which consisted of getting together an army and throwing it upon the coasts of Normandy. The Emperor was quite willing to mass troops upon the frontier for the purpose of assisting Louis XVI. to get away from Paris, but not to reinstate him there by a victory in arms,

Too complete a success would have defeated his own secret hopes.

Gustavus was, in fact, beating the air. In vain did he address to Count Fersen a *Memorandum for the inhabitants of Normandy*, and *Instructive Notes upon the most commodious and suitable point for the landing which it is proposed to effect on the coast of Lower Normandy;* not a voice in Europe responded to his appeal, and the mission of his envoys failed everywhere.

Fersen sorrowfully admits the fact. "I beg of you, my friend, to tell the King (of Sweden) how much I grieve that I have succeeded so ill," he wrote to Baron Taube on the 20th of September; "the hope that I may be useful to him at Brussels is a little consolation to me."

His longing for news from France had much to do with his readiness to return to the frontier. Several weeks had elapsed since any intelligence had reached him, and during that time serious events had occurred. The Assembly had completed the Constitution, and had presented it to the King. In order to allow him to make a thorough examination of the document, the restrictions under which he lived were relaxed to a certain extent, and some measure of liberty was granted him.

After a few days of reflection, Louis wrote to the Assembly that he accepted the Constitution, and undertook to have it carried out. This was the result of advice which had been given to him by Lafayette, Barnave, Duport du Tertre, the Lameth brothers, and Prince Kaunitz. The advice of the latter conveyed the secret desire of both the Emperor and himself. Count Fersen would probably have been more indignant than surprised if he had known this.

The news of the King's action raised a chorus of protest, and caused great displeasure abroad. Since Louis had sanctioned the Constitution, some said there was nothing for it but to let him try the experiment; while the more active partisans of the Princes asserted that he was not entitled to renounce his rights, and talked of nominating the Comte de Provence Regent without further delay. Thus we see that the emigrants went faster than the Revolutionists; they were the first to propose the deposition of the King of France.

They were so glad to lay hold of any plausible pretext for the justification of their conduct in their own eyes, that they accumulated grievances against the royal family, and spread the report, which Fersen notes in his journal, that the Queen "allowed herself to be led by Barnave."

Appearances might indicate this, but it was not the case. The Queen was, in fact, playing a double game, which was not dangerous only at that crisis of affairs.

It is well known that Barnave, formerly an adversary of the Court, had been won over to the side of royalty rather by the woman than by the Queen. But whatever may have been the motives of a conversion which had taken place during the return from Varennes under the eyes of Pétion (who had seen nothing of it), Barnave was sincere in the counsel and the support which he gave to Louis and Marie Antoinette. The Queen accepted both his counsel and his support with the private intention of using them to divide her enemies, but it was far from her mind to conform to the policy he laid down. She did not disguise this from her familiar friends. Speaking of Barnave one day to Mme. Campan, she said :—

"A feeling of pride, which I cannot blame in a young man of the Third Estate, has led him to approve of everything that smoothes the path to honours and renown for the class to which he belongs. If power ever comes back again to us, Barnave's pardon is *written beforehand in our hearts.*"

Barnave's pardon! That was all she promised to him who was sacrificing himself for her sake! It was apparently a sufficient reward for the devoted service of "a young man of the Third Estate."

The Queen's attitude with respect to Barnave was consistent in every way with her previous conduct. She was married to the Dauphin when a child; she could not love her new country except through the husband who had been given to her, and he was not capable of making the little Austrian princess love either himself or France. The sentiments with which she was regarded by his nearest of kin as well as by the majority of the Court were not calculated to modify her first impressions.

And so it was that the daughter of Maria Theresa continued to be a docile instrument, at first in the hands of the Empress of Germany, and afterwards in those of her brother Joseph. On two occasions she gave striking proofs of this; perhaps it may be well to recall these incidents of political history in this place.

In 1778, during the affair of the Bavarian succession, which her brother had brought about, and in which the army under his command had not been successful, Marie Antoinette made several attempts to sound the King, or his Ministers, Maurepas and Vergennes, so that she might communicate the projects and the despatches of the French Cabinet to her mother. When Maria Theresa solicited the mediation of France, Marie Antoinette wrote to her: "I have every motive for acting, for I am quite persuaded that the glory of the King and the good of France are concerned in this, *without reckoning the welfare of my dear country*" (October 1778).

Her dear country! Austria.

In 1784, when her brother Joseph laid claim to the mouth of the Scheldt and the possession of Maëstricht, she again put herself forward and endeavoured to influence her husband and the Ministers in his interests. She kept him acquainted with what she was doing. On the 22nd of September 1784 she wrote: "I will not contradict you about the short-sightedness of our Ministry. I have spoken of it more than once to the King, but it would be necessary to know him to understand how I am restricted in means and resources by his character and his prejudices. He is naturally taciturn; when I reproach him with not having spoken to me about certain matters, he does not get angry, but he seems embarrassed, and sometimes tells me simply that it did not occur to him to do so. M. de la Vauguyon alarmed him about the control his wife would try to exert over him, and, moreover, his black soul took pleasure in frightening him with all sorts of phantoms conjured up against Austria. M. de Maurepas thought it to his advantage to keep up these ideas in the King's mind. M. de Vergennes pursues the same plan, and probably makes use of his Foreign Office correspondence to employ treachery and lying. I have spoken of this to the King plainly and more than once. He has sometimes answered me with displeasure, and, as he is incapable of discussion, I have not been able to persuade him that his Minister was either self-deceived or deceiving him."

M. Geffroy makes the following remarks upon this quotation :—

"In concert with Mercy, she besets Louis XVI., deceives the Ministers, does all she can to get promises and agreements out of them in the presence of the King, whom she had previously persuaded, delays the couriers while she informs her brother of the decisions which they will bring, and so gives him time to guard against them. And when Joseph II. accepts our mediation, it is she who makes the conditions to be proposed to France more onerous, and she does this in a quick, business-like way, indicating the obstinacy of a rather crafty mind. This sort of thing goes on uninterruptedly for eighteen months, and certainly cannot be called a refusal to interfere in political matters, an attitude of impartiality with respect to the interests of the Austrian Court."—(*Marie Antoinette et les documents authentiques.*)

And yet, at this period, the Queen of France was the mother of a Dauphin, a sweet child, popularly known as *Chou-d'Amour*, so pretty was he, and whose precocious intelligence was remarked by all who approached him. Baroness Oberkirch has related a pleasant anecdote of the little Dauphin. On one occasion, he wanted to buy some costly toys, but he was not allowed to do so. In the evening, when he was sleepily lisping his prayers, the old servant who had charge of him thought proper to administer a little lesson.

"Monseigneur," said he, alluding to the incident of the toys, "you must ask God for wisdom rather than for wealth."

"My dear Joseph," replied the royal child with a sly look, "now that I am about it, I am going to ask Him for both."

His mother dearly loved the poor little boy, who died of decline in 1789, just as the evil days set in, leaving an inheritance of woe to his younger brother, the Duc de Normandie; and yet Marie Antoinette, as we see, seems to have preferred the land of her birth to that over which her own son was destined to reign.

Her state of mind being such as we know it was, is it surprising that she should have welcomed the succour from abroad that was offered to her, especially at a period when the howls of the populace and their demonstrations of hatred had transformed the French nation, in her sight, into a formidable assemblage of rebels and ruffians? She knew only what she had been taught of the rights of kings, of the rights of peoples she was wholly ignorant; and this being so, she might very naturally consider herself in an attitude of legitimate defence, and be unconscious that she was guilty of high treason against the country in calling the arms of foreign sovereigns to her aid.

Many excuses may, indeed, be made for her, but that excuse which ought to absolve her completely before impartial posterity is that the King of France was her accomplice—he, who could not plead that he was of foreign birth, and whose very title indicated the plain path of his duty.

As for Count Fersen, he had no scruples to overcome; although he was colonel of a French regiment, he had never regarded himself as in the service of the nation, but solely in the service of the King, and his nationality entitled him to act against France at his own risk and peril. Even though his ever-living love for Marie Antoinette had not induced him to make every effort to save the Queen from the terrible fate which threatened her, his high sense of honour would have driven him into action. On the

20th August 1791 he wrote to his father from Vienna as follows:—" The confidence with which I have been honoured by the King and Queen of France makes it my duty not to abandon them under the present circumstances, but still to serve them so long as my services can avail. I should be condemned by everybody were I to act otherwise. I alone have been admitted to their confidence, and I can still serve them, because I am in full possession of their position, their intentions, and the affairs of France. I should everlastingly reproach myself with having contributed to place them in their present unfortunate situation, if I did not employ all the resources I possess to rescue them from it. Such conduct would be unworthy of your son."

For two years after this, Count Fersen, faithfully adhering to his intention, was the chief secret agent between the Tuileries and foreign Courts. He was the centre of correspondence; it was he who held all the threads of the schemes, interventions, and negotiations in which the captive royal family were concerned; and his action—completely unknown at that period, and hardly suspected twenty years ago—but now clearly revealed, through the publication of his papers, or at least such of them as his descendants have thought proper to make known—throws an entirely new light upon this period of our history.

When we recall the precautions that were taken against the King and Queen and their surroundings, it seems almost impossible that they could have corresponded with their friends on the outside. The watch kept over them was not limited to their persons; it extended to everything that came into the Tuileries, and everything that went out of the Tuileries. How then did they contrive to receive and send out letters which escaped the eyes, the search, the suspicion, and the inimical activity of their guards?

Human intelligence has wonderful resources, and the prisoner is almost invariably more clever and more cunning than his jailer. This was proved in the case of the Queen. Before she was separated from Count Fersen she had arranged a cipher with him; their letters would have kept the secret of their contents, even had they fallen into the hands of their enemies. They also adopted the device of writing with invisible ink between the lines of an insignificant correspondence.

The modes of despatch were of various sorts. Sometimes the letters were confided to trustworthy persons, like Baron de Goguelat, who had recovered his liberty under the terms of an amnesty granted to the King in exchange for his acceptation of the Constitution, the Chevalier d'Eclans, a gentleman of Franc-Comtois, and a Constitutional deputy, or his friend Terrier-Monciel. Sometimes the papers were hidden in a box of biscuits, in a packet of tea or chocolate; in the lining of a garment, or in the binding of revolutionary works. The persons for whom they were ostensibly destined were mostly foreigners. At Brussels it was Colonel Crawford, or "his pretended Madame Crawford" (Mrs. Sullivan). Sometimes they were addressed *poste restante* to "M. l'Abbé de Beauverin." It was the same thing in Paris, but during the whole of this correspondence, the safest messenger and the most often employed was Goguelat.

We have read the notes that were exchanged between Marie Antoinette and Count Fersen a few days after the Varennes incident.

Two months elapsed, during which they had no news of each other, then communication was re-established, and the half-political, half-private correspondence began. A great many passages of this are missing. Some of these were suppressed by Fersen himself, who was imprudently discreet in this matter, for it allows more than the truth to be suspected. The following letter from Marie Antoinette, written on the 26th September, is interesting from more than one point of view :—

"Your letter of the 28th has reached me. For two months I have had no news of you; no one could tell me where you were. I should have written, if I had known her address, to Sophie (Sophie was Countess Piper, Count Fersen's sister); she would have told me where you were." (Here eight lines are obliterated from the deciphered copy.) "Our position is changed since the King's acceptance (of the Constitution). To refuse it would have been more noble, but this was impossible under our circumstances. I would have wished the acceptance to be simpler and shorter, but it is our misfortune to have only scoundrels about us. Yet I can assure you the measure which has been passed is the least of evils; you will be able to judge of this one day, for I keep for you all that has . . . (here a passage is missing) been there. I am happy to recover, since there are papers of yours.

"*The follies of the Princes and the emigrants have also forced our hand.* It was essential to remove all doubt of our good faith by accepting. We think that the best means to weary them out with all this is to seem to enter fully into it; that will show very soon that nothing can be done. And then, notwithstanding the letter which my brothers have written to the King, and which, by-the-bye, has failed to produce the effect which they hoped from it, I do not see, especially from the declaration of Pilnitz, that the foreign succour is so very prompt. This is perhaps as well, because the more we advance, the more these wretches will feel their misfortunes. I fear that the hot heads may induce your King to do something which will compromise him, and consequently us; a great deal of prudence is necessary. I am going to write to M. de Mercy.

"So soon as you arrive at Brussels, let me know. I will write to you quite simply, for I have a sure means always at my disposal. You could not believe how much all that I am doing just now costs me, and besides, these wretched men who say they are attached to us and have never done us anything but harm, are quite mad at the present time. *At this moment they are furious.* It seems that one's mind ought to be base enough to take pleasure in what one is obliged to do; . . . it is their (obliterated line here) . . . and their conduct which has dragged us into our present position. I have only one happiness; it is seeing all those gentlemen who were imprisoned for us, especially M. de Goguelat, who is perfectly reasonable; his head has grown cool in prison. Adieu!"

Count Fersen received this letter on the 8th October. Two days afterwards he replied to it:—

"I have at length come back. I am sorry that you have been forced to sanction (the Constitution); but I feel your position; it is dreadful, and there was nothing else to be done. The Imp. (Empress of Russia), the Kings of Prussia, Sardinia, Norway and Sweden are all right, especially the three first. Sweden will sacrifice herself for you; England has assured us of her neutrality. The Emperor is the least willing; he is weak and indiscreet." Then he goes into the means to be taken, and puts several questions to the Queen. " 1st. Do you intend to go sincerely into the Revolution, and do you think there is no other course open? 2nd. Do you wish to be assisted, or do you wish that all negotiations with the Courts should be relinquished? 3rd. Have you a plan, and what is it? Pardon all these questions. I flatter myself that you will recognise in them only my desire to serve you, and a proof of my unbounded attachment and devotion."

The accusation of allowing herself to be led by Barnave and some of the Constitutionalists is distinctly repelled by Marie Antoinette in her letter of the 19th October.

"Make your mind easy; I am not going over to the extremists. If I see or have relations with any of them, *it is only to make use of them. They inspire me with too much horror for me ever to belong to their party.* You say nothing to me of your health; mine is good." (Here a passage is suppressed.) Then the Queen resumes. "*The French are atrocious on every side; we must take care that if those who are here get the advantage, and that we have to live with them, they cannot reproach us with anything.* We must also bear in mind that if those from the outside become masters, neither must we displease them." This phrase is curious to quote, for Marie Antoinette reveals her real thoughts in it. But what skill it would have required to act up to this view of things! What marvellous dexterity always to pursue a double line of conduct, so as to puzzle everybody and enable her to prove to the conqueror, whomsoever he might be, that she had been for him, and had striven for his success from the first! This was a miracle of astuteness and equilibrium far above the power of Louis XVI., and Marie Antoinette, although she saw the necessity of it, was incapable of carrying it out.

The danger, in fact, was great on the side of France, but it was not less formidable beyond the frontier. For the moment, in a pause, during which his acceptance of the Constitution had restored some power and an appearance of popularity to the King, and had given the people some confidence and tranquillity, the least thing happening outside might react unfavourably on the interior, and cause great embarrassment to the Princes and the emigrants.

"I fear everything from their folly," writes Fersen; "they are greatly excited, for they believe themselves forsaken. I can no longer answer for anything on their part."

This complication was not his only cause for anxiety. His sensitive mind had been profoundly disturbed by the unpleasant rumours which had reached him, and he could not refrain from mention of these to Marie Antoinette. "Staël says horrid things of me; he has bribed my coachman, and taken him into his service; this annoys me. He has turned many people against me, who blame my conduct and say that I have acted from ambition solely, and that I have ruined you and the King. The Spanish ambassador and others are of this opinion—they are right. My ambition was to serve you, and I shall all my life regret that I did not succeed. I desired to discharge a part of the obligation which was so dear to me, and I intended to prove that a man may be attached to personages like yourself without any interested motive. The rest of my conduct would have proved that this was my only ambition, and that the glory of having saved you was my best reward." Then he relates that his horses have arrived, those horses which drew the fugitives from the Port-Saint-Martin to Bondy. This was a sad remembrance, if it be true as Dante says:—

> "Non è maggior' dolore
> Che ricordarsi dal tempo felice
> Nella miseria."

"I know that you have seen the wife of my valet-de-chambre," he adds. "How good you are! but I ought to be accustomed to that. They say that you prefer remaining as you are to making use of the Princes. You are quite right; but take care; this must not be said; it would be dangerous to you."

Yes indeed, and it was dangerous. Marie Antoinette knew this. At all times she had found her worst enemies in her husband's family: misfortune had not disarmed them, and they continued to carry out their selfish policy, heedless of the harm which they did her. They had allies almost everywhere, even close to the Queen herself, for Madame Elizabeth was in the conspiracy. It would be difficult to believe this if Marie Antoinette had not confided the fact to Count Fersen. She writes:—

"M. de Breteuil's letter astonished and shocked us, but we must have patience and not show any anger at this moment. I am, however, going to copy it, so as to show it to my sister. I am curious to know how she will justify it in the midst of all that is happening. *Our home-life is a hell; it is impossible, with the best intentions in the world, to say anything. My sister is so indiscreet, so surrounded by schemers, and, above all, so entirely ruled by her brothers from the outside, that there is no use in talking—it would be nothing but quarrels all day.* I see that the ambition of the people about Monsieur will entirely ruin him. At first he thought that he was everything; but no matter what he does, he will never play any real part. His brother will always have the confidence of all parties and the advantage over him, because of the consistency and the invariability of his conduct. It is most unfortunate that Monsieur did not come back immediately on our being stopped; he might then have taken the course which he always proclaimed he would take, that of never leaving us: he would have spared us much pain and trouble, as we shall probably be forced to summon him to return. To this we know he cannot consent, especially if recalled in such a fashion. *We have been lamenting for a long time the number of emigrants; how bad this is, no less for the country than for the Princes themselves.* It is frightful the extent to which all these good people have been deceived, and are being deceived, so that they will soon have no resource but that of rage and despair. Those who have sufficient confidence in us to consult us have been stopped, or at all events, if they have thought it consistent with their honour to go, we have told them the truth.

But what would you have? The system is to say that we are not free in order not to do what we advise. This is quite true; but it is also said that consequently we cannot say what we think, and that action must be taken in the contrary sense. This explains the fate of the document sent to my brothers, and which you saw and approved. ... It is as much as to say, 'Do all we wish and then we will serve you, but not otherwise!'" She then explains her view of the line of conduct that ought to be taken, as follows :—" We must show what is our real situation, and what are our desires, by proving to them that the only course for us to follow is to gain the confidence of the people here at this present time; that, in fact, it is necessary to do this, in view of any plan whatsoever; that in order to do this we must all act together, and that, as the Powers will not be able to come to the succour of France in great strength during the winter, the only resource is a Congress, which would collect and unite all available resources for the spring. But, in making this communication, their extreme indiscretion must be guarded against. It is only from abroad that our salvation can come, *for nothing is to be done with this Assembly; it is a mob of scoundrels, madmen, and fools.*"

A few days later she reverts to this idea, and adds a memorandum from the King to her private letter to Count Fersen. She is careful to give her correspondent notice of this. "There is not . . . for you inside, therefore leave the decipherment to B." (meaning Baron de Breteuil). The King's note contains this sentence: "The firm and uniform language of all the European Powers, backed by a formidable army, would have the happiest consequences; it would temper the ardour of the emigrants, whose part would henceforth be only secondary, factions would be disconcerted, and confidence would be restored among good citizens, friends of order, and the monarchy."

How fallacious were such hopes! How little did the King know the "factions" on the one side, or the "good citizens" on the other, if he could believe that the assembling of a Congress would disconcert the former and consolidate the latter! How little did he understand the sentiments of the emigrants if he could believe that such a prospect would cool them down! Perhaps he knew still less about the state of mind of the sovereigns of Europe, when he flattered himself that a sincere and serious common understanding would ever unite them in any task.

At the same moment innumerable schemers were busy in the service of private interests, and as diplomatists will apparently stop at nothing to gain their ends, they spread a report that Marie Antoinette was carrying on an active correspondence with her brother, with the purpose of inducing him to separate himself from the common action of the other sovereigns.

The King of Sweden, without taking the trouble to inquire into the truth of such an accusation, wrote to Count Fersen on the 11th

November 1791, expressing his anger unreservedly. "The equivocal conduct of the Prince," he writes, alluding to Leopold, "with his foreseen continual tergiversation, was a presage of the part which he has been taking for a long time, and all that he did was for the purpose of preventing the other Powers from acting, by causing them to lose time. *But it is true that the shameful conduct of the Court of France has marvellously favoured his projects. . . . The conduct of the Court of France has surely surpassed in cowardice and in ignominy all that one could have presumed from it, and that the past has indicated.*

"If the Queen prefers the subjection and the peril in which she lives, to dependence on the Princes her brothers, of which she seems to entertain a greater dread, although very wrongfully, I ought to tell you that the Empress (of Russia) is very much displeased at this conduct, *and especially that the Queen of France writes letter upon letter to the Emperor to prevent him from acting.*"

Great was Count Fersen's grief on receiving such missives. Living at Brussels in the midst of the emigrants, he knew better than anybody whence these false rumours proceeded. Why, indeed, should those gentlemen, who had fled their country, restrain themselves? They were accustomed to hear the Comte de Provence speak of his brother in cruel, contemptuous, mocking terms. Had he not called him "King Log" when railing against him and the Queen? They were merely following an illustrious example.

However painful it was for him to have to apprise Marie Antoinette of the accusations made against her, Count Fersen did not shrink from that duty. His letters contain the proof of his courageous fidelity in this respect. The Queen, being informed of these calumnies, was enabled to defend herself.

"What is said of my letters to the Emperor," she writes, "is incomprehensible. For some time past I have suspected that my hand is imitated in communications to him. I must clear up this fact."

Whether the letters existed or not, what did it signify? The mischief was done; the Emperor did not act. The other sovereigns acted without any mutual agreement, and the Princes kept up diplomatic correspondence with the European Courts as if Monsieur had been king. As for the emigrants, with the exception of a few short-sighted persons, whose royalism, to quote the expression of Madame Swetchine, was only patriotism simplified, they were more furious against the King and Queen because they had not rejected the Constitution, than touched by their unhappy position in a kingdom in revolt.

That they were not the stronger was resented to the unfortunate King and Queen as a crime. Marie Antoinette felt the desertion of their former friends profoundly. Occasionally her indignation breaks out in vehement words, and in a letter to M. de Mercy she writes of the emigrants as "cowards." What an existence for the unfortunate woman! Nevertheless she did not break down, her pride sustained her, pride and hope, notwithstanding all, remained intact in her heart. She was a mother, too, and on that side she found some alleviation of her pain. "As for myself, I keep up better than I could have expected, considering my prodigious fatigue of mind, and that I go out very little. I have not a moment to myself, between the people that I must see, my writing, and the time that I am with my children. The latter occupation, which is not the least, is my sole happiness, and when I am very sorrowful, I take my little boy in my arms, I kiss him with all my heart, and that consoles me for a moment. Adieu, adieu once more."

CHAPTER VIII.

Gustavus III. renews his efforts for the deliverance of the royal family—A scheme of flight—Count Fersen is commissioned to communicate with the King and Queen of France—Obstacles to his return to Paris—The Queen consents—Difficulties concerning passports—His journey, postponed at first, is accomplished in February 1792—Departure from Brussels—Disguise—Arrival in Paris—First visit to the Tuileries—Interview with the King—Departure from Paris—Incidents of the return—Fersen's report to the King of Sweden.

AT the end of the year (1791) three policies were contending for adoption by the unfortunate King, who was face to face with revolution.

The first was the policy of the Constitutionalists, inspired by Barnave, the Lameth brothers, Duport, and others. This policy consisted of rejecting all connivance with foreigners or emigrants, and giving a trial to the new order of things which France had created for herself.

The second was the Queen's policy; this consisted of inducing the sovereigns of Europe to make an armed demonstration in order to strike terror into the factious nation.

The third was the policy of the Emigrants. The only means of salvation it recognised was the active intervention of the foreign Powers, and it contemplated, without scruple or regret, the idea of making war against France by a European coalition.

Louis, who was always undecided, naturally did not know which of the three policies to adopt; he inclined first to one, then to another, and so came to the worst condition of all, that of having no will of his own.

In the meantime, in spite of difficulties, in spite of rebuffs, the King of Sweden was not disheartened. He was proud of the part he felt himself called upon to play; his eyes were always fixed upon France, and his mind was constantly engaged upon schemes for the rescue of the royal family.

The plan of a descent upon Normandy having come to nothing in consequence of the downright refusal of the Emperor to take part in it, Gustavus fell back upon the idea of assembling an armed Congress at Frankfort; this had been suggested by Marie Antoinette. But on giving full consideration to the difficulty of realising this project, he relinquished it in favour of a fresh attempt at flight. He was afraid that the people of Paris might revenge themselves upon the King and Queen for warlike demonstrations from without; and he also desired that the royal persons should be out of the reach of popular fury, in order that the coalition which he contemplated might have greater freedom of action.

He therefore advised Louis to "regard himself as in the case of Henri IV. after the death of Henri III., or Charles VII. after the death of Charles VI., and, accordingly, to occupy himself solely with the means of wresting his kingdom from the usurpers, also to treat the latter as Henri IV. treated Mayenne and the League, or as Charles VII. treated the Duke of Burgundy and the partisans of the English."

In writing these lines the King of Sweden displayed a more profound knowledge of history than of the character of Louis XVI., although he had thought it well to enhance the effect of his counsel by addressing himself equally to the Queen. It was with good reason that he wrote to her : " Your position is desperate ; you must be got out of it by desperate means. However great the danger that you will have to confront, it will be less than that of abandoning your fate to the course of events, and leaving the opportunity and merit of saving the kingdom to others. But I think it right to speak of the danger that exists, and also to endeavour to lessen it in the eyes of that princess who, on the 8th of October, showed herself with such intrepidity to a furious and misled people, and who has ever since been, so to speak, fed on peril only."

But Marie Antoinette, however ready she might be to encounter necessary and useful danger in her own person, was unable to influence her husband, and she might have answered the King of Sweden in the melancholy and disconsolate words which she addressed to Mme. Campan a few months afterwards—words that reveal her thoughts plainly, but in which she tries to combine a stern judgment of her husband with the external respect due to the King of France.

"The King," she said, "is not a coward; *he has great passive courage*, but he is overpowered by shyness and distrust of himself, and this is due as much to his education as to his character. He shrinks from commanding, and dreads beyond everything having to speak to an assemblage of men. . . . A Queen who does not reign must, under these circumstances, remain inactive and prepare to die."

There was then very little chance that Louis XVI. would consent to repeat the Varennes attempt, and the chances of success in a second attempt to escape were still less.

The scheme formed by Gustavus III. seemed simple enough to his Majesty, but it was very complicated.

Starting with the fact that all the roads leading to the frontier were closely watched, he advised that the sea-coast should be the destination of the fugitives this time: an English ship, stationed in a small port, was to await them, and convey them to Ostend, or else to England. The plan for getting out of Paris was that the King, under the pretext of hunting, should escape by the woods, and be guided by an Englishman to the coast. An Englishman was to be chosen for this confidential mission, because it appears "these people are bold in action and also generous." The Queen, the Dauphin, and Madame Elizabeth were to take another route.

By travelling separately, the fugitives would attract less attention, and their meeting could be more easily effected at the selected seaport.

The conception of this scheme was obviously absurd; its practical execution was of course impossible.

Neither the King of Sweden nor Baron Taube, to whom he confided his idea, recognised any difficulty, and it was decided that the project should be laid before Count Fersen, who was to be sent to Paris to communicate with the persons concerned.

Count Fersen, who was usually more reasonable and cautious, made no objection to this chimerical plan. It may be that his longing to be with the Queen, to pass a few days with her whom he had feared he should see no more, overrode every other consideration. He accepted the mission intrusted to him without hesitation, although it stretched his fidelity to the full, and taxed all his tender interest to induce him to brave the danger to which such a mission must inevitably expose him. He had been indicted with the accomplices of the flight to Varennes, but his absence had saved him from arrest; he was, however, still "condemned as contumacious," for he had not been included in the amnesty, which affected actual prisoners only. His relations with the royal family, his participation in the Varennes scheme, were well known; he had everything to fear if he were recognised. On this venture he staked his head.

Although he did not hesitate, Marie Antoinette took a different view of his generous imprudence, and at first opposed the dangerous and foolish enterprise. However, she longed to see her friend once more, and, trusting in the precautions which he would take, she yielded at last to his urgent pleading. On the 21st of January Count Fersen writes in his journal, "The Queen has consented to my going to Paris."

He began immediately to prepare for his mission, fixed his departure for the 3rd of February, and announced it to Marie Antoinette; but a vexatious occurrence obliged him to alter his intention. A report was spread that the King intended to escape by way of Calais, and Paris was in commotion. The Queen wrote to Fersen to postpone his journey until the decree respecting passports had been issued, and tranquillity was restored. Then, a few days later, she again wrote to him to the effect that passports "for the individual" were required for everybody; that the rumour of the King's intended escape had caused the watch kept upon the royal family to be much more strict, and that he (Fersen) must relinquish a journey which had now become impossible.[1]

Count Fersen, however, thought otherwise. He had resolved to brave all possible risks. Could he not procure a passport from Sweden,

---

[1] These letters, to which Count Fersen alludes in his journal, are not to be found in the two large volumes of Extracts from his papers. Did he destroy them with his own hand, or did the editors object to publishing them? The answer to this question would evidently be of great interest.

and pass, under an assumed name, as a messenger from Portugal? Travellers had recently passed the frontier without any difficulty; he had just seen M. de Simolin, who was newly arrived from Paris, and had met with no obstacles.

It was not merely the sight of the former Ambassador from Russia to the Court of France, safe and sound at Brussels, that had redoubled Count Fersen's anxiety to cross the frontier. Baron de Simolin, who was devoted to the royal family, had seen the Queen in secret during his stay in Paris, and gave his friend terrible news concerning her. The situation was dreadful; the danger was growing greater every day. He repeated the Queen's own words—

"I would rather submit to anything than live longer in the state of degradation I am in, for anything seems preferable to the horror of our position."

Baron de Simolin added that he had been moved to tears by hearing the unhappy woman speak thus, and that he was then going to Vienna to plead the cause of the Queen, and as the bearer of letters from her to the Emperor, the Empress, and Prince Kaunitz. In relating all this to Count Fersen, he again gave way to keen emotion, which was shared by his friend. This scene confirmed his resolution; he must go—he would go!

He set about his final preparations at once, and by the 10th of February he was ready to start. On the 11th, at half-past ten in the morning, he took his place in a (literal) "post-chaise."

He did not take a servant, from the prudent consideration that a valet-de-chambre, however faithful he might be, might involuntarily betray both himself and his master. He had, however, a travelling companion, one Reutersvaerd, a Swede, who was a trustworthy person, frequently employed by Gustavus to carry secret missives.

Fersen himself relates the precautions that were taken to put the French police off the scent, should they exhibit an indiscreet curiosity concerning the travellers. He was provided with a letter of credit as Minister of the Queen of Portugal. Letters, and a memorandum from the King of Sweden to the King of France were placed under cover, and addressed to him in that capacity; a detailed report was signed "*Franc*," and the whole was "sealed with the arms of Sweden, made here" (in Brussels).

They arrived at eight o'clock in the evening at Tournay, where they slept. At half-past three in the morning they set out again (this was Sunday, the 12th of February), being only moderately easy in their minds, for Reutersvaerd had been talking with a M. d'Aponcourt, who had told him "he could not reach Paris for a full fortnight, as he would be stopped everywhere."

M. d'Aponcourt was wrong; they crossed the frontier unmolested. "At Orchies nothing was said to them." They breakfasted at Bouchain and dined at Bonavy, were detained four hours at Péronne by an accident to their carriage, and reached Gournay, where they remained until the next day, at half-past one A.M.

Notwithstanding the facility of their journey, the travellers were very prudent; and Count Fersen, who was effectually disguised by a big wig, avoided the blunder that had betrayed Louis XVI.; he kept himself well hidden in the carriage, and as much as possible avoided showing himself on any occasion.

On Monday the 13th they stopped at Louvres to dine, and at half-past five they entered Paris, well pleased to have reached the end of their journey.

They were now in that city on which the attention of the world was fixed. What must Fersen have felt on looking around him—what recollections of every sort must have crowded upon him! He had not seen those streets since that eventful night of the 20th of June, on which he had played coachman to the royal family when "they broke prison."

The times were changed, the position also was changed. Marie Antoinette, whom he had tried to liberate, and to save from the wrath of the people, was still more closely imprisoned in the palace of the monarchy, now her gaol, and he himself stood in peril of his liberty —nay, more, of his life, as an accused and contumacious person.

The travellers alighted in the Rue de Richelieu at the Hôtel des Princes, and Fersen leaving Reutersvaerd without entering the hotel, got into a hackney-coach, giving the driver the address of Baron de Goguelat, Rue Pelletier.

The driver did not know that street, and said he was afraid he could not take his fare to it; fortunately, another driver gave him instructions, and Fersen was deposited at Goguelat's door. But the Baron was not at home. Fersen waited for him in the street; time passed, and he became uneasy. Goguelat had been told to expect him. What had happened? After an hour's waiting, he lost patience, and returned to the Rue de Richelieu, to rejoin Reutersvaerd. At the Hôtel des Princes, no Reutersvaerd. There was no room in the hôtel. He inquired whither his friend had gone, but nobody could tell. Fersen went back to the Rue Pelletier;—no Goguelat. He summoned up his patience once more, and resumed his watch in the street.

At seven, Goguelat appeared, and explanations ensued. The letter of advice had arrived only at noon on that same day. Goguelat was not at home, and there was no means of finding him, so that the important missive had to wait for his return.

The two gentlemen could not linger over retrospective memories at that moment; they took their way to the Tuileries without delay. They were expected; they got into the palace, and once more Fersen stood in the presence of Marie Antoinette!

We have no details of that first interview, and are obliged to be content with two lines in Fersen's journal, who again proves himself "a hero of romance, but not of a French romance," by his discreet reserve. Here is the entry: "Went to the Queen; passed by my usual way; fear of the National Guards; not seen the King."

On the morrow—"the weather was very fine and warm"—he waited until it was dark to return to the Tuileries. It was about six o'clock when he saw the King and Queen. "The King wore the red ribbon."

The situation was discussed, with its imminent danger and its possible developments. Count Fersen communicated to their Majesties the plan for their flight which the King of Sweden had formed; but the King stopped him after he had said a few words, declaring that he would not go away, and that were he willing to attempt such a thing, it would be folly, and could not have a chance of success, so close was the watch kept upon them. The Queen, although she acknowledged that to escape would be an immense advantage to them, and while she assured her distressed hearer that the failure of the first attempt should not deter her from a second, was of the same opinion, and united with Louis in absolutely refusing to adopt the views of the King of Sweden on this point.

Count Fersen was, however, convinced that the words of Louis were inspired by another motive than the material impossibility of the undertaking. "The truth is," he writes, "he made a scruple of it, having so often promised to remain, for he is an honest man." Fersen's entreaties failed to obtain anything more than the King's promise that he would betake himself to the woods, on the approach of the united armies, and allow himself to be guided by smugglers to a place where he would be met by troops detached for this purpose.

On the question of the Congress, the King required that immediately upon its meetings it should deal with his demands, and especially, in case of the Assembly's being disposed to treat, should insist upon his being permitted to leave Paris, and to proceed to some place of abode, where he would have the necessary freedom to follow the course of the negotiations, and, if need, to ratify them, secure from coercion.

If, on the contrary, the Assembly should prove intractable and refuse all discussion, he would no longer oppose the action of the Powers, and he submitted himself beforehand to the dangers which he must necessarily incur in such a case.

Count Fersen entered fully into the nature of those dangers, placing various cases which might arise before the King and Queen. Had it not been reported that the King was to be taken to the Cevennes, and placed in the midst of an army of Protestants? To meet this emergency, he proposed that a trustworthy person should be employed "to write a pamphlet, stuffed full of demagogic ideas, and invectives against the King, and especially against the Queen, in which the project of taking them to the Cevennes should be represented as a device of the aristocrats to get them out of Paris and conveyed to the foreign armies."

Then he added that the Powers who were disposed to come to the aid of the King, according to the belief of the King of Sweden and the Empress of Russia, "would only do so in order to re-establish the monarchy and the royal authority in all its fulness, and not to organise a mixed government in France."

The Queen took up this idea warmly, but the King, while approving, declared it to be impossible. Fersen still insisting, Louis answered with unusual animation :—

"Ah! here we are by ourselves, and we can speak. I know that I am taxed with feebleness and irresolution; but no one has ever been in my position. I know I lost the opportune moment; it was the 14th of July. I should have gone away then, and I wanted to do so; but what was I to do when Monsieur himself begged me to remain, and Marshal de Broglie, who was in command, answered me, 'Yes, we can go to Metz, but what shall we do when we get there?' I missed the opportunity, and it has not come again. I have been forsaken by everybody."

This outburst of feeling had made it easy for the poor King to speak, and he continued the confession of his weakness. Yes, he had sanctioned the decree for the sequestration of the emigrants' property, but it was to preserve it; if he had not done this, all would have been pillaged and burned. Then he hoped by that concession to secure the passing of his "veto" upon the decree concerning passports. Besides, he was not in a position to refuse any of the demands of the rebels, and he begged Count Fersen to warn the Powers that they must not be astonished by anything, by any concession, any weakness on his part.

"They must put me on one side altogether," he said simply, "and let me alone."

The Queen did not take any such humble attitude. Pride was more natural and easy to her. She mentioned to Fersen the confidants she had made among the former Revolutionists; of course, she was only trifling with them. These men themselves were beginning to say "This cannot last," and they admitted that they had gone farther than they intended, but laid the fault upon the aristocrats who had opposed them. She was not deceived by these tardy protests, however, and she attributed them to two sentiments which were neither noble nor generous—enmity against an assembly in which they were nobodies and totally without influence, and fear that things were about to change. Their real motive was the desire to escape punishment. Accordingly, she did not trust them, and continued to see them only because it was useful to do so.

She then described the political *personnel;* with the exception of Bertrand de Molleville, who was "good," but powerless to do anything, all the Ministers were "traitors." The worst was Cahier de Gerville, a "wretched little lawyer at seven hundred francs a year;" he was always ready to denounce his colleagues. Lessart and Narbonne thought solely of themselves, not at all of the King. She had already told Fersen in one of her letters about Narbonne and his intrigues with Mme. de Staël. What was to be expected from such people?

In the brief happiness of being once more with the friend of her prosperity, she made him the confidant of her evil days, and dwelt upon certain details of the disastrous flight which they had planned together. Mdlle. Rocherette, the waiting-woman, whom they had suspected, was really Gouvion's mistress, and she told him everything. On the day after their departure she was questioned, and had said "horrors" of the Queen. When she was asked whether she had heard a noise near the door, she had the audacity to answer that "she so often heard going and coming when the King had gone to bed, that she paid no attention to it."

M. de Valory had confided the plan to his mistress, who had another lover, "M. X., a fanatical 'patriot.'" Including the three body-guards in a sweeping censure, she declared that they had been "good for nothing."

As for the return, it was awful. She recalled every incident of it, the murder of M. Dampierre, the man who accused her of wishing to poison him, the cries, the insults, all, all was told to her friend. Then she gave her opinion of the Commissaries sent by the Assembly: "Latour-Maubourg and Barnave were 'very well,' Pétion was indecent."

Pétion boasted of knowing everything. He told her that they took a hackney-coach close to the Tuileries, and that it was driven by a Swede named ———? pretending not to know the name—and then he asked if she could tell him. She answered, "I am not in the habit of asking the name of hackney-coach drivers."

And the sufferings of that last day: thirteen hours in the carriage in intense heat, without daring to lower the blinds! And the six weeks that followed, what a watch was kept over them! And the spying! The officers of the National Guard always in the room adjoining theirs, and wanting actually to sleep in their room! It was with difficulty that they were made to remain between the double doors. They even came in during the night, to make sure that she was in her bed; and one night the officer finding she was not asleep, took a seat by the side of her bed and began to talk! But this was not all; a camp was formed under their windows, and day and night a constant racket and noise was kept up. As the Queen recapitulated all these wrongs and miseries, her thoughts turned to those who had forsaken, and those who had served her. She could not refrain from owning that in general the former owed everything to her, and the latter nothing. So much ingratitude and so much fidelity aroused many and deep emotions in her, and Count Fersen, sharing all her feelings, was moved to tears. Among those who were devoted to her she did not forget the King of Sweden, and she charged his ambassador with the expression of her gratitude for his "friendship and interest." Why could she not say the same of her own brother, the Emperor Leopold?

Thus ended an interview which did not lead, and could not lead, to any practical result, but which at least gave Marie Antoinette a brief moment of happiness. She retained so vivid an impression of it that she recalled it, as we shall see hereafter, in one of the most bitter hours of her existence.

Count Fersen might have returned direct to Brussels, but he had announced himself as a "messenger" from Portugal, and was therefore obliged to go to some distance from Paris, if not so far as the Spanish frontier, in order to avert suspicion. He set out for Tours, and came back by Fontainebleau on the 19th of February.

He did not venture to go to the Tuileries, but it was painful to him to abstain from doing so. He wrote, asking whether there were any commands for him. The answer was an order to come and take leave of the King and Queen. Accompanied by Goguelat, he entered the château for the last time, while his companion, Reutersvaerd, waited for him below in the square. He supped with the King and Queen, took tea with them, and did not leave them until midnight. Fersen had beheld Marie Antoinette for the last time.

On coming out of the château he failed to find Reutersvaerd, and this made him anxious, for he could not postpone his departure. After a while the Swede reappeared; they quickly regained their hôtel, which was at no great distance, and at one o'clock in the morning they were off.

Their carriage was a light one and drawn by three good horses; they went at a smart pace. At half-past two they reached Senlis without any difficulty; at a place which Count Fersen calls *Pons* in his journal, and which must be Pont-Saint-Mazence, they saw some National Guards, but the latter took no notice of them. They stopped because snow was falling heavily; but the weather having cleared up, they went on again, much more slowly on account of the slipperiness of the roads, so that it was seven o'clock in the evening before they reached Bonavy. They supped badly, and slept worse, for the only accommodation they could procure was a wretched bedroom which belonged to a carter, and they lay down in their clothes.

Hitherto they had experienced only some ordinary inconveniences, but on the following day, Thursday the 23rd, several exceptional incidents marked their progress. The roads so far as Cambrai were so bad that the postilions refused to go on, and the postmaster backed their refusal, saying they were within their right, and he could not force them.

At last, by dint of persuasion, a postilion, with more "pluck" than the others, consented to take them on their way, in consideration of the lightness of the vehicle. The travellers were overpowered by cold and fatigue, and Fersen fell asleep. All of a sudden he was awakened; the carriage had been abruptly stopped, and a man was demanding Reutersvaerd's passport. Fersen leaned back in the carriage, and feigned profound sleep. Reutersvaerd held out the passport; the man looked at it, read it, examined it for five minutes, and then declared that it was worthless, inasmuch as it bore the words *de par le roi*, and not *de par la loi*, and, moreover, did not contain any personal description (*signalement*).

Although this incident occurred in a little village consisting of ten houses only, within half a league of Marchiennes, it was important to the safety of the travellers that they should not be delayed, still more so that they should not be stopped. Reutersvaerd tried the highhanded method; he waxed indignant, and said angrily, "But it is the Minister's passport; he knows how it ought to be, and our Minister would not have given us a passport if it had not been all right."

The man was not convinced. "It is not on the pattern that we have; it is no good," he repeated.

Fortunately the postilion came to the aid of the travellers by saying, "Sir, do you not see that these gentlemen are messengers? You have no right to stop them."

"Certainly we are messengers," said Reutersvaerd, "and Swedish messengers; that is in the passport, and here is our Minister's."

"The fool," adds Fersen, "had not yet discovered that;" and as he saw Reutersvaerd growing polite, he grew insolent. However, after he had re-read the passport, he made up his mind to let the travellers go on, but not without warning them that they would certainly be stopped at Marchiennes, a prediction that was strictly fulfilled. The sentinel "in a grey vest," and the officer "in a brown coat," with whom they had to deal, proved, however, very good-natured, and they were allowed to proceed.

Before they reached Orchies they were stopped once more "at a National barrier," set up for the purpose of searching for money. This was one of the measures inspired by popular suspicion for preventing the enemies of the people from taking the money of the country out of France. The keepers of the "National barrier" treated them with politeness; they did not even search them.

They passed through Orchies, crossed the frontier, and arrived safely on Belgian territory. They might throw away their cockades, as the postilion himself took care to tell them. They were most fortunate in having escaped the perils of their dangerous journey, and they felt this keenly. Nevertheless Count Fersen cannot refrain from reverting sadly to the past, after his characteristic fashion, in one sentence: "At four o'clock we were at Tournai; we dined there well, *and in the room we slept in on our way. What a difference!*"

At half-past five they started again. "The evening and the night were excessively cold; the wheels creaked as they creak only in Sweden.

We arrived at Brussels at three o'clock in the morning."

Count Fersen went immediately to the King, and gave him an account of his journey. He left nothing undone that could fire the soul of Gustavus and make him work hard for the rescue of the prisoners. In dwelling on the "touching feeling" with which Marie Antoinette had spoken to him of the King's efforts to liberate her, and having expressed her gratitude towards him, he seems to have had the future rather than the past in view. Fate was about to put all these hopes to rout; by an unforeseen event the Queen was destined to be deprived of her best and bravest champion. At that same moment a band of conspirators were assembled to select the assassin who was to slay their victim. In the cold North also regicide was looming on the horizon.

CHAPTER IX.

Sudden death of Leopold II.—Rumours of poison—The emigrants rejoice at the death of the Emperor—Francis II.—News from Sweden—Convocation of the Diet at Gefle—Dissatisfaction of the Swedish nobility—Superstitious credulity of Gustavus III.—The vision of Charles IX.—In the Haga Park on an evening in January 1792—Plot against the life of the King—The conspirators—Ankarstroëm—Lieutenant-Colonel Liliehorn—The 16th of March—At the masked ball—" *Bonjour beau masque* "—Gustavus is wounded by a pistol-shot—His last hours—His death—The doom of Ankarstroëm—Count Fersen's grief.

"WHAT will the brother do if they kill the sister?" asked the Comte d'Allonville of the Prince de Condé.

"Perhaps he may venture to wear mourning for her," was the reply.

Both question and answer testify to the slight esteem that was generally professed for Leopold II., Marie Antoinette's brother, he whom Baron Taube had called "that accursed Florentine." It must be owned that the conduct of the Emperor Leopold had not realised the very natural hopes of the Court of France. Leopold was bound beyond any other of the sovereigns to come to the aid of the royal authority that was attacked and destroyed in the person of Louis XVI.; for that unhappy monarch was his own brother-in-law, and his own interests as Emperor and King were deeply concerned in his family interests.

In this fact we find the explanation of the severity with which he was judged by some of the French, and by those foreigners who were more particularly anxious about the fate of the King and Queen of France. Nevertheless, impartial history must not forget that the action which was required of Leopold was not truly politic. The real family of a prince is the nation he reigns over, and for the interests of that nation alone he is bound to care. Perhaps Leopold II. was withheld from entertaining the projects of Gustavus III. by his desire to save his people from the scourge of war; in any case, it is meting out too hard measure to him to make a crime of his having considered first the greatness of the House of Austria, and put the policy of sentiment into the background.

Even though the validity of these excuses be admitted, it is none the less true that the friends of the royal family had some right to reproach the Emperor with having deceived them, by letting them hope for support which always failed them, and succour which never came. If it be true that hypocrisy is a homage to virtue, Leopold's duplicity was a homage to family feeling, and it must be borne in mind that if it were politic for him to assume a selfish attitude towards the Court of France, it was really very difficult to do this with complete frankness, which would have been instantly transformed by public opinion into odious cynicism. The great misfortune of false positions is that they beget falsehood.

Leopold could not escape from that fatal consequence.

Meanwhile, however pacific his disposition may have been, circumstances were beginning to be too strong for him. France was growing tired of the noise that the emigrants and their foreign friends were making all about the frontier, and began to want to silence this vexatious buzzing. The nation was becoming warlike.

"You are very lucky," said the Elector of Mayence to the Marquis de Bouillé, "that the French are the aggressors, otherwise we should never have had war."

At last Leopold was about to yield, and although hoping to the last that he might elude the necessity of throwing himself into the fight, he signed the treaty of alliance with Belgium; but death came to relieve him from the responsibility of a decision which he dreaded. He was attacked suddenly by an illness which the physicians could neither diagnose nor check, and in a few hours he was at the worst. He suffered from excruciating pain in the bowels, accompanied by vomiting. Some relief was afforded by bleeding him, but the respite was brief; he was soon seized with convulsions, and expired in the arms of the Empress, who had just arrived. Such a death, so sudden, and under the actual circumstances, gave rise to sundry interpretations and to grave suspicion. Rumours of poison were spread immediately, and the declaration of the doctor who made a postmortem examination of the body confirmed them.

The Emperor died on the 2nd of March; on the 8th the event was made known to the public at Brussels in a singular way. It was announced by an actor on the stage of a theatre. The play was interrupted, and the crowd dispersed about the city spreading the news. The Bishop, who was promptly apprised of the fact, called on Count Fersen at half-past seven with the information.

The news not only failed to produce any feeling of regret, or even the moderate emotion generally excited by occurrences of public importance, but it was received with a general manifestation of satisfaction. At the theatre some of the audience had actually applauded the actor's announcement!

"The Emperor is dead; well, that is a good thing," said one of Fersen's friends to him.

This was the feeling of all the generals. The soldiers themselves rejoiced. It is on record that in the evening a sentinel, seeing some unusual stir, asked what it meant. When he was told that the Emperor was dead, he exclaimed—

"Ah! ah! Dead is he? Well, then, long live François, the soldier's father!"

The emigrants, as may be supposed, were of a similar way of thinking. They might, however, being persons of good-breeding, have been more reserved in the expression of their sentiments. Count Fersen, who witnessed their conduct, was shocked. "The French," he writes to Gustavus, "display an indecent joy on this occasion, and their remarks are unguarded for persons to whom hospitality is being granted; but misfortune does not correct them."

Fersen himself was not inclined to waste sentiment upon the fate of a man whose "feeble and uncertain conduct had alienated all from him." He gave his opinion in the discussions which arose upon the rumour of poison. Almost all those who spoke of it held that the bolt was shot from Paris, and generously attributed the deed to the Jacobins, as though such a crime were possible at that distance, even admitting that the Jacobins, who were letting Louis live, should think it to their interest to kill Leopold.

It is, however, interesting to observe the different conclusions which were drawn by the disputants. While some of them eagerly argued that the crime "was a proof of the danger of meddling in the affairs of France," Fersen wrote in his journal—"So much the better; this will prove the necessity of exterminating the monsters in France."

His eyes were fixed on France, therefore he spoke thus. Before long, facts were to give him a cruel contradiction, teaching him that in other lands there were "monsters" preparing to prove themselves bolder and more prompt of action than the Jacobins of France, in their enmity, if not to royalty, at least to kings.

Baron de Goguelat came to Brussels towards the end of March 1792. He was explaining in detail the position of Louis and Marie Antoinette, which was becoming more painful day by day, when news arrived from Sweden that struck terror to the hearts of the two friends. Gustavus had been fired at by an assassin and severely wounded.

Was the King to live or die? None knew that as yet; all was confusion and uncertainty, except the terror that the possible death of the royal victim, coming so soon after the sudden death of Leopold, inspired in the friends and supporters of the monarchical system. Was this crime also the work of the abominable Jacobins? How great must be the power of that odious sect!

By degrees the truth came out. The Jacobins were entirely innocent of the murder of Gustavus III. The assassins bore the greatest names in the kingdom, and it was not certain that the nearest kinsman of the victim—one standing on the very steps of the throne—would not have to be reckoned among the accomplices.

This catastrophe astonished and horrified everybody, and yet there were many things to explain it, and it might even have been foreseen.

Gustavus III., in his desire to play a great part, in imitation of the object of his admiration, fancied that he might equal Louis XIV. In the first place, he imitated not only the splendour, but the prodigality of the Sun-King. Forgetting that Sweden was not France, and would be much more rapidly ruined by a reign of display, he expended money lavishly, money that he did not possess, and had to procure at any price. He resorted to all sorts of vexatious measures to fill the coffers of the Treasury; but excessive taxation frequently defeats its purpose, and exceptional measures can only meet temporary exigencies.

The expenditure was continued, the deficit was increasing, and resources were diminishing. Nevertheless, it was at this critical moment that the King, full of his chivalrous ideas, proposed to place himself at the head of a European coalition against the French Revolution. It would take money to attack the Jacobins; Gustavus resolved once more to ask his people for supplies, and made up his mind to summon a Diet.

He did not disguise from himself that his fresh demands would meet with formidable obstacles. He found that universal discontent prevailed among his subjects; nevertheless he was more afraid of the opposition of the nobles, or a certain number of them, than of the objections of the other classes. He then bethought him of a notable device for diminishing the number of the members who would respond to his tardy summons, and instead of fixing upon Stockholm as the place of assembly, he named the little town of Gefle, whither most of the opposition could not, or dared not, come, and where it would be easy for him to have them watched, or to intimidate, and even, if necessary, to "suppress" them for a time.

These measures availed nothing; the Diet

lasted hardly a month, and the King, notwithstanding the precautions he had taken, did not venture even to put forward his designs against France. The only result obtained was an increase of that smouldering enmity against himself, which was ready to burst into flame so soon as a head could be found sufficiently daring to plan the assassination, and an arm sufficiently firm to strike the blow.

Sweden seemed ripe for such events. Never at any period had the extravagance of men's imagination reached such a height. The cool heads of this Northern people passed, so to speak, at a bound, from apathetic calm to transports of madness.

At that period the majority of men's minds were disturbed by strange dreams, by extraordinary ideas. Illuminism had made great ravages among them, and the King himself, yielding to the current, was perhaps the most ridiculously credulous person in the kingdom. Every day he consulted a female soothsayer, and the two passed whole hours in examining coffee-grounds for rules of government and the secrets of the future!

The belief that space is peopled by mysterious and invisible beings, and that malignant or benevolent genii have sovereign power over the events of life, is calculated to inspire vague superstitious terrors in even the strongest minds. Gustavus III. had not escaped such fears. Various predictions were circulated among the people—one, stranger than all the others, had attracted universal attention; this was a so-called vision attributed to Charles XI., who had died nearly a century before.

The story had been current in Sweden for a hundred years. It is now popular in France, thanks to Mérimée, who has told it after his own inimitable fashion, arranging it, dramatising it, and, above all, treating it with the certainty of a prophet who speaks forty years after the event.

Who is there that cannot recall the simple and dismal beginning of the tale? Charles XI., in dressing-gown and slippers, was seated near the fire, in a wing of the old royal palace overlooking Lake Mœler, on an autumn evening. Count Brahé, his chamberlain, and Baumgarten, his doctor, were with him. The conversation was dull and monotonous. All of a sudden a strange and surprising spectacle presented itself. The great "Hall of the Estates" in front of them, situated in another wing of the palace, was shining brightly. The windows seemed to be lighted up. It was not a fire. What was the meaning of this illumination?

"I will go into the hall myself," said the King.

He was pale, but composed. Brahé and Baumgarten followed him, each carrying a candle.

They roused the porter, and entered the gallery, which formed a sort of antechamber to the "Hall of the Estates;" the walls were entirely hung with black.

"By whose orders was this gallery hung with black?" inquired the King.

"By no one that I know of," replied the bewildered porter, "and the last time I had the gallery swept, it was panelled just as it has always been."

The King went on. A confused noise came from the great hall.

"Stop, stop, sire!" exclaimed Brahé.

"Let me go and fetch twenty of your life-guards," said Baumgarten, whose candle had just been blown out by a gust of wind.

"Let us go in," said the King.

He took the keys from the shaking hands of the porter, opened the door, and entered the Hall of the Estates.

The bravest of men would have shrunk from the sight that met his eyes. The hall was entirely hung with black, and lighted by an immense number of torches. A numerous assembly occupied the benches. Every man there was dressed in black. On the raised throne where the King usually sat lay a bleeding corpse, wearing the insignia of royalty. On the right of the corpse stood a child, on the left an old man. Below the throne was a block, and beside it an axe.

"The individual who presided made a sign, a door was opened, and several young men appeared. Their hands were tied behind their back. The executioner followed them. The first of these young men stopped in the middle of the hall in front of the block, at which he looked with supreme scorn. At that moment the corpse seemed to quiver convulsively, and fresh ruddy blood flowed from its wound. The young man knelt down and stretched out his head; the axe glittered in the air, and fell with a dull thud. A jet of blood spurted out upon the steps of the throne and mingled with that of the corpse, and the head, rebounding upon the bloodstained pavement, rolled so far as the feet of the King, and stained them with gore."

At this moment King Charles recovered his speech, and, addressing the President, said—

"If you are of God, speak; if you are of the other, leave us in peace!"

The phantom answered him slowly :—

"Charles the King, this blood shall not flow under your rule, but five reigns later. Woe! woe! woe! to the House of Vasa!"

Then the forms became indistinct and slowly vanished; the torches went out, the black draperies, the severed head, and the block all disappeared. The King's slippers only retained some stains of blood.

This sinister prediction had been near to realisation in 1792.

One evening in January two men were walking in the Haga Park. The place was deserted, and they were free to examine the lie of the grounds, and to measure the distances at their pleasure. The two men were, respectively, Count Horn and Jean Jacques Ankarstroëm, a former sub-officer in the body-guard. They, with some others, had formed a plan for restoring its old liberties to Sweden by "suppressing" the King. The first intention was

A NARROW ESCAPE

only to carry him off, and to keep him out of sight during the time that would be required for the establishment of a new Constitution and a new government.

As they were approaching the château, a lighted window attracted their attention. They then saw Gustavus, who had just returned from hunting, throw himself wearily into an arm-chair. The King was alone; the victim actually presented himself to receive the deadly stroke, and flight seemed easy. Perhaps the temptation to deliver themselves from him whom they regarded as their enemy may have seized upon them; at all events, they stealthily advanced.

At that moment, by a strange coincidence, Gustavus rose, opened the window, and showed himself to the conspirators, whom he did not see. The King's face was so expressive of care and melancholy, his attitude was so full of mournful self-abandonment, that the assassins took pity on their victim, and, for a moment, enmity was extinguished in their minds by the unconscious fraternity of misfortune. They withdrew softly.

A few days afterwards the King set out for Gefle, from whence he returned at the end of February.

Like Cæsar, whom he resembled in the breadth of his ideas and in his habits, and whom he was destined to resemble in his tragic fate, the Ides of March were formidable to him. Dark rumours, forerunners of great disasters, indicated that especial danger to him was threatened at this period, and these rumours were not fallacious. A conspiracy against the life of the sovereign was formed, and the time was approaching when its fell purpose was to be carried out.

A great number of the nobles were vaguely initiated into the plot; they were ignorant of its details, but they approved of its object. Certain personages of high station were the soul of it.

Chief among these was Baron Pechlin, an old man of seventy-two, who still cherished in his heart the passions of the epoch of the civil wars, which he had survived owing to the clemency of the King. He had been imprisoned after the first *coup-d'état* in 1772, but was amnestied five months afterwards, although Gustavus was aware of his fierce enmity, and called him *the first Republican of Sweden.* Pechlin hated him with a savage hatred, and he had inspired several young men with a similar sentiment; among these was Count Horn. The latter was a handsome man, not quite thirty years of age, and a distinguished horseman; a very unfit person, to all appearance, for the deed of blood from which he had recoiled in the Haga Park; but his father had been imprisoned and threatened with death, and he had begged the favour of being allowed to share his fate. This was not permitted, and his father was not executed; but the recollection of his filial fears had made him fierce against "the tyrant." He had lent a ready ear to the first proposals, and afterwards he had frequently given his country-house for the meetings of the conspirators, to whose number Ribbing belonged.

Count Ribbing had reason to complain of the King, it was said. He had been in love with a rich heiress, and was cut out by a rival who was favoured by Gustavus. Disappointed love was the cause of his enmity; he hardly attempted to hide it, but took pleasure in heightening the King's superstitious terrors. Gustavus, being a good-natured "tyrant," put up with his insolence, and dreaded Ribbing less as a man who might kill, than as a "porte-malheur."

Lieutenant-Colonel Liliehorn, the captain of the body-guard, was also a conspirator. It would be impossible to account for the co-operation of this man, whom the King loaded with favours, if we did not know what havoc ambition can make of the minds which it rules.

Liliehorn aspired, not, like certain of his accomplices, to high destinies for his country, but to a high position for himself, and the rôle of Lafayette seemed to him the most enviable for a soldier—a conception which can only be explained in the actual case by the axiom, *Major è longinquo reverentia.*

Among the active members of the conspiracy Baron Bielke must be reckoned; but however active they were, the arm capable of striking was not of their number: they were but the heads that planned the deed. He to whom the detestable honour of its achievement was to fall was Ankarstroëm, one of the two who had walked in the park.

Ankarstroëm, who had been successively page, sub-officer in the guard, and ensign in the body-guard, had left the service in 1788, when he was only twenty-two years old.

He was of a bold and resolute temper, both morose and passionate, and strongly attached to the prerogatives of his caste. From that time he was a malcontent. He retired to the country with his wife, and became more and more embittered by solitude. Regardless of restraint, he spoke with reckless hostility against royalty, brought prosecutions upon himself, and, in fact, his whole life was a battle.

This man was then in a state of mind which rendered him singularly sensitive to the ills of his country, which seemed greater and more terrible to him when seen through the medium of his own grievances. He was ready for vengeance, that is to say, for murder.

He himself has related before his judges the reasons which impelled him to assassinate the King. Confronting the block, he dared to frame the indictment of his victim. The grievances which he invoked were many. From 1789, pamphlets of a nature insulting to the nobility were circulated without interference, and the King "had attempted" the liberties of members of the Diet. Then came the "Act of Security," which destroyed the last barriers that had been opposed to the royal "all-power." With this were cited the insensate prodigality that was emptying the treasury and ruining the nation. In order to extract further sums, the King threatened the Diet; the hall was surrounded by soldiers, and almost invaded by a mob incited by him. Notwithstanding this terrible pressure, the majority rejected the proposition of the King: the latter declared it accepted. Nor was this all: had he not declared war without having the assent of the Estates, which was required by the Constitution?

"Kings," said he, "who are but poor sinners like other men, have no authority except through the confidence of the nation, and that confidence is theirs only so long as they continue to deserve it by their respect for law and liberty.

"These are the reflections that have decided me. My heart was hardened when I saw exile, and punishment, and all sorts of taxes and subsidies multiplied, to supply the expense of luxury and foreign travel. Nor was this all; a Diet was announced only three weeks in advance, so that there was hardly time for the necessary elections; it was summoned in a little town far from the capital, so that it might be difficult to come to it, and to stay.

"In the presence of such facts, I asked myself: 'Shall this man continue to be our king—this man, capable of violating the oath which he took to the people, to observe, maintain, and bequeath to his successors the Constitution of 1772, *a Constitution drawn up by himself, and accepted without amendment by the Swedish nation?*'

T

"According to my conviction, this man has become a perjurer; he has ceased to be king. The compact between the nation and himself is broken. Moreover, it is written in the law that he who shall endeavour to change or to destroy that fundamental law shall be regarded as an enemy of the kingdom. Now, by his 'Act of Security,' King Gustavus has become a public enemy, and *as in an organised society there must be mutual defence and protection, the hand that desires to arm itself, in order by force to repel the force that was threatening the community, ought to be permitted to do so.* I had then resolved, immediately after Christmas, to kill the King; the shortest way appeared to me to give my life for the public good. To live, unhappy, for ten years more or ten years less, was nothing to my mind in comparison with the hope of restoring happiness to my country."

Ankarstroëm, devoutly believing his cause to be good, accepted the rôle of justiciary, which his accomplices awarded to him, without hesitation. It has been said that he received a sum of money, and the thing is possible, but he was not actuated by the greed of gain. He had made the sacrifice of his life in anticipation, for the chances of his escaping the penalty of his deed were small. Resolved as he was, it was not a few riksdalers that would have nerved his arm; the money, if he did receive it, was a provision for his wife; and if it was the price of blood, it was the price of his own blood rather than the King's.

The arrangements being made, the murder decided upon, the doer of the deed selected, it remained to choose a propitious opportunity. One presented itself very soon ; it became known that the King would attend the masked ball at the opera on the 16th of March 1792. In the midst of the crowd the conspirators could approach their victim, and their masks would protect them from recognition. The complicity of Liliehorn (the captain of the King's bodyguard) secured their means of escape.

In the meantime, a vague and uncertain rumour warned the King of the danger that threatened him. He would not pay any heed to it ; the torment of perpetually trembling for fear of a bullet, a dagger-stroke, or poison, seemed to him worse than the attempt itself. He resolved to carry out his intention, and to go to the ball.

A few hours previously, when he was supping with his favourite, Baron Essen, a note which had been mysteriously brought was handed to him. The King opened it, read it twice attentively, and, without saying anything, slipped it into his pocket. The note, written in pencil in French, warned him that a plot had been formed against him, entreated the King not to go to the ball, and advised him to govern in another fashion thenceforth, and thereby disarm the anger of his enemies.

This denunciation, whether true or false, deserved attention. The King despised, not the warning, but the danger. He was determined to have done with the matter ; so he went to the opera, and passed into a little room, where he put on a domino. Not until then did he let Essen see the note. Essen, greatly alarmed, besought the King not to go down on the stage, but Gustavus would not listen to him.

"Let us see whether they will dare to kill me," said he.

Essen followed him, keeping close upon his footsteps; he felt the full extent of the danger, for, in spite of their masks, they had been recognised. A general whispering had announced the King.

Presently the crowd gathered around them; a group separated them and surrounded Gustavus. A man tapped him on the shoulder, saying—

"Bonjour, beau masque!"

This was the signal. At these words, uttered by Count Horn, Ankarstroëm drew a pistol from his pocket and fired point-blank at the King.

"I am wounded! Arrest him!" exclaimed the King.

But a cry was instantly raised on all sides—"Fire! Fire! Save yourselves!" Utter confusion prevailed. Nevertheless, Baron Armfeldt had the presence of mind to have the doors shut. None of those present could get out without unmasking and giving his or her name. The crowd therefore dispersed slowly, and after a while only one person remained. He walked in a leisurely manner towards the door, slowly removed his mask, and said carelessly to the officer on duty—

"As for me, sir, I hope you will not suspect me."

"You are mistaken; I believe that it was you," replied the police officer at hazard.

The individual showed some perturbation, but he was allowed to pass. It was Ankarstroëm.

Gustavus did not die on the spot, although the whole charge had been lodged in his side. He was carried into an adjoining room and laid on a sofa; there the wound was dressed. The King retained complete presence of mind, and issued his commands with perfect clearness. He sent for his brother, the Duke of Sudermania, although his conduct had been most suspicious. It was said that the Duke, who was extremely ambitious, and believed in a prediction which had promised him the throne, had been aware of the plot. The page who was despatched to him found him dressed, booted, and ready to mount his horse.

Gustavus III. did not believe in his brother's complicity. He did not know whose was the hand that had struck him, or whom they were that directed it; but was fully occupied by the main subject of his thoughts for a year past, and solicitous above all about the effect of the news upon Paris.

"This shot will rejoice your Paris Jacobins," he said to the Duc d'Escars, a French gentleman who was by his side; "but write to the Princes that, if I get over this, my feelings and my zeal for their just cause will be in no wise altered."

The murderer had thrown away the pistol,

but it was picked up, and the gunsmith who had sold it shortly before was found immediately. Ankarstroëm was discovered by this means, and arrested on the following day.

He was asked the names of his accomplices, but refused to give them. The conspirators betrayed themselves. Liliehorn, that singular traitor who wrote the letter which Gustavus received a few hours before the ball, was taken the same day, and shortly afterwards Horn, Ribbing, Bielke, and Pechlin were arrested.

The King appeared to be recovering; the wound was doing well. As it happens in such cases, the crime had simply reversed its intention. The powerful sovereign was hated; when struck down, he regained the sympathy of all.

Among his former adversaries were the representatives of the most illustrious families in the kingdom, Count Brahé and Count Frederick Fersen. These gentlemen, his loyal opponents, did not choose to be supposed to be instigators or accomplices, or even approvers, of a murder; and they made it a point of honour to declare this loudly—a proceeding by which they regained the alienated regard of their king.

"I do not regret this accident," said Gustavus to them, "since it procures me the pleasure of a reconciliation with the representatives of the nobility."

The "instruction" preliminary to the trial began. Each day new accomplices were dis-

THE VISION VERIFIED

covered. Did the danger of being unmasked in which certain high personages stood in their turn suggest a guilty resource to some of them? We do not know, but it is certain that a sudden change in the state of the wounded King took place on the 25th March. His convalescence was checked, high fever set in, and after four days of agony the unfortunate monarch died, leaving a son thirteen years old as his heir, and as Regent the Duke of Sudermania, his brother.

Gustavus displayed admirable courage and coolness during his last days. He requested that the actual murderer only should be put to death, and that mercy should be shown to his accomplices. His injunctions were observed. Count Horn, Ribbing, and the others were banished; only Ankarstroëm paid for his crime with his life.

He was as brave in the face of death as his victim; he refused to name those who had aided or urged him to commit the deed; he proudly assumed the entire responsibility of it, and no threats, no ill-treatment availed to move him from his haughty attitude. Without any apparent emotion he listened to the sentence that condemned him to be beaten with rods on three successive days, conveyed to the scaffold in a common cart, and beheaded after his right hand had been cut off.

He endured these tortures, and met his death with the same sombre courage.

Thus was the prediction realised to the letter;

the bleeding corpse was that of Gustavus III.; the boy standing on the right of the throne was Gustavus IV.; the middle-aged man on the left was the Duke of Sudermania; the young man brought thither and beheaded was Ankarstroëm.

The Swedes were under no mistake concerning the causes of their King's death; but a different impression prevailed in Europe, where Gustavus, like Leopold, was regarded as a victim of the Revolution. This was not the case; as yet the Revolution threatened royalty only, and not kings.

Count Fersen had been kept informed of all these tragic events, but the better news, sent after the crime of the 16th of March, had completely relieved him from any fear of its consequences; he believed in a speedy cure, and continued to write long political letters to his King, who was never to receive them. At length, about the middle of April, he learned the truth by a letter despatched from Stockholm by Baron Taube on the 29th of March. In his answer (18th of April) he gave full expression to his grief: "I cannot be consoled for the dreadful loss that we have sustained. Every day my grief is renewed by the remembrances of his kindness—that remembrance will never leave me, and my gratitude will end only with my life. Good God! why can I not offer him the homage of that life? You will know what pleasure it would give me to have his portrait, if that may be so. . . ."

He had written immediately to Marie Antoinette: "You will have already heard the sad and overwhelming news of the King's death. In him you lose a strong support, a good ally, and I a friend and patron. This is a cruel loss."

It might be thought that the death of this chivalrous and disinterested King would have had great weight in the decisions of the sovereigns of Europe, and that the cause of Louis XVI. and Marie Antoinette had lost its best and most effective support in losing him who was actively seeking champions for the royal family of France. But human fears as well as human previsions are constantly contradicted by events which control men instead of men controlling them. The proof of this was not long delayed. Gustavus dead, his idea was realised, and war, which he had vainly desired to let loose in his lifetime, broke out of its own accord.

CHAPTER X.

The situation in France—Isnard's words—A summons to the Electors of Trèves and Mayence, and to the other Princes of the Empire, to put an end to the massing of troops upon the frontier—The reply of Francis, King of Bohemia and Hungary—Declaration of the "State of War"—Satisfaction of the Queen and Count Fersen—Correspondence in cipher —M. *Rignon*—The 20th of June—The Queen's despatches —"It is said, but I do not believe it"—Lafayette proposes a plan of flight—The arrival of the Marseillais—A manifesto by the Duke of Brunswick—M. de Limon's text modified by Count Fersen—It is proposed to ask for a declaration by the King of England in favour of the royal family of France—The 10th of August—The National Assembly and the Temple—Lafayette is made prisoner—The September massacres—The death of Mme. de Lamballe—Manuel's words—M. de Mercy—Dumouriez—Valmy (20th September 1792)—Sufferings of the troops and the emigrants—The Duke of Brunswick's retreat—Count Fersen leaves Brussels —Jemmapes (6th November 1792).

FOR some months War had been in the air of France, troubling and agitating her. The dwellers in fortunate countries which have enjoyed a long era of peace and tranquillity are enabled to devote themselves to labour, commerce, and industry, and they ask no better than the perpetuation of the benefits of their condition; but for those peoples who are subjected to interior disturbances, and whose existence is highly feverish, there is in the perils and the hoped-for results of war a powerful stimulant, which they long for and demand.

In 1792, the masses, who suffered, and who

attributed the excess of their ills to the Emigrants assembled upon the frontiers, and to the foreign Governments their accomplices and support, regarded war as the only possible solution of the situation.

It was a curious thing that the political parties were not opposed to war, with the exception of the Jacobins, who probably dreaded victory more than defeat. The Feuillants and the Girondists willingly accepted the idea, and in their hearts the faithful Royalists, who divined the secret wishes of the King and Queen, ardently desired it, for they believed in defeat, and reckoned upon the victorious armies of the coalition to destroy the Revolution and re-establish order in France.

Even the Humanitarians, those to whom the shedding of blood was hateful, and whose dreams were of universal brotherhood, did not recoil from so grave an eventuality. Who could say what might be the result of the meeting of the armies, of the contact of the poor soldiers, sent out by the sovereigns to kill in their cause, with the free defenders of the French nation? Isnard, the deputy, speaking from the tribune, had given utterance to that hope in language worthy of it, full of the pretentious naïveté of the period.

"If," he said, "at the moment when the enemies' armies shall meet ours in conflict, philosophy reveals itself to them (*frappe leurs yeux*), the peoples will embrace before the face of the dethroned tyrants, the consoled earth, and the glad heaven!"

The prospect of so fair a spectacle, due to the triumph of philosophy, captivated the Assembly, and urged it to a decisive step. The "executive power" was charged to demand that the Electors of Trèves and other Princes of the Empire should renounce their culpable toleration of the Emigrants, and disperse the assemblages of such persons upon the frontiers.

The natural result of this summons was "to set fire to the powder." Far from returning a satisfactory reply, the Princes only increased their "toleration" of the Emigrants, and Francis, who had taken the title of King of Bohemia and Hungary on the death of Leopold, before being proclaimed Emperor of Austria, replied by a note demanding "the re-establishment of the French monarchy on the bases fixed by the royal declaration of the 23rd of June 1789;" that is to say, the re-establishment of the three Orders, the restitution of the goods of the clergy, the retrocession of the county of Venaissain to the Pope—in a word, the abolition of all the measures voted by the Constituent Assembly.

This demand was sufficiently audacious. By what right did the King of Bohemia and Hungary meddle in the affairs of France? He might have been answered at once by an ultimatum requiring him to refrain from any such domineering demands, and this would have been equivalent to a declaration of war. No such conclusive step was taken; the parties hostile to the Court were reluctant to rush into a war in which they saw that the King wished to engage.

It was decided that the "state of war" should be declared, with the idea that, by going no farther than stating a fact, responsibility for a rupture would be placed upon the foreign Powers (20th April 1792).

Since the return from Varennes, Marie Antoinette was convinced that the only way of salvation for the royal family lay in the armed intervention of Europe. This alone would have power to reduce the rebellious subjects of the King to submission—this alone could restore its legitimate authority to the monarchy. She was rejoiced at the declaration of the "state of war." On the 19th of April she wrote to Count Fersen :—

"The Ministers and the Jacobins make the King declare war on the House of Austria to-morrow, on the pretext that by the treaties of last year the treaty of alliance made in 1756 has been broken, and that no categorical reply to the last despatch has been made. The Ministers hope this proceeding will create fear, and that negotiations will be opened in three weeks. *May God grant it may not be so, and that at last vengeance may be taken for all the outrages of this country.*"

Count Fersen was no less pleased. Immediately on receiving the news, he addressed a letter containing his impression on the subject to the Queen; this letter was conveyed to her in a box of biscuits.

"M. de Thugut has told the Baron (Breteuil)

that the King of Hungary had stated that
he was weary of all that was going on in
France; that he was resolved to put an end
to it, and to act; that he was about to set
his troops in motion in concert with the King
of Prussia; that if the French attacked, they
were to be amused for six weeks or two months
until the armies could arrive; that if they
did not attack, he was resolved all the same
to attack them, and that they must be cajoled
by appearances of peace until the moment at
which he could act.

"I received the news of the declaration of
war yesterday, and I am very glad of it. It is
the best and the only means of bringing the
Powers to a decision at last."

The object was to make the ardently desired
intervention, now at length obtained, produce
the happy results that were expected from
it. The invading forces, if conquered, would
not only be unable to co-operate for the
deliverance of the royal family, but would inevitably ensure their destruction. Nobody was
under any mistake on this point; accordingly,
we find Count Fersen setting to work with
indefatigable zeal and activity to avert such
a misfortune, and Marie Antoinette sparing
no pains on her part. Both were fully aware
that they were playing a very dangerous game,
and they took every possible precaution for the
safety of their mutual communications. We
already know, by a despatch addressed to M.
de Mercy on the 29th of March 1792, and
published in the Arneth collection, that the

Queen did not hesitate to reveal the political and military plans of the French Government; but it was not known until the papers left by Count Fersen were brought to light how active was the part she took in the events of that particular period. Her correspondence may be described as incessant. She usually employed Goguelat's hand, and she arranged a complete plan of correspondence with Fersen, so contrived as to mislead suspicion, if by any mishap one of her letters were to fall into inimical hands.

The means she had hitherto employed—cipher, invisible ink, missives hidden in boxes of tea or biscuits, or in the cover of the *Moniteur*, no longer sufficed, and she resorted to a very clever stratagem. She was to dictate to Goguelat business letters, which a friend was to be supposed to send to a M. Rignon. A number of things were to be mentioned, but at a spot indicated by a sign, the fictitious correspondence was to cease, and important news was to be conveyed in a manner previously arranged according to a key—in short, what we should now call a code.

On the 5th of June the Queen writes on this plan. The letter is worth reproducing, for it is a good example of the method.

"I received your letter No. 7, and proceeded immediately to withdraw your funds from the Boscaris firm. There was no time to lose, for the bankruptcy was declared yesterday, and this morning the matter was made public at the Bourse. It is said that the creditors will lose heavily. Here is a statement of the various matters which I have in my hands."

Then follows the coded portion, written out by Count Fersen:—

"*Orders are given that Luckner's forces shall attack at once; he is opposed to this, but the Ministry will have it. The troops are in want of everything, and are in the greatest disorder.*"

Then the letter is resumed:—

"You will instruct me what I shall do with these funds. If I had the decision, I should invest them to advantage in some of the fine domains of the clergy. This is, according to what I hear, the best way of investing money," &c., &c.

She skilfully contrives to convey the news concerning herself even in the "padding" portion of the missive. The allusions in the passage which ends the letter are obvious, and easy to be understood: "Your friends are pretty well. The loss they have sustained grieves them much. I do what I can to console them. *They think the re-establishment of their fortune impossible, or at least very far off. Give them, if you can, some consolation in respect of this; they have need of it; their position becomes more dreadful every day.* Adieu. Receive their compliments, and the assurance of my entire devotion."

The next day but one she sends him the following: "My Constit. (Constitutionalists) are sending a man to Vienna; he will pass through Brussels. M. de Mercy must be instructed to treat him as if he were announced and recommended by the Q. (Queen) to negotiate with him in the sense of the memorandum which I have sent him. It is desired that he write to Vienna to announce him (the envoy), to urge that it be carefully concealed from him that I have ever sent there, and to say that we hold by the plan made by the Courts of V. and B. (Vienna and Berlin), but that it is necessary to appear to enter into the views of the Const.; and, above all, to urge that it is according to the desires and demands of the Q.: these measures are very necessary. . . .

"Tell M. de Mercy that we (*on*) cannot write to him, because we (*on*) are too closely watched."

All this was wrapped up in details of the Boscaris bankruptcy, advice to buy confiscated church property, &c., &c.

At this point, and in order to meet a possible objection, perhaps it may be well to prove that these letters really did emanate from the Queen, although they were not signed or written by her own hand: the matter is of importance, considering the gravity of the information which they contain.

Their authenticity might be taken as proved by the simple fact that Count Fersen deciphered them, and classed them in the collection of his correspondence with Marie Antoinette; but conclusive evidence is afforded (as the editors of *M. de Fersen et la Cour de France* point out) by a passage in a letter of Fersen's to Baron Stedingk, who was at that time Swedish Ambassador at St. Petersburg. This passage contains the clearest possible statement :—

"*The Queen, in sending me the mandate of this Constitutional Ambassador who was to pass through here, says to me: 'Instruct M. de Mercy,' &c.*"

The whole passage already given is re-copied by him, and he adds :—

"I have communicated all this to the Comte de Mercy, who has promised me to write to Vienna to the same effect." Beyond this, he wrote in his journal: "*Sunday the* 10*th. . . . Letter from the Queen of France. Orders to Luckner to attack*," &c.

It is therefore impossible to cast any doubt upon the authenticity of the quoted documents.

Count Fersen employed a certain Madame Toscani, who was a confidential person in the service of Mrs. Sullivan, to convey the answers to these letters. It will be seen that he endeavoured to encourage the unfortunate Queen.

"How deeply I grieve for your position; my mind is strongly and painfully impressed by it. *Try only to stay in Paris and they (on) will come to your help.* The King of Prussia is resolved upon this, and you may count upon it" (11th June).

But would the promised succour arrive in time? The Revolution moved more quickly than did the monarchies, and only a few days had elapsed after the interchange of these letters when Count Fersen received distressing and alarming news.

"Dreadful account of the attempt at the Tuileries on the 21st," he writes in his journal. "Horrible! it is appended to this; the ensuing events make one shudder. . . ."

The narrative had been sent to him by the Swedish Chargé d'Affaires at Paris, M. Bergstedt. It told that the Tuileries had been invaded by a crowd of nearly 50,000 persons armed with pikes, and shouting "Down with Monsieur Veto! Madame Veto, and all their brood!" The doors, either ill-guarded or not guarded at all, had afforded free passage to this mob, which spread itself tumultuously all over the palace. The King had sought to resist the torrent by taking refuge in the deep bay of a window, and was surrounded by a few faithful grenadiers. He had been exposed to great dangers, and had confronted them with cool courage. The details that were given afford proof of this. An individual approached him, brandishing his pike and shouting, "Where is he, that I may kill him?" but the perfect composure of the King daunted the ruffian. Louis, however, while steadfastly refusing to withdraw his *veto* on certain decrees of the Assembly, had thought proper to yield to a popular whim, and consented to put a red cap on his head.

The Queen was in the Dauphin's apartment. Hearing the shouts, she ran to the spot, but she was separated from the King, and had to stand alone against vile abuse and threats. "The Queen heard her head demanded several times, and her face never changed."

We find among Count Fersen's papers a note without a date and without a beginning, which must bear reference to this period. It had been brought to him by Leonard, the Queen's hairdresser.

"*Do not torment yourself too much on my account.* Believe me, courage will always make itself felt. The line which we have just taken will, I hope, give us time to wait, but six weeks is a very long time. Adieu! Hasten, if you can, the succour which is promised us for our deliverance."

(*Written in invisible ink.*)

"I still exist, but it is a miracle. The 20th was an awful day. It was not I who was the chief object; it was my husband's very life they sought to take; they no longer conceal this. He showed firmness and strength, which made an impression upon them for the moment, but our danger may be renewed at any minute. Adieu! Take care of yourself for our sake, *and do not distress yourself about us.*"

In this repeated injunction "not to torment himself on her account," we trace all the refinement of friendship which grieves at the thought of the friend's distress. Poor woman! she deserves praise for having kept up any courage and composure under the terrible circumstances, for she was but feebly sustained by her surroundings.

Louis XVI., who had borne himself nobly, with passive resignation, in the face of the howling crowd, had fallen back into his habitual apathy. It is heart-sickening to read in his journal what he says, in the fewest possible words, about those terrible events :—

"*Wednesday, the 20th of June.*—Affair of the Tuileries."

On the following days he finds only one word to write—"*Nothing.*" On the 25th he merely notes :—

"Walked after Mass in the courtyard and the gardens with my son, to see the National Guards."

Meanwhile, the King's brothers beyond the frontier were losing no opportunity of augmenting his danger by their attitude and their talk. They had already replied with charming involuntary modesty to a letter from Louis XVI., in which, according to the new Constitution, they were styled "French princes," that "this title did not belong to them." After the 20th of June they issued a manifesto, which Count Fersen describes as "stupid, and insolent towards the King."

They sent it "to all the Courts." A clever thing to do by way of stimulating the zeal of the sovereigns in favour of Louis XVI. ! But it is very likely that they were well aware of what they were doing. Their conduct under other circumstances had been so egotistical, so obviously selfish, that we may question, without calumniating them, whether they were not very glad to decrease the distance that lay between them and the throne by acting thus.

Marie Antoinette, notwithstanding the perils of the hour, and aware of the urgency of the need for help, proved herself to be a woman with brains, or rather the man of the family.[1] She misjudged the situation; she was not a politician, but believing that there was a chance of safety in foreign support, she carried out her idea on that point. She, at least, was persevering, and she acted. It was otherwise with her husband.

On the 23rd of June, she again sent secret intelligence to Count Fersen: "*Dumouriez starts to-morrow for Luckner's army; he has promised to raise Brabant. Saint - Huruge is also setting out to accomplish the same object.*"

The rest of the letter went on with the pretended correspondence on the affairs of *M. Rignon*; but it comprised several easily detected allusions. "Your friend is in the greatest danger. Let his relations know of his unhappy position."

On the 26th she wrote: "You will immediately receive particulars relating to the purchase I have made, on your account, of the goods of the clergy.

"I am sorry that I cannot reassure you concerning the position of your friend. During the last three days the malady has not made progress, but none the less the symptoms are

[1] As Napoleon said afterwards of her daughter, the Duchesse d'Angoulême.

alarming; the most skilful physicians give him up. Only a speedy crisis can save him, and of this there is no sign as yet; so that we despair. Inform the persons who have business with him of his condition, so that they may take precautions; time presses. . . ."

Count Fersen understood this with his intelligence, but how keenly did he feel it with his heart! If the matter had depended upon him only, Europe should have fallen upon France, and taken her victim out of her clutches; but he was not master, and he had to await events. He exhorted and encouraged the unfortunate Queen to patience.

"I received the letter of the 23rd yesterday; there is nothing to fear so long as the Austrians are not beaten. A hundred thousand Dumouriez will not make this country (Brabant) revolt, although it is well enough disposed to do so.

"Your position gives me incessant anxiety. Your courage will be admired, and the firm conduct of the King will have an excellent effect. I have already sent the statement of affairs everywhere."

He communicates the plan of the Duke of Brunswick to her.

"He is marching straight upon Paris, leaving the combined forces on the frontiers to mask the forts, and to prevent the troops that are there from acting elsewhere and opposing his operations.

"The Austrians have done a foolish thing in attacking Luckner on his entrance. . . .

"You ought to make Gog. (Goguelat) write me on Sundays and Wednesdays to give the particulars of all that is taking place. When he shall say to me: *It is said, but I do not believe a word of it*, then I shall know that the thing is certain.

"Our position is frightful; but do not disquiet yourself too much. I feel strong, *and I have in me something which tells me that we shall soon be happy and safe. This idea only consoles me*. . . .

"Adieu! When shall we see each other again in tranquillity?"

However impossible such a thing may seem to us now, they actually did think that the moment was approaching. Count Fersen wrote on the 10th of July: "They are hurrying the operations as much as possible; the arrival of the Prussians is already a little accelerated, and in the first days of August they can begin. . . ."

The Queen sometimes yielded to hope, even in those sad days; this correspondence kept her up. Mme. Campan gives a curious proof that it did so. Speaking of Marie Antoinette, she says: "She was always awake at dawn of day, and desired that neither the outside shutters nor the blinds should be closed, so that her long sleepless nights might be less wearisome.

"About the middle of one of these nights, when her room was lighted by the moon, she gazed at it and said to me that *a month hence she should look at that moon when she should be loosed from her chains and see the King at liberty.* Then she confided to me that all was going on well for their deliverance, but that the opinions of their close and trusted advisers were alarmingly divided; that some guaranteed the most complete success, while others pointed out insurmountable dangers. She added that she knew the order of march of the Princes and the King of Prussia; that on a certain day they would be at Verdun, on another in such and such a place; that Lille would be besieged. . . ."

She was, however, very anxious about what might happen in Paris before the entry of the allies, especially as a plan had been formed for removing the King from the capital.

"The Const., who have joined Lafayette and Luckner," she writes on the 11th July, "want to take the King to Compiègne on the day after the Federation. The two Generals are coming here for that purpose. The King is disposed to agree to the plan; the Queen opposes it. No one knows as yet what will be the issue of this great enterprise, of which I do not at all approve. Luckner takes the army of the Rhine, Lafayette that of Flanders, Biron and Dumouriez the army of the centre."

It was true that the Queen strongly opposed the removal of the King, first, because she did not wish to be replaced in the hands of Lafayette, to whom she had not forgiven any part of the past; also, and above all, because Count Fersen urgently begged of her to use every effort to remain in Paris.

The project which was formed with the object of saving the royal family was succeeded by an analogous scheme, but the latter originated in the enmity of the Jacobins, who wanted to put the King out of the reach of the foreign armies. The Queen communicated it to Fersen, employing the formula that was to confirm the authenticity of any statement to which it was opposed.

"The rumour runs, *and I forewarn you that I do not believe a word of what I am going to tell you,* that the Jacobins are planning more than ever to get out of Paris with the King, and gain the southern provinces. . . .

"All in whom you are interested are well. Adieu, my dear Rignon. I embrace you tenderly."

Time passed, and hostilities were not begun. Marie Antoinette imagined that a strong declaration by the Duke of Brunswick would have a great effect in frightening the excited patriots, and would make up for the lack of action for a time.

"The manifesto must be sent at once . . . it is expected with extreme impatience; it will necessarily bring over many to the King, *and will place him in safety.*"

The Queen draws a vivid picture of the danger of the royal family.

"The life of the King has been threatened for a long time past, as well as that of the Queen. The arrival of nearly 600 men from Marseilles, and a number of other deputies from all the Jacobin clubs, greatly increases our anxieties, which are unfortunately too well founded. Precautions of every kind are taken for the safety of their Majesties, but assassins skulk continually about the château, emissaries excite the people, a part of the National Guard is disaffected, and other parties are either weak or cowardly. The only resistance to the enterprises of the ruffians would have to be offered by a few persons resolved to make a rampart of their bodies for the royal family, and by the regiment of the Swiss Guards. The affair that took place on the 30th, between 180 picked grenadiers of the National Guard and some Marseilles Federals, after a dinner at the Champs-Elysées, has clearly proved the cowardice of the National Guard, and the little reliance that can be placed upon that force, which is really impressive only by its bulk. The 180 grenadiers ran away. . . .

"For a long time past the factious party have taken no pains to hide their intention of annihilating the royal family. . . . *If they* (the foreign forces) *do not come, nothing but Providence can save the King and his family.*"

At last, at the moment when she was writing these almost despairing lines, the Queen received the famous manifesto which she so ardently desired. She might have rejoiced in it, if facts had realised her fancies, and if the fear which she imagined would be struck to the hearts of the patriots on reading it had not given place to fierce anger. Never had such threats been addressed to a whole people.

"Any National Guard taken when carrying

arms shall be treated as a rebel; all inhabitants who shall dare to defend themselves shall be put to death and their houses burned; all the members of the National Assembly, of the department, of the district, of the municipality, and of the National Guard of Paris, are rendered responsible for all events, to be judged by military process, without hope of pardon; it is declared that *if the least outrage be done to the royal family, and if their safety be not immediately provided for, their Imperial and Royal Majesties will hand Paris over to a military execution and to total overthrow.*"

" To avoid this fate, the French nation must submit on the spot to the King, its legitimate sovereign."

This extravagant manifesto, published in the name of the Duke of Brunswick, was not his; we now know who were the authors, or rather who was the author. A draft of a manifesto had been made in the first instance by M. de Limon, a Frenchman who had formerly been in the service of the Duke of Orleans and had gone abroad; this draft, which was firm but moderate, was submitted to Count Fersen. It was the latter who, moved by the piteous cries of distress which reached him from Paris, and agonised by his utter powerlessness to save her whom he loved, poured out his wrath in this document, and by his influence induced the chief of the allied troops to adopt threats which he, Fersen, had often longed to fulminate. Such an exaggeration was excusable in him, but stupid and ridiculous on the part of the

General who had to accept the responsibility of the manifesto before all Europe.

The effect quickly revealed the extent of the error that had been committed. Shouts of fury were the answer returned from all parts to these intolerable pretensions; the people, threatened by common foes, rose up with one common purpose of resistance, and as though a secret instinct had apprised them that these insensate declarations had found their inspiration in the palace of the kings of France, they rushed forth against the Tuileries. The manifesto was intended to beat them down; it drove them mad instead.

The manifesto bore date the 28th of July; on the 3rd of August the deposition of the King was demanded. In vain did poor Louis deny all complicity with the foreigner; his word was no longer believed. The people wanted to have done with royalty. On the 9th of August the city rose, and an outbreak was organised for the morrow.

Stupefaction prevailed in the château. General Viosménil's measures of precaution were so ridiculous, that M. de Jarjayes warned Madame de Campan of the sure and certain issue of the coming conflict. The King lost his head; he was incapable of forming a firm resolve, and could not act. Nevertheless, being urged by the Queen, he tried to arouse the zeal of his defenders by appearing among them on the morning of the 10th. He was received with acclamation by some gentlemen who had remained faithful, and by the Swiss Guards;

then he went on to the battalions of National Guards massed around the château.

A resolute king, on horseback, might perhaps have rallied these waverers; but Louis XVI., on foot, his wig awry, his face puffed and weary, did not awaken even pity in their ranks. They let him pass, silently at first, then murmurs were heard which rose to shouts, base insults were flung at him by patriot lips; he was hooted, and had to re-enter the château hurriedly, pursued by abusive cries, amid which "Down with the fat hog," was repeated several times.

It was all over; the monarchy was lost. Its friends had quite as great a share in its ruin as its enemies.

While the King and Queen of France, accompanied by the Dauphin, Madame Royale, Madame Elizabeth, and a few devoted friends, including the faithful Goguelat, abandoned the royal palace for the dangerous hospitality of the reporters' room, accorded by the National Assembly, and afterwards for the captivity of the Temple, Count Fersen, full of his fixed idea, searching the world for saviours for the Queen, bethought him of asking the King of England to proclaim that "he would avenge in a striking manner every attempt against the royal persons;" and on this same 10th of August he notified this to Marie Antoinette.

His delusion still existed; his journal contains the following significant note:—

"10th, *Friday*.—The news from Paris is very encouraging."

In three days news from Paris arrived, to falsify his forecast utterly, and to destroy his last hopes at a blow.

"13*th, Monday.*—Terrible news from Paris. On Thursday morning the château was attacked; the King and Queen escaped to the Assembly; at one o'clock fighting was still going on in the courtyards and the Carrousel. Blood was shed profusely, many were killed and hanged, the château was forced in every part, eight pieces of cannon were turned upon it and fired. . . . A thick smoke led to the belief that the château had been set on fire. . . . What horror!"

"15*th, Wednesday.*—News from Paris; the royal family are at the Hôtel de Noailles, closely watched; not allowed to see any one. . . ."

"17*th, Friday.*—News from Paris; the King and his family are confined in the tower of the Temple; Mme. de Lamballe and Mme. de Tourzel are shut up with them. . . ."

Events followed events with marvellous rapidity. Every post brought most serious news. One day it was the announcement that Lafayette—the hero of "the Independence," the favourite of the National Guard of Paris, the popular general—Lafayette had left his army, had left France, and had just been taken, with his friends Latour-Maubourg, Lameth, Bureau de Puzy, &c. Another day, the news was still worse: the city was given over to blood and fire. The passions of the populace were let loose, and the mob proceeded to massacre those whom they believed to be the enemies of the people.

At first there were only rumours. It was said that "the people judged, and execution was done on the spot." Presently the details became known, and the alleged atrocities were confirmed. Fersen learned with horror that the gentle Princesse de Lamballe was among the victims, that her corpse had been carried under the windows of the Temple, that the King had been forced to look upon it, and that Manuel had said to him (using the *tutoiement*)—

"Look here! There may be a counter-revolution, but at any rate you shall not enjoy it; this is the fate that awaits you."

The terror which Fersen had hoped to see let loose upon the French nation was now the lot of its enemies, and he also trembled. "I have never been so much afraid," he writes on the 6th of September.

He had good reason to be afraid. Paris was in the power of the mob, and, through either weakness or complicity, the Government carefully abstained from interference with their acts.

What an answer to the famous manifesto? All the adversaries of the Revolution were equally surprised and dismayed by it. The facts went beyond their most gloomy forebodings, and M. de Mercy, who "saw black," used the language of a madman in his turn, actually saying to Count Fersen that "much severity was needed," and that "*there was no other means than this: fire must be set to the four corners of Paris.*"

To set fire to the four corners of Paris, however, it was necessary to reach those four corners; now, the Prussians were a long way off them. The French army, placed under the command of General Dumouriez, an adventurer of genius, did not seem disposed to yield the ground so easily. The affair of Valmy (20th of September) had done more than arrest the march of the enemy.

That check, although slight in itself, was accompanied by other calamities which rendered its results disastrous. The Duke of Brunswick's troops, being badly victualled, fed on unripe fruit, and were decimated by dysentery. And besides, the weather was bad and the cold premature.

Letters sent by the emigrants gave disheartening reports. While they stated that Dumouriez was in an unassailable position, they acknowledged that the troops were in want of everything. "Houses are demolished to warm them (the troops); it has been necessary to take grain out of the barns, and this is effected in so slovenly a fashion that a great part has been lost and entire villages consumed, to the great detriment of the harvests. The country presents a spectacle of devastation and is like a desert. The Vicomte de Caraman draws a terrible picture of the misery of the inhabitants; he relates that in a burning village he saw an old man and his wife sitting before their house, which was in flames, and contemplating the destruction of all they possessed. Their dog lay on the ground close to them howling dismally.

x

"Vauban's letter to his wife draws a terrible picture of the plight of the emigrants. They are in bivouac for the last ten days, without tents, without means of conveyance, afflicted with dysentery, without medical aid or means of relief, absolutely without victuals; he had eaten his last pound of bread, and knew not where to find another.

"These two letters throw doubt on the success of the enterprise, and say, '*God only knows what the end will be.*'"—(*Fersen's Journal*, 1st October.)

What everybody did know just then was that the Duke of Brunswick was beating a retreat, to the great displeasure of all the enthusiasts. Baron de Breteuil, who was generally more reserved, severely condemned him:—

"*This astounding conduct reflects great blame on the Duke of Brunswick; he is a man in the mud.*"

During this time the success of the French was continuous. Dumouriez had got his plan—the conquering of Belgium—adopted, and the victory of Jemmapes proved that he was in the right (6th of November).

And now the situation was becoming very grave, the danger was drawing nigh to Brussels. It was time for Count Fersen to leave that city. With Colonel Crawford, M. de Simolin, and Mrs. Sullivan, he started for Düsseldorf at noon on the 9th of November.

What he saw on that journey filled him with profound sadness. "A heartrending spectacle," he writes, "was that of the unfortunate emigrants; young men and old men of the Bourbon corps lagged behind, being hardly able to drag themselves along with their muskets and knapsacks, carrying the little that they had managed to take away. There were even women of the upper class, with or without their waiting-women, going on foot, this one with a child on her back, the other with a small bundle. I wish I could have had carriages to pick up all these poor people; the sight of them inspired horror and pity."

The hopes of the month of July had receded into the far distance. France and the Revolution did not seem disposed to lower their crest before Europe and Royalty.

CHAPTER XI.

News from Paris—The trial of the King—The 21st of January—The Will of Louis XVI.—Attitude of the Princes and emigrants—Indifference of foreigners—Attempts to escape made at Paris—Toulan and Jarjayes—The Stamp—Agreement arrived at between Dumouriez and the Prince of Coburg—Hopes of Count Fersen, appointed Ambassador ·to King Louis XVII.—Note of the 8th of April 1793—The defection of Dumouriez—Interview of the General with Count Fersen at Brussels—Inaction of M. de Mercy—Hostility of M. de Thugut—Drouet—The Queen transferred to the Conciergerie—The Chevalier de Rougeville—Details of the captivity of Marie Antoinette—A last effort in favour of the Queen—Novere, the dancing-master, and Ribbes, the banker—The trial of the Queen—Marie Antoinette at the National Window—Count Fersen's grief.

It is regarded as an indisputable proof of the courage of a general that he has slept well the night before a battle. It is a pity that no one has ever thought of ranking the fact of having eaten largely in great crises, among the proofs of intrepidity of soul, for, if this were so, Louis XVI. would have left quite a different mark upon the memory of mankind. In that case, we should quote with admiration, not mere curiosity, the bill of fare of his Majesty's supper on a certain evening in December, as reported by Albertier, the commissary. "Louis ate six cutlets, a large piece of fowl, some eggs, drank two glasses of white wine, and one of Alicante, and then he went to bed."

And yet that evening was an important one

in his existence: the King had just returned from the Convention, where his counsel, M. de Sèze, had pleaded for him courageously and in vain.

The eagerness with which Louis satisfied the demands of his formidable appetite was already notorious. In the stenographer's gallery, during the massacre of his Swiss Guards and the loyal gentlemen who had remained with him at the Tuileries, he had greedily torn a roast fowl to pieces with his fingers, and devoured it, under the indignant eyes of the Queen, and amid the scornful glances of the deputies.

Why should he have restrained himself? Louis XIV. had left him traditions of gluttony which excused him. And besides, wherefore should he trouble himself? Louis did not believe in his danger, especially when he was a prisoner in the Temple.

In the Tuileries, on the Champ de Mars, whither he had been obliged to go for the Fête of the Federation, he might have to dread that an enthusiastic fanatic, passing from revolutionary theory to practice, might aim a dagger-thrust or a bullet at him; but now, in shelter behind the walls of the Temple, he might indeed be exposed to insult and to oppressive measures, but what appearance was there of the Convention's going any farther? They would never dare. Cléry puts this false security strongly. "I was far from fearing for the King's life," he says. "The Queen was equally inapprehensive, and her husband governed himself by her only."

A similar delusion prevailed abroad. Count Fersen wrote to the Duke of Sudermania about the end of November :—

"We have no fresh news from Paris. We only know that the trial of the King is imminent. The Abbé Fauchet thinks his Majesty sufficiently punished by all that has befallen him, and hopes they will let him go; others want to have him tried and executed, and the penalty of death abolished afterwards. *There is reason to believe that the intention is to try the King, to condemn him, then to have him pardoned by the nation, and a sum of money assigned for his support and that of his family;* but it is not known whether he is to be kept in prison or left at liberty to go where he may please."

The result did not justify this optimistic forecast. The cause of Louis XVI. was lost by the discovery of papers in "*the iron press,*" after its existence had been uselessly denied by him. He was unanimously found guilty by the voters, and condemned to death by the majority of the Assembly.

Count Fersen received the news of the execution from the Archbishop of Toulouse, on the 27th of January, with such details as the latter had been able to procure.

"On the 21st, at half-past nine in the morning, the King was brought out of the Temple, escorted by 400 cavalry and 1200 infantry. He was taken, in the midst of profound silence, by the boulevards of the Temple, St. Martin, and St. Honoré, to the scaffold, which was erected on the place formerly called Place Louis XV., now called Place de la Révolution, between the spot where the statue stood and the entrance of the Champs-Elysées.

"At the back of the carriage, and by the King's side, was his confessor, an Irish priest; on the front seat were two officers of the gendarmerie.

"Having arrived at the foot of the scaffold, he submitted to the binding of his hands with the utmost composure, and mounted the steps bravely.

"He wished to speak to the people, but the roll of the drums overpowered his voice. Nevertheless, those who were close to the scaffold heard these words, uttered in a firm tone—'*I pardon my enemies, and I desire that my death may be the salvation of France.*'

"He breathed his last sigh at a quarter to eleven o'clock; his severed head was held up to the people, and at the same moment the air was rent with cries of 'Long live the Nation! Long live the French Republic!'

"Several volunteers steeped their pike-heads in his blood, and others their handkerchiefs. His head and body were carried to the Madeleine (cemetery) and buried."

These sad details of the King's death affected Count Fersen profoundly, "renewing all his grief, and presenting the most heartrending pictures to his imagination."

The reading of the Will drawn up by the King "on Christmas Day, 1792," disturbed him to the extent of making him write in his journal: "Will of Louis XVI.—superb."

Superb in resignation, perhaps; and yet, could it be admitted that a prince, placed at the head of twenty-five millions of men, had nothing better to do than to contemplate the evils by which himself and his subjects were assailed, then patiently to bear his own, and the sight of theirs? The merit of the King in refusing to shed blood for the defence of the rights which he held by tradition and from his ancestors, is greatly diminished by the fact that he refrained equally from defending the rights of the nobility and the clergy, and even those of the simple honest folk whose sole desire was to live peacefully under a protecting Government. As a fact, never was there so much blood shed, and the weakness and incapacity of Louis, ill-concealed under merit of a certain kind, caused greater misfortunes, brought about more numerous catastrophes, and gave greater opportunity for crime than would have resulted from an armed resistance.

As for the Will itself, it must have grieved the true friends of legitimate monarchy. Did it not contain the following sentences:—" I desire my son, *if he should have the misfortune to become king*, to consider that he owes himself altogether to the welfare of *his fellow-citizens* . . . that he can make the people happy only by reigning according to the laws; but at the same time that a King cannot ensure respect for those laws, and do the good that he has at heart, except in so far as he has the necessary authority, and that otherwise, being restricted in his operations and not inspiring respect, he is more harmful than useful."

The subjects of former times, now called the "fellow-citizens" of his son, who was no longer king by birth, but only liable to "the misfortune" of becoming king, was not this the theory of the Revolution recognised by its victim?

Louis XVI. was not mourned by his own. The Comte de Provence, whose ambition was gratified by the abridgment of the space between himself and the throne, hastened to display the outward sign of his power by proclaiming himself Regent until the majority of the little Louis XVII. The consequences of his conduct speedily ensued.

"There are already parties among the French," writes Fersen, alluding to the French emigrants. "One set approves of the regency of Monsieur, the other bears in mind the rights of the Queen, and it is much to be feared that their difference of opinion will have evil results one day. *The Princes already are going to make a thousand blunders.* It is said they are about to nominate a Chancellor, but Barentin was appointed on the death of Maupéou by the late King, and he will object."

The emigrants were but lightly impressed. "The death of the King has not produced any great effect upon them; they console themselves with the regency of Monsieur. Some of them even went to the play and the concert."

Count Fersen was indignant at the sight

of such indifference, such apathy, so little care, in a word, for the safety of the unhappy Queen, who was still a captive, and on whom the popular vengeance might wreak itself in her prison by heaping outrage and suffering of every kind upon, and even—who could tell?—by killing her also, as her husband had been killed.

They did not believe, however, that such a fate could be in store for a woman. Louis XVI. had paid the debt of royalty; the life of Marie Antoinette would be respected. Their confidence excused the inaction of the oldest friends of the Queen, but Count Fersen could not be content with such barren attachment; he was not satisfied merely to condole with the royal widow.

But what was he to do? how was he to act? There was the difficulty, and his perplexity was great. Incoherent, and sometimes contradictory ideas were seething in his troubled brain. His letters reflect his indecision and embarrassment. He writes to M. de Mercy, owning that "the more he considers all that has taken place, the more he is confirmed in his opinion that they can serve the Queen only by doing nothing for her." He adds, "It is dreadful to have to limit one's zeal to inaction."

Then he passes on to another idea: "A simple step for the Emperor to take, and entirely in conformity with his dignity, would be to claim the Queen." Yes, but if this step should be injurious to her? "Might it not bring about a discussion upon the trial of the

Queen, which had been decreed at the same time as the King's, but had not yet been mooted, and which one party probably desired to have forgotten? Might it not hasten the condemnation of the Queen? . . . If the Emperor were to manifest interest in the cause of his aunt, would not this furnish the factions with a cry of which they would avail themselves, and be the means of working her destruction, by rekindling enmity against the Austrians, and *representing the Queen as a foreigner and the accomplice of the King in the crimes imputed to him?*"

No, there was danger in this plan; he must think of another. "A more efficacious means of saving the Queen would be, in my opinion, to employ intelligent agents from England, who should gain over the leaders of the Orleans party, such as Laclos, Santerre, Dumouriez, by money and promises. The Duc d'Orléans himself must not be approached; his dulness and incapacity are on a par with his rascality and poltroonery."

He might indeed be believed when he affirmed, in conclusion, that "his zeal and attachment for the Queen had solely dictated these reflections." Unhappily for him and for Marie Antoinette, there was nothing practically possible in them; all his efforts were neutralised by the reluctance of the foreign sovereigns to see a monarchical government re-established in France. The policy that schemes to enfeeble France by condemning her to be republican is not new.

Princes were relied on to save the Queen: men sufficed.

While there was a stir and agitation more or less sincere on all sides, while troops were being assembled and formidable preparations were being made, two men, almost unknown, without resources, without power, coolly made up their minds to do what so many others merely dreamed of vainly — to save the royal family. Toulan, the municipal, and the Chevalier de Jarjayes conceived that heroic project, and it was not their fault that it failed on the very brink of success.

I have related elsewhere in detail the story of this marvellous attempt, which was inspired by pity and sincere attachment.[1] That strange personage, Toulan, deserves to be rescued from oblivion, he was in his dry manner so bold a conspirator, always good-humoured, a right generous Gascon, who, contrary to the ways of his compatriots, was much more ready with deeds than with words.

When the plan laid by him, and adopted by M. de Jarjayes, was on the point of being carried out, the vacillation of a man whom they had been forced to take into their confidence ruined everything; flight was rendered impossible, except for Marie Antoinette only, and the Queen nobly refused to separate herself from her children.

She then wrote a note which Toulan passed on to Jarjayes. A copy of it exists among Fersen's papers. It is truly touching:—

---

[1] See *Un Complot sous la Terreur* (*Marie Antoinette, Toulan, Jarjayes*).

"*Adieu! I think, if you have decided upon going away, it is best that it should be done promptly.*

"*How happy I should be if we might soon meet again . . . Never can I sufficiently acknowledge all that you have done for me.*

"*Adieu! That word is cruel!*"

If the word was cruel, the thing was still more so. Notwithstanding her strength and her resolution, Marie Antoinette suffered from the anguish which is caused by every parting, every breaking of relations with a faithful and devoted friend. And yet there was an alleviation of the bitterness of the separation: in leaving France, M. de Jarjayes would be able to convey the captive's tender remembrance to Count Fersen.

This episode in the life of Marie Antoinette was entirely unknown until a fortunate circumstance placed me in possession of the original of another note addressed to the Chevalier de Jarjayes in that terrible month of February 1793, which had brought her consolation and hope, too quickly followed by disappointment.

The note contains a sentence which we know, from our information concerning Count Fersen, can only bear reference to him. Here it is in its eloquent simplicity: "*The Stamp which I send with this is quite another thing. I desire that you remit it to the person who came from Brussels to see me last winter, as you know, and that you say to him at the same time that the motto has never been more true.*"

"The person who came from Brussels last winter," that is to say in 1792, was Count Fersen. We know all about that expedition; no doubt on the point is possible. Now, what was that "Stamp"? Only the inheritors of Count Fersen's papers can now answer that question, if, indeed, the Count himself did not destroy the last token which had come to him from her who seems to have been his only love. The latter hypothesis is not likely to be correct, considering the care with which he had translated, classed, and preserved the Queen's letters; unless, indeed, he may have thought that such a token, brought to light one day, would be too significant, and hoped by destroying "the Stamp" to conceal the secret of two hearts for ever.

He well deserved that Marie Antoinette should think of him, for he never for an instant ceased to think of her.

Even at that very moment hope entered into his soul. Political news reached him by which he learned that treason was coming to the aid of the cause he was defending. The general to whom the French Republic had intrusted the command of its forces, the victor of Valmy and Jemmapes, was meditating dark designs. Bolder than Bouillé, less of a patriot than Lafayette, he did not intend to deprive France of his own sword only; with his troops he meant to turn against the Convention, and, aided by his late adversaries, to march upon Paris, there to re-establish a King.

Such was the agreement formed between

Dumouriez and the Prince of Coburg. Count Fersen did not doubt for a moment that the French general who came forward in such fashion was certain that his troops would follow him. He was overjoyed, and immediately despatched "an express to carry the news to Sweden."

His imagination set to work actively; so readily do we believe what we ardently desire! He "no longer has any fear for the Queen." Nor was this all; he pictures to himself the remaining members of the royal family set free, and takes the precaution of inquiring of Baron Taube "whether he ought still to abide by the instructions which he has, in the event of the King's being at liberty (he is speaking of Louis XVII.), or wait for others," and in the latter case, he begs that these "*may be sent to him as early as possible, for this may go very fast.*"

How should Fersen have had any doubts? Marshal de Broglie announced that he had received information that "Dumouriez was marching alone on Paris with a force of 50,000 men, all wearing the white cockade, and that the Prince of Coburg remained at the frontier, quite ready to support him, if necessary."

Fersen's assurance was sufficient for the Duke of Sudermania. The Regent of Sweden replied to him by a letter overflowing with enthusiasm and confidence :—

"It has come, then," he wrote, "that much-desired moment when the delirium of France and her tragic and sanguinary triumphs are about to cease; when at last she will be placed in subjection to her lawful masters, and the unfortunate family of Bourbon, our old and true friend, will enter into its ancient rights; when we shall see Louis XVII. re-established upon his father's throne, and guided by a tender and estimable mother, receiving the homage of a guilty but misled people, and at the same time punishing the enemies of his father with a terrible hand, restoring the tranquillity of Europe by avenging outraged royalty, by crushing that impious sect whose execrable principles threatened to infect the world with universal barbarism. . . .

"You are a Swede, you love your country; I am your friend, and I have rights over you; I cannot better intrust the interests of my country than to your hands, and *I constitute you ambassador from the King to Louis XVII.* You will be a better judge than I of the time and the propitious moment for proceeding to Paris, to your destination."

And Count Fersen, taking his *rôle* quite seriously, prepared a "note" for the Queen of France, in which he repeated the hopes that he had built upon the treachery of Dumouriez, but also gave his opinion of that personage with the severity of a gentleman of ancient race pronouncing upon an adventurer of plebeian birth, thus revealing the aristocratic article of faith that gratitude is due between equals only.

"The position in which you are about to find yourself is going to be very embarrassing; *you will have incurred great obligations to a knave*, who, as a matter of fact, has only yielded to necessity, and did not want to behave well until he saw the impossibility of resisting any longer. *This is the whole of his merit as regards you;* but the man is useful; he must be used, and the past forgotten; you must even appear to believe what he will say of his good intentions; you must even deal frankly with him respecting the things that you may desire, and for the re-establishment of the monarchy in its entirety as you would have it, and as circumstances permit. With regard to Dumouriez you have nothing to fear. You must try not to pledge yourself too deeply to him, and as far as possible to keep off all the other schemers whom he will want to place and recommend.'. . . He is a vain and covetous man."

It was on the 8th of April 1793 that Count Fersen wrote this note. When we think of what was going on in Paris, we are amazed at the delusion to which it gives expression. That delusion was not to last long, and even at the very moment events were exposing its vanity. France was not displaying a disposition to receive "her lawful masters" again, and her army had no desire to resume the white cockade.

The "note" had hardly been written before the Bishop of Pamiers, who was mixed up in these schemes, came to Fersen, and in a sentence announced the overthrow of all his hopes. The "knave" had indeed endeavoured to fulfil his agreement with the Prince of Coburg, but his soldiers had refused to obey him. He had fled before their threats—they fired their muskets after him—and reached the frontier with only a few officers of his staff. He had time, however, to give up to the Prince of Coburg the four commissaries who had been sent by the Convention to watch him; this was the sole advantage his treachery had obtained.

This news affected the emigrants, who so little expected it, very painfully. "The consternation among the French," wrote Count Fersen in his journal, "was as great as their joy had been; they believed all to be lost." His own "fears for the Queen were born again;" yet he was not entirely disheartened; he cherished the notion that the French army, being deprived of its chief, was in a state of disorganisation, and he was still determined to hope on.

In the meantime, General Dumouriez had arrived at Aix-la-Chapelle. Count Fersen wished to see the man who had missed the playing of so great a part, and who could give him information, and the details of the position. On the 17th of April, he proceeded, with his friend Simolin, to the military station, and there the General made his appearance at half-past two in the afternoon. Fersen describes their interview as follows:—

"We made our way through a crowd, and found him in a lower room. The windows were besieged by people. Three aides-de-camp were with him. He recognised Simolin; I introduced myself, and he paid me a compliment, saying that he ought to have known me by my handsome face.

"I said that I was very glad to see him *here;* he replied that he had intended to come for a long time. He then told us that . . . fear was abroad in Paris. . . .

"I said: 'Explain to me, Monsieur, what has happened with regard to the Duc d'Orléans.'

"'I cannot give you an explanation, M. le Comte, for I have never had any relations with the Duc d'Orléans, whom I have always despised and regarded as a scoundrel. I know, however, that the contrary has been stated; but as this report is the only stain with which my character can be blackened, I am about to issue a proclamation which will prove that I have never had any dealings with him.'

"I asked him for particulars of the circumstances of his flight. He gave them just as they are narrated in his proclamation, and added that Baptiste, his aide-de-camp, who was present, had had his horse killed under him.

"He highly praised the Duc de Chartres,[1] who did not resemble his father, he said, in anything.

"He assured me that Biron and Custine were behaving well, and said that he was going to the neighbourhood of Mayence, in order to consult with him (Custine), and

[1] Louis Philippe.

would probably go to Vienna; and that he had a plan in his head. He complained of the slowness of the Austrians, said that with greater activity in dealing with these people they would be put down; that there was no longer an army, that all the troops of the line would pass over as soon as they could. . . .

"He complained greatly of Dampierre, who had betrayed him, and in whom he had placed confidence, because, as he said, he was a man of quality, and ought to belong to the right side; that his plan was to seize on Lille, Condé, Valenciennes, and Meubeuge, making hostages of the commissaries who were there; that this plan had failed through the imbecility of those whom he had intrusted with the execution of it; that it had already been proposed to exchange the four commissaries for the royal family; that in his opinion, everything ought to have been granted in order to secure possession of the royal family, and no faith kept afterwards with these knaves."

The epithet was ironically happy; but if Dumouriez thought to ingratiate himself with his present audience by such language, his mistake was great, and proved his ignorance of the law of human nature which ordains that while men freely avail themselves of treachery, they always despise the traitor, and that the contempt which he inspires shall be the greater in proportion to the non-success of his treason.

In a few lines, Count Fersen tries and condemns Dumouriez, but while treating him fairly, he contrives to be unjust to the French.

"In everything," he writes, "I consider him a true Frenchman; *vain, confident, and feather-headed; clever, but possessing no judgment.* The whole of his plan failed through excess of confidence in his troops and in his own influence over the army. He had not sufficiently organised the affair.

"He was very uneasy, and upset by every sound from the crowd who surrounded the door and windows; he seemed to be afraid of some mishap. His lackey came to complain of having been insulted by an '*émigré.*' He sent him away, and said to us—

"'*If these gentlemen push matters too far, I will show them that I can still make myself respected.*'

"On getting into his carriage, he received some verbal insults."

Dumouriez did not remain long at Brussels; he went to England in search of a warmer welcome, and a few hours after his arrival a crowd assembled under his windows shouting, "To the lamp-post with him!" This manifestation probably reminded him of his own country, where the same cry was in high favour. He had to fly, and now we may dismiss this personage, merely mentioning that he was reduced to wandering about from kingdom to kingdom, always being turned out, and living like a beggar on the meagre alms which his importunity extracted from various persons here and there.

The French Revolution, which ought to have been crushed out a hundred times over by the armies which Europe could put in the field, so superior in number and in discipline were these, had on its side that marvellous occult power which seems to watch over the destinies of nations—in reality an unknown force, sometimes called chance, a force which, in the present instance, it would be rash and irreverent to describe as Providence.

Nothing that was devised against the Revolution succeeded, and it marched on without a stumble, notwithstanding that its feet were bathed in blood. The reason was that its real allies were those who professed to be its enemies. Those who are faithful to the principle of royalty cannot possibly have to make a more painful admission than this.

Setting aside Monsieur and the Comte d'Artois —those French princes of whom even Fersen said, "Their folly led them always to reject useful people"—we must acknowledge that the oldest friends of the royal family, and of the Queen herself, evinced very little solicitude for the interests of the prisoners of the Temple.

The conduct of M. de Mercy affords more than one example of this indifference, to use a mild expression.

He had been sent as Ambassador to France, honoured with the twofold confidence of Maria Theresa as Empress and as mother, and for years he had corresponded with his sovereign, making a show of zeal and devotion which were believed to be sincere. No sooner was the muttering of the storm heard, no sooner did the times change, than he left France and retired to Brussels. Did he, from the safe shelter of that city, ever use his influence to secure allies against the persecution of the Queen? Did he imitate the conduct of Count Fersen, who had forgotten nothing, and strove with desperation to save Marie Antoinette? We should like to be able to believe that he did, but the documents are there, and they render any doubt of the pitiful part which he acted impossible. We have only to consult Count Fersen's journal. There we read, at the date of the 20th of April 1793—" There have been proposals to exchange the royal family for the four commissaries taken by Dumouriez, but beyond this a demand is made for an unlimited suspension of hostilities and the recognition of the Republic. The Prince of Coburg has called for a full explanation of the vague declaration of an undefined truce, and demands that the royal family shall be brought to the frontiers, that the four commissaries shall also be brought thither, and that the parties shall then treat."

Negotiations had been opened with the Prince of Coburg, and at that very moment, on the 3rd of May, Count Fersen records that "the Comte de Mercy has been ordered to join the Prince of Coburg, in order to guide his political conduct. . . ." This is not all. "M. de Mercy said to Crawford that he should go once a week to see the Prince of Coburg; *that he had full powers for the affairs of France in the widest sense.*"

It is, then, quite certain that it depended upon M. de Mercy to give a turn to the negotiations, just begun, which would bring about the exchange of the royal family for the four commissaries.

But this was not M. de Mercy's purpose. His advice was that no negotiations with the French should be carried on, that no proposition should be listened to, for—so he declares beforehand—he believed "it would lead to nothing. Absolutely nothing but force must be employed."

From such an attitude terrible consequences might ensue, and certain persons regarded it with just alarm. Baron de Breteuil endeavoured on one occasion to bring M. de Mercy to bay, and put the question to him plainly—

"But if, by a possible chance, the King and Queen of France were free, what would you do? Would you receive them?"

One would think that an answer should come spontaneously from the lips of the diplomatist. Not at all: he reflected a moment, and said—

"Well, that is a theme . . ."

He meant by this "a supposition." He deigned, however, to consider it, and his conclusion was, that "if it were proposed to liberate them outside the kingdom, it would be necessary for their own safety to refuse!"

It was impossible to be more cynically

DE MERCY'S BASENESS

insensible to the fate of the victims whose quarrel was ostensibly embraced. Baron de Breteuil perfectly understood the motive which led M. de Mercy to speak thus; it was the fear of the allies "having to confront a power with which it would be necessary to treat, and being hampered in the arrangements they reckoned on making."

This mental reservation of the sovereigns could not escape the faithful friends of the unhappy captives, and Count Fersen himself was obliged to recognise and own it.

In the note which he had drawn up for Marie Antoinette on the 8th of May (a passage from this has already been quoted) he wrote:—"Your will concerning the re-establishment of the monarchy will still be hindered by the influence of the coalised powers. *There is no longer any doubt that the partial dismemberment of the kingdom is decided upon.* ... M. de Mercy cannot, and ought not, to give you advice except on this basis."

Light was let in upon the selfish policy of the sovereigns; then came testimony more overwhelming still, that if M. de Mercy was indifferent, M. de Thugut, the Austrian Minister, was hostile to the idea of receiving the royal family.

The Maret-Sémonville mission was charged, in July 1793, to negotiate an "understanding" with the Governments of Venice, Florence, and Naples. (See, for a detailed narrative of this episode, *Un Complot sous la Terreur*.) "It was thought certain," says Maret, "that if the three States I have named made *the safety of the Queen and her family a condition of the continuance of their alliance, it would not be refused."*

That was precisely what Thugut did not wish, and accordingly he resorted to a very simple expedient for cutting short the mission. This son of a Danube boatman gave orders for the arrest of the two plenipotentiaries at Novale, in violation of the law of nations, and had them thrown into prison.

There is no doubt that the exchange of prisoners was a genuine desire, and this was afterwards confirmed by Drouet, the hero of Varennes, who was made prisoner at Maubeuge. Being questioned by Count Metternich, he stated that "the Queen and her family would have been given for the four commissaries delivered up by Dumouriez; *that was decided."* Drouet was a member of the Convention; it was not surprising that he should be aware of the intentions of the Government.

It is, then, evident that the responsibility for the fate of the royal family ought not to be thrown solely and entirely upon the Revolutionary party, and that, although the foreign sovereigns made a show of zeal in their cause, this was mere hypocrisy on the part of most of them. In reality, they desired an event which they would regard as a triumph for their own policy, and a means of gratifying their greed.

What of the Queen in Paris? how did the days pass with her, while her false friends were making believe to bestir themselves beyond the frontier?

Under strict and unremitting guard in the Temple, she saw her true friends fail in each successive effort to deliver her from her terrible bondage; after Toulan and Jarjayes came Michonis, the municipal, Cortey, the grocer, and the famous Baron de Batz, who all conspired to save her, but whose plans were defeated at the last moment by the most extraordinary and mysterious of chances. Yet these cruel disappointments grieved her less severely than the anguish that was inflicted upon her through her son. About this time she was separated from the little King, by an order equally senseless and inhuman, and he was removed to another floor of the Tour du Temple.

"What a dreadful grief for the Queen! Unhappy princess!" exclaims Count Fersen on learning this news (12th July).

There was worse to come soon. The foreign armies were victorious in a few fights, and the Convention retaliated by voting on a motion by Barère for a series of ultra-revolutionary measures. Among these was the transfer of Marie Antoinette from the Temple to the Conciergerie. The decree was executed without delay, and the Queen of France, parted from all who were left to her, awaited her trial in a prison cell!

Every scrap of information that reached him increased the misery of the unhappy Count. What would his anguish have been had he then known the details which he learned afterwards and recorded in his journal! Some of these are heartrending.

"They say that the hackney-coach which brought the unfortunate Queen to the Conciergerie was filled with blood; that the driver did not know, but that he suspected whom she was, having had to wait a long time; that on arriving at the Conciergerie, it was some time before they alighted; that the men got out first, and the woman after; that she supported herself on his arm, and that he found his coach all filled with blood."

In vain does he add, "But all this is not very authentic." Perhaps he strove to deceive himself. It was authentic; these sad details were only too true.

The Chevalier de Rougeville, who fortunately eluded the warrant for his arrest which was issued after his abortive attempt and his visit to the Conciergerie, gave Count Fersen other particulars of the Queen's captivity. He records these in his notes with the reverential compassion of a faithful friend.

"Her room was the third door on entering to the right, opposite Custine's; it was on the ground-floor, the window opening on the courtyard, which was crowded all day with prisoners, who looked in through the glass and insulted the Queen.

"The room was small, damp, and ill-smelling; there was neither stove nor chimney; there were three beds: one for the Queen, the other, by the side of hers, for the woman who served her; the third, for the two gendarmes, who never left the room *on any occasion or under any circumstances whatsoever*.

"The Queen's bedstead was, like the others, of wood, the bedding consisted of a straw mattress, a woollen mattress, and a worn and dirty blanket, which had been used by prisoners for a long time; the sheets were of coarse grey linen, the same as those on the other beds; there were no curtains, only an old screen.

"The Queen was dressed in a black loose jacket (*caraco*), her hair was cut short on her forehead, and quite grey at the back; she was so thin that she could hardly be recognised, and so weak that she could scarcely keep herself upon her legs. She had three circlets on her fingers, but no jewelled rings.

"The woman who served her was a sort of fishwife, of whom she complained very much.

"The gendarmes told Michonis that Madame did not eat, and that if this went on she could not live; they said her food was very bad, and one of them brought a small stale chicken, and showed it to Michonis.

"'*There*,' he said, '*is a chicken which Madame has not eaten, and it has been served to her these four days.*'

"The gendarmes complained of their bed, although it was exactly like the Queen's.

"The Queen always slept fully-dressed, in black, expecting every moment to be massacred or led to the scaffold, and wishing to go thither in mourning. Rougeville says that Michonis wept while confirming the statement of the hæmorrhage from which the Queen suffered, and told him that when it was necessary to procure the black jacket and some indispensable linen for the Queen from the Temple, he could not go until after a 'deliberation' of the Council."

The announcement that Marie Antoinette was about to be brought before the Revolutionary Tribunal threw Fersen into a state of acute distress; but he was not one of those friends who are to be beaten by failure. Notwithstanding the defeat of all his previous efforts for the deliverance of the Queen, he still contemplated a fresh attempt.

Deep and powerful indeed must have been the feeling that nerved him to such endeavour, for he received but slender support from those whom he would fain have made his accomplices.

He placed little reliance upon the zeal of M. de Mercy, but was obliged to apply to him in the first instance, because only Mercy had sufficient influence to second his efforts. A fresh disappointment awaited him. "The Count received him like a man of ice. He saw only impossibility in his ideas. *He believed the royal family to be lost, that nothing could be done for them.*"

However, Count Fersen still persevered; he communicated his plan to Count de la Mark, and succeeded in inspiring the Count with his own ardour. They made a second joint-appeal to the former Ambassador.

There was nothing to be done, according to their present view, in the way of political action, of setting the incapable diplomatists of the warring nations in motion, and intrusting them to fresh negotiations destined to pitiable failure. No, they must address themselves directly to one of the men who were then leading France, and obtain help from him to take the Queen out of prison and set her at liberty, by promises, at need by money, and even by the threat of future reprisals. Finally, M. de Mercy accepted this idea, but the way in which he carried it out permits us to doubt his sincerity. The two men he selected to fulfil this delicate mission were not persons whom we should expect to find engaged in such a matter. One was Novère, a ballet-master, the other was Ribbes, a financier, who having hitherto managed all parties in the interests of his own particular operations, was no more worthy of the confidence of those who sent him, than of those to whom he was sent.

Neither this selection nor the mission seemed very promising, especially to Baron de Breteuil, who feared lest this proceeding should excite rather than check the " scoundrelism " of the demagogues. But Fersen had none of these scruples. He thought, rightly, that although there might have been grounds for such a fear while the Queen was still in the Temple with her son, and not directly threatened, the moment was now past. What was the risk? In the existing state of things, the position of the person for whom they were interested could not be made worse, and there was apparently some chance that it might be improved.

At Fersen's urgent entreaties, Baron de Breteuil consented to see Ribbes. They regarded Danton as the person whose influence was at that time greatest in France, and decided upon addressing themselves to him. Ribbes was to have him asked by his (Ribbes') brother for an interview near Paris, at which he would treat for the ransom of the Queen. Danton's reputation justified to a certain extent their hopes of the possibility of buying him; they did not take so much into account the chance of Danton's recommencing the game he had already played with the Court. That game was to take the money, and always to put off the support he promised in return for it until a later day. Moreover, supposing Danton to be bought, to be willing, would he have the power to do what they wanted?

Before the project had reached this point, other obstacles, always of M. de Mercy's making, arose to hinder its execution.

The Count began by declaring that it was not necessary to promise money; that it would be sufficient to offer "favours, security, protection, and pardon." This was childish. He was made to see that it was so by such sound reasoning that either he could not persist in the idea, or he pretended to yield, at the same time putting forward fresh objections.

He formally opposed Ribbes's presenting himself to Danton as coming in the Emperor's name to treat for the ransom of his aunt. He said that the men to whom they would have to apply would very likely be delighted to divulge their overtures, and in that case the Powers who had not been informed might take umbrage, and thereby the already great difficulties of the coalition would be complicated.

He advised that Ribbes should approach Danton in the name of certain speculators interested in the political affairs of Europe.

"This was a miserable device," writes Count Fersen, "and the change in M. de Mercy's ideas surprised and grieved me. La Mark himself, without saying so, seemed to disapprove. *I was so much the more pained because I thought I could perceive that M. de Mercy's second objection arose from his doubt as to how far the Powers, and even Austria, truly desired the freedom of the Queen;* for as the basis of the negotiation was to be the laying aside of every political idea, and demanding the Queen as a simple individual, the aunt of her nephew, that demand could not influence the political operation, or embroil the coalition. M. de Mercy had also added—

"'*I am obliged to say it with regret, but if the Queen were on the scaffold, that last atrocity could not stop the Powers or change their march.*'"

Such a sentence uttered by a diplomatist was assuredly very significant. It made Baron de Breteuil indignant, and Count Fersen also, but the latter, who was more anxious about the fate of Marie Antoinette than hurt by the cynical saying of Mercy, tried to profit by that small amount of good-will which the Count did not as yet venture formally to withhold.

It was not easy to do this. Ribbes having come to him, highly discontented with the hindrances put in the way of his mission, Fersen saw clearly that the prospect of figuring as an important personage, and posing as a plenipotentiary, had charmed the financier, who was vexed at being prevented from playing a part which flattered his very real vanity more than it gratified his hypothetical ardour in the cause.

Fersen begged him not to distress himself, but to accept the mission, or rather the commission, proposed to him. Ribbes ended by accepting, and set out on the 4th of September. But he did not go far, and a few days afterwards he came back. "He had adopted the plan of writing to Danton in a manner unintelligible to all but himself, and had sent him the letter."

What could a letter do under the circumstances, and in the midst of the events that were hurrying on?

"I fear it will arrive too late," says Fersen, "and how bitterly will M. de Mercy have to reproach himself, he who has caused eight days to be lost by staying away in the country, and four more since his return by all the difficulties he has made!"

And in his pain he adds: "This is horrifying to think of. May God preserve her, and give me the satisfaction of seeing her again some day."

In God only did he hope at this dark hour: the news from Paris was bad, very bad! The Queen's trial was imminent; she had already been subjected to a first examination before the Committee of General Safety. What was known of the sentences pronounced by the Revolutionary Tribunal was well calculated to appal him.

The days passed with terrible rapidity. The beginning of October had come, and at that moment chance brought Fersen in contact with a man who had had a tragic influence upon the fate of the Queen—a man who had frustrated all the Count's former efforts: this was Drouet, who had been made prisoner at Maubeuge.

The sight of the man who had stopped the berline at Varennes which he, Fersen, had got safely out of Paris, enraged the Count:— "The sight of that infamous wretch put me into a fury," he writes; "and the effort which I made not to say anything to him, on account of the Abbé de Limon and the Comte de Fitz-James, who were with us, made me ill."

An officer, who was captured with Drouet, declared that the Queen was in no danger, and that she had all she wanted! Fersen did not believe a word of this. "The infamous scoundrels," he says, "how they lie!"

The terrible moment was approaching. Count

Fersen felt it, although the news from Paris was contradictory, and restored him to hope or plunged him into despondency by turns. He was no longer the cold and correct personage whom some of his contemporaries have depicted. His misgiving, or rather his misery, is apparent in the brief notes he makes in the pages of his journal. Now comes the moment of supreme anguish.

The Queen had appeared before the Revolutionary Tribunal on the 13th October, and, as it was to be expected, she had been condemned to death. The execution was to follow close upon the sentence.

Couched in terms of irony, hideous in its grossness, came the awful news to the wretched man : he was handed a letter which had been written from Paris, and contained the following atrocious sentence :—" *This morning Marie Antoinette is to appear at the National Window.*"

"Although I was prepared for it," he says, "and, since she was transferred to the Conciergerie, have been expecting it, the certainty overcame me; *I had not strength to feel anything.* I went out to speak of this misfortune with my friends Mme. de Fitz-James and Baron de Breteuil, whom I did not find. The Gazette of the 17th speaks of it. It was on the 16th, at half-past eleven, that this execrable crime was committed, and the Divine vengeance has not yet fallen upon the monsters!"

He no longer thinks of hiding his grief, and he speaks in profoundly touching words of her whom he loved so faithfully.

THE END

"*Monday*, 21*st*.—I can think only of my loss. It is dreadful not to have any positive details. That she should have been alone in her last moments, without consolation, without any one to speak to, to hear her last wishes! That is horrifying! The monsters of hell! No, without vengeance my heart will never be content."

Until the end of his life he had to bear in his heart the grief of that death; it was not granted to Fersen's love either to save Marie Antoinette or to avenge her.

CHAPTER XII.

Consequences of the Queen's death—The Regent of Sweden deprives Count Fersen of his diplomatic post—Recognition of the French Republic—The son of Gustavus III.—Reactionary policy—The majority of Gustavus IV. is proclaimed (6th November 1796)—Count Fersen at the Congress of Rastadt—General Bonaparte's speech to Fersen —Return to Sweden—The strong protest of Gustavus IV. against Napoleon is attributed to Count Fersen—The fall of Gustavus IV.—The Duke of Sudermania is proclaimed King under the name of Charles XIII.—Adoption of Prince Christian of Holstein-Augustenburg—Sudden death of the Prince—Rumours of poison—Accusations against Count Fersen, and against his sister, Countess Piper—Popular excitement—Moral complicity of the King—Funeral ceremony of the 20th of June 1810—Popular feeling against the Grand Marshal—Count Fersen is massacred in the courtyard of the Hôtel-de-Ville.

COUNT FERSEN, struck to the heart by this frightful catastrophe, found his only solace in talking incessantly of the dead Queen with those who had known and loved her. The arrival of Baron de Goguelat, who had fortunately got out of France, where his life was not safe, was a consolation to him; they could speak to each other of "the unhappy princess" whose remembrance was ever living in their hearts. These conversations, which rekindled their sorrow, also increased it, and the hope of avenging that august victim of the French Revolution excited their enmity against both the Revolution and France.

The information received from Paris, the

accounts of the captivity of the royal children and Madame Elizabeth, served to intensify their purpose of conflict with the abominable Convention.

"How horrible!" wrote Fersen, "and how is it that Divine justice does not avenge such deeds?"

He appealed in his wrath to God more than to men, for he began to see clearly that the latter were powerless to execute the task of justice. His delusion was all over; the whole truth had come home to him now, and on this point his mind had recovered its cool and complete lucidity. "It is painfully plain, through all these intrigues, how little the sovereigns know concerning the affairs of France, *and how little they feel the danger that threatens them all if this fire be not trampled out.*"

He draws a melancholy contrast between the enemies in array: on one side, France, without generals, destitute of all the necessaries of war, with troops hastily gathered together, without resources, without money, suffering from dearth, torn by civil war, obliged to defend herself at almost every point of her territory; on the other side, the great Powers, provided with numerous and well-disciplined troops, free to move as they will; and, in spite of all these advantages, he records that "after an eight months' campaign by the Austrian, Prussian, English, Spanish, Sardinian, Italian, and Imperial armies, the territory intact, except at two points only, and for three or four leagues, and winter quarters have not been established in France."

What friend of the French nation, what fervent adherent of the Revolution, has ever passed a more eloquent eulogium on either or both? Does not this testimony prove the singular vitality and strength of the nation that was hailing a new principle of existence?

Fersen did not, indeed, understand, but he instinctively hated, those hitherto unknown elements which were forcing their blood-stained way into the worm-eaten fabric of the old social systems, and he could not tolerate their formidable attacks upon the established order of things. Still less could he forgive them the victims—*the victim*—whom they had immolated.

The "Divine vengeance" which he invoked was apparently no more disposed to punish the death of Marie Antoinette than the assassination of Gustavus III., and the French Revolution, despite Fersen's invocation of the lightnings of Heaven and the armies of the kings, seemed to defy and defeat fortune. It found friends where it was believed to have enemies. Sweden was of this number, and the Duke of Sudermania, who had for some time pursued the policy of Gustavus III., began to detach himself from it, and was evidently about to come to an understanding with the Government of the Republic.

Count Fersen was becoming troublesome; for, his principles being immutable, like his affection, he would not countenance any concession. The first pretext that could be found was eagerly used to get rid of a representative whose mission, formerly conferred upon him in a moment of enthusiasm, had become embarrassing and slightly ridiculous. He was accused of having regarded a conspiracy formed by Baron Armfeldt, one of his friends, to proclaim the majority of Gustavus IV. prematurely, and deprive the Duke of Sudermania of the regency, with a favourable eye, and he was deprived of his diplomatic functions, also of the title of "Ambassador to King Louis XVII."

Fersen understood the full bearing of his dismissal. That incident took place in March 1794. A year later, M. de Staël, who had resumed his functions in Paris, recognised the French Republic in the name of Sweden.

The "Friend of the Queen" was too devout a worshipper at the shrine of memory, he cherished in his heart too keen a longing for vengeance, to own himself beaten and relinquish the strife. There still remained a good chance that he might recover his influence, and once more get his country governed according to the political theories of the murdered King.

The young Gustavus Adolphus would soon attain his majority; on him Fersen built his hopes. He endeavoured to breathe his own sentiments and ideas into the heart and mind of the youthful prince, and he had the satisfaction of succeeding in this. On the 6th of November 1796, the majority of Gustavus IV.

was proclaimed; he assumed the reins of government, and the Duke of Sudermania went into retirement.

Count Fersen's restoration to favour was promptly made manifest, and when the Congress of Rastadt (1797) was opened, it was he whom the young King sent as plenipotentiary. His *rôle* in the Congress was likely to be very subordinate, since the attitude of Sweden towards France was again altered to such an extent that all diplomatic relations between the two countries were broken off; but an incident occurred which brought him forward in an equally unexpected and disagreeable manner.

General Bonaparte, travelling by Piedmont and Switzerland, arrived at Rastadt. The General, who had just made himself illustrious by his campaign in Italy, the victor of Arcola and Rivoli, the signatory of the Treaty of Campo-Formio, had no notion of dealing with the plenipotentiaries of the great Powers otherwise than as he dealt with their generals; that is to say, he meant to talk to them as their master.

Count Fersen appeared to be unaware of this, and let it be openly known among his colleagues that he intended to defend the Treaty of Westphalia, although that treaty had been torn up at Campo-Formio.

This was not all. Montgaillard had made overtures to General Bonaparte, immediately on his arrival, in favour of a restoration of the Bourbons, and, rightly or wrongly, a report was spread that Count Fersen had instigated that proceeding.

General Bonaparte, who entertained a well-founded antipathy to Louis XVIII., and who proposed to himself to do something very different from restoring the throne of France by his own hands, and then placing that prince upon it, was profoundly irritated by these overtures and pretensions, and he skilfully availed himself of the first opportunity to give vent to his anger.

When Count Fersen presented himself at the General's hotel to pay his compliments, Bonaparte asked him to have the goodness to inform him what Minister from Sweden was then in Paris.

There was none. Count Fersen made an embarrassed answer.

Bonaparte replied sharply that it was surprising the Court of Sweden should so conduct itself towards a nation with which it had had friendly relations for a long period; then, making a direct thrust at his adversary, he added that the Court of Sweden seemed to take pleasure in sending on all occasions agents, ministers, and ambassadors *who were personally disagreeable to every French citizen;* that no doubt the King of Sweden would regard a French Minister who had tried to raise the people of Stockholm against him, with disfavour; and that the French Republic likewise ought not to suffer *men too well known for their connection with the former Court of France to be sent to mock the Minister of the first nation of the earth.* . . .

Fersen could not fail to understand the

personal allusions of this apostrophe; but what was he to say in reply? He maintained his apparent composure, and said only that "he would make known to his Court what he had just heard," thus saving his dignity by dint of diplomatic reserve and coolness. He then retired without another word.

Such an adventure was certainly not calculated to diminish his dislike to the political doctrines whose triumph permitted a victorious general to treat one of the representatives of the oldest nobility in such high-handed fashion. On his return to Sweden he advised the young King to the most reactionary measures more urgently than before, so that when Gustavus IV. thought proper to put forth a strong protest against Napoleon in 1805, the inspiration and the composition of the document were alike attributed to Count Fersen.

But what could proclamations or oppositions do against the Emperor of the French? He replied to them only by victories. Austerlitz defeated all the hopes of the enemies of the Empire.

In vain did Sweden, still impelled by Count Fersen, give a kindly welcome to the French refugees, in vain did she place herself in touch with the secret agents of the House of Bourbon, such as Fauche-Borel; these petty plots came to nothing. Other hands were needed to seize and subdue the steed and the horseman who were galloping about the world, trampling under foot all that resisted them as they passed.

By degrees, Fersen came to recognise the uselessness of his efforts, and the despondency that attended this conviction, added to his successive bereavements, turned the "handsome Fersen" of former days into a moody and melancholy man. His eldest sister, the Baroness Klinckowström, had died in 1792; Count Frederick, his father, in 1794. In 1800 he lost his mother; Baron Taube, his best friend, the confidant of his political hopes, had died a year previously. On that grieving heart, which for ever mourned the beloved Queen in faithful silence, each of these losses inflicted a fresh wound.

Meanwhile the King loaded him with favours. He made him Chancellor of the Academy of Upsala, a peer of the realm, a Knight of the Order of the Seraphim; he gave him every proof of the esteem in which he was held. These were distinctions which might have satisfied his vanity, if small passions could hold any place in a heart laden with great sorrows.

Very soon a fresh revolution broke out in his own country and once more overthrew the plans of Count Fersen. King Gustavus IV., an inept ruler, so seriously displeased his subjects, both nobles and people, that he was obliged to abdicate (13th March 1809), and the son of Gustavus III. had to tread the path of exile. His posterity were deprived of all their rights, and the crown reverted to the Duke of Sudermania, the former Regent.

The King's fall deprived Count Fersen, who was even more unpopular than his sovereign, of his last stay. A numerous party had been persistently inimical to him, and would not now be satisfied by the overthrow of Gustavus IV. unless an end were also made of his detested favourite ; and an incident occurred very soon which let loose the storm that had long been gathering over his devoted head.

The Duke of Sudermania, proclaimed King under the name of Charles XIII., had no child. In order to secure the succession to the throne, and to render the exclusion of the posterity of Gustavus IV. more certain, the new monarch adopted Prince Christian of Holstein-Augustenburg. A few months afterwards Prince Christian had an apoplectic stroke while reviewing some troops in Scania, and died suddenly on the 28th of May 1810. The very circumstances of his death forbade it to be attributed to anything but an accidental cause ; but political passions are beyond reason. A rumour was spread that the Prince had been poisoned, that the deed had been done by the partisans of the fallen dynasty, and Count Fersen and his youngest sister, Countess Piper, were frequently mentioned in ominous connection with the matter.

The leaders of the party which had overthrown the elder branch of the Vasas were very desirous once for all to rid themselves (while effectually frightening the last remaining followers of that dynasty) of so highly placed a personage as Count Fersen, whose position, wealth, and great name made him a rallying-point for the nobility, and who might again become dangerous to his adversaries. The opportunity to "suppress" him was propitious; they did not allow it to escape.

The populace, which finds consolation for its exclusion from the direction of affairs in a ready belief in secret transactions of every kind, has an innate taste for the mysterious, and is ready to adopt all sorts of opinions, provided only that people will take the trouble of suggesting them.

After a few days' circulation of these insinuations, no doubt was entertained of the guilt of Count Fersen, his sister, and a few other great personages, and the popular wrath against those enemies of the people rose high. This was kept up by distributions of money and brandy, and, rapidly reaching its paroxysm, it threatened to vent itself in deeds of violence. Count Fersen, who was warned of the fact, did not dread, while the dastardly King desired, such deeds. It is recorded that Charles XIII., being informed by the competent authorities that a disturbance was to be expected on the day of Prince Christian's funeral if the Grand Marshal should be present, merely answered, "It would not be a bad thing that this proud lord should receive a lesson."

These imprudent and cruel words were repeated, and they contributed to bring about a popular tumult, which did not stop short at "a lesson," and was aggravated by the prearranged omission of any military precautions.

The date of the royal obsequies had been fixed for the 20th of June 1810.

What remembrances must that anniversary have awakened in Count Fersen! On the same date, nineteen years before, the Queen's friend had attempted to wrest the royal family of France from their enemies, and from that moment their misfortunes and his own had begun. The coincidence might have daunted a superstitious nature, a mind less finely tempered, less utterly detached from the things of life than his; but since he had lost all that he loved, since he had witnessed the defeat and renunciation of the principles he cherished, and the objects he revered, what did life matter to him? He had none of these fears; he despised insult, and of death he had no dread.

Therefore, on the day when the body of the deceased prince was brought back, with solemn pomp, from Liljeholm to Stockholm, "Count Fersen, in full ceremonial dress, entered the gilded coach, drawn by six white horses, which was to convey him to the place where he was to meet the funeral procession, and from thence to the city. The escort set out at eleven o'clock in the morning, with the Grand Marshal and some members of the Court in coaches, going before the coffin. The Light Horse of the Guard advanced at the head of the procession, which was closed by the squadron of cavalry that had accompanied the mortal remains of the Prince from Scania.

"The procession was received, almost before

it entered the capital, with insulting shouts from the populace; they even spat upon Count Fersen's coach. In the Hornsgatan (Horn Street) copper coins were flung at the coach; the windows were broken and Fersen's face was cut. At the Kornhamn (Grain-Market) the populace abused and threatened him, and tore up stones from the pavement to fling at his carriage. The coachman was hit so hard that he fell upon his knees. In the Stora Nygatan (New High Street) the shouts and stone-throwing were continuous, and at last, at the top of the square in which the 'House of the Nobles' stands, almost at the end of the Stora Nygatan, at the moment when the escort was turning to the right towards the château, an immense crowd prevented Count Fersen's coach from passing.[1] That moment was decisive; if the armed force allowed the furious crowd to begin its work of death, who could stop it? The crowd encountered no obstacle.

The people flung themselves on the coach, unharnessed the horses, and dragged out Count Fersen. The Grand Marshal made an effort to shake himself free, and escaped for an instant from the hands of the ruffians who swarmed about him; he darted into the first door in front of him—it was that of a café—and ran upstairs to the first floor, where he took refuge in a room. At that moment, General Silfversparre, who had been informed of Count Fersen's danger, came bravely to his aid; but

[1] See the Introduction to *Le Comte de Fersen et la Cour de France*, by Baron R. M. von Klinckowström.

he had only sixteen men and one officer with him. What could that little troop do against the howling and threatening crowd?

The house was invaded; the wretches, who feared for a moment that their prey had escaped them, avenged themselves by insulting the unfortunate man. Blows followed insults; they tore off his decorations, his cloak, his sword, and flung them out of the window, to prove to the populace that they still had possession of their victim, and induce them to have patience.

General Silfversparre, being powerless to repel the crowd by force, adopted a stratagem in the face of the growing danger: he offered to arrest Count Fersen, and to hold him prisoner until his trial could take place. Much they cared for a trial! Sentence had already been passed by popular fury, and was about to be executed. They struck the Grand Marshal, they tore his hair out, they wounded him in the head, they dragged him from his precarious refuge. He was now in the square. A battalion of Guards was there, with Generals Adlercreutz, and Vegesach. The crowd wavered for a moment before this armed force; that moment was propitious for the rescue of the prisoner.

The Generals turned back and rode off at a trot, under pretext, as they afterwards pretended, "of facilitating the deliverance of Count Fersen from the hands of his tormentors!"

Then the mob was at liberty to indulge its cruel instincts, and it played with its victim. The crowd passed before the soldiers, who looked on stolidly, and drove the wretched Fersen before them to the Hôtel-de-Ville.

"There, although surrounded by the mass of his tormentors, he had a moment's respite. They seemed to grant him this breathing-space from an impulse of pity. Seating himself upon a bench, he asked for a mouthful of water; it was brought to him by a soldier of the City Guard. But the mob began again to threaten him with death, and to reproach him with having poisoned the Crown Prince. They struck him with their fists and their sticks, they tore out his hair, and also his earrings, with pieces of the flesh.

"The people outside, closely packed in the courtyard of the Hôtel-de-Ville, shouted to them to give up Count Fersen. . . ."

Again they dragged him out; they flung him down on the staircase, and there, in the courtyard, the ruffians completed their crime. At length the victim, trampled under the feet of these bloodthirsty brutes, uttered his last groan.

Their fury was not slaked by his death; they fell upon the corpse, stripped it, mutilated it, and carried the fragments about the town.

Does not this story remind us of one of those sanguinary scenes which made the early record of the Revolution so horrible? And yet the deed was done between twelve and two o'clock in broad day, in the city of Stockholm, under the regular government of a legitimate King.

Printed by BALLANTYNE, HANSON & Co.
Edinburgh and London

www.ingramcontent.com/pod-product-compliance
Lightning Source LLC
Chambersburg PA
CBHW030348230426
43664CB00007BB/576